M000198008

Joe Hescnmeyer

POPE PETER

Defending the Church's
Most Distinctive Doctrine
in a Time of Crisis

Catholic
Answers
Press

© 2020 Joe Heschmeyer

All rights reserved. Except for quotations, no part of this book may be reproduced or transmitted in any form or by any means, electronic or mechanical, including photocopying, recording, uploading to the internet, or by any information storage and retrieval system without written permission from the publisher.

Published by Catholic Answers, Inc.
2020 Gillespie Way
El Cajon, California 92020
1-888-291-8000 orders
619-387-0042 fax
catholic.com

Printed in the United States of America

Cover and interior by Russell Graphic Design

978-1-68357-180-3
978-1-68357-181-0 Kindle
978-1-68357-182-7 ePub

To Paul and Barbara Heschmeyer,
for raising me to be a shameless papist.

ACKNOWLEDGEMENTS

This book originated with a series of blog posts that I wrote that sparked a lively debate amongst Catholics, Protestants, and at least one Eastern Orthodox reader in the comments as well as numerous private e-mails. The feedback, particularly the critical feedback, was invaluable, and I hope that the final product reflects this. "Iron sharpens iron, and one man sharpens another" (Prov. 27:17).

Over the next several years, I periodically attempted to turn this idea into a book before getting distracted or giving up. Special thanks to Kara Beth Vance, Darin Tuck, and Mary Beth Baker for aiding me in this stage of the journey.

Special thanks also to Todd Aglialoro and Drew Belsky, for their extensive help in editing and polishing. Todd was the one who convinced me to finally do something with the idea, and the book might never have happened without that push, or without his patience in the face of numerous missed deadlines.

Jason Kirklin, a Presbyterian pastor who was on his way to becoming a Catholic, was a great resource for matters both theological and grammatical. Welcome home, Jason!

Last and certainly not least, I would like to thank my wife Anna. In what were probably the busiest two years of her life (moving to Kansas City, getting married, getting pregnant, and having a baby), she encouraged me and gave me the space to write, and then edited the first (and worst) drafts of each chapter. This book and I would be much the worse without her.

CONTENTS

Introduction:

THE POPE FRANCIS PROBLEM

"Remember Zika?" the *New York Times* asked recently. "With measles and Ebola grabbing headlines, it is easy to forget the health panic of 2016, when Zika was linked to severe birth defects in thousands of Brazilian newborns whose mothers were infected while pregnant, striking fear across the country and much of the Americas."[1]

It's helpful for us to step back into that world that was panicked about Zika and its threat to mothers and babies, because it was in that climate that, aboard a plane headed from Mexico back to Rome, a Spanish reporter named Paloma García Ovejero asked Pope Francis what should have been a simple softball question:

"Some authorities have proposed abortion, or else avoiding pregnancy. As regards avoiding pregnancy, on this issue, can the Church take into consideration the concept of 'the lesser of two evils'?"[2]

The answer is likewise simple, albeit controversial, and has been declared by the Church repeatedly. In 1931, a year after the Anglicans officially declared an openness to contraception "where there is such a clearly felt moral obligation to limit or avoid parenthood, and where there is a morally sound reason for avoiding complete abstinence," Pope Pius XI clarified:

> *No reason*, however grave, may be put forward by which anything intrinsically against nature may become conformable to nature and morally good. Since, therefore, the conjugal act is destined primarily by nature for the begetting of children, those who in exercising it deliberately

frustrate its natural power and purpose sin against nature and commit a deed which is shameful and intrinsically vicious (*Casti Connubii* 54, emphasis added).

In his answer, though, Pope Francis said something that sounded closer to the opposite. While condemning abortion as "an absolute evil," he seemed to open the door for contraception to avoid conceiving a child with birth defects:

On the "lesser evil," avoiding pregnancy, we are speaking in terms of the conflict between the Fifth and Sixth Commandment. Paul VI, a great man, in a difficult situation in Africa, permitted nuns to use contraceptives in cases of rape. . . . Avoiding pregnancy is not an absolute evil. In certain cases, as in this one, or in the one I mentioned of Bl. Paul VI, it was clear.[3]

Both García Ovejero's question and Pope Francis's answer were somewhat ambiguous (for example, "avoiding pregnancy" is a term vague enough to include abstinence, natural family planning, and contraception), but the Vatican quickly clarified that Pope Francis *did* mean contraception. Vatican spokesman Fr. Federico Lombardi explained that the pope was declaring that "the contraceptive or the condom, in cases of particularly [sic] emergency and seriousness can also be objects of a serious discernment of conscience."[4]

Both the pope's answer and the subsequent clarification were stunning. As recently as four days earlier, the *New York Times* had reported, "Catholic Leaders Say Zika Doesn't Change Ban on Contraception."[5] The new headline read: "Francis Says Contraception *Can* Be Used to Slow Zika."[6] This apparent about-face confirmed non-Catholics' long-held suspicions that the Church's opposition to contraception is arbitrary. The *Guardian*'s Barbara Ellen and others quickly asked, "Why is 'permission' being granted to safeguard against one virus, Zika, but not against HIV and AIDS?"[7]

It's a fair question. If it's okay to contracept because you don't want to conceive a child with microcephaly, then why not because you don't want to conceive a child with AIDS... or conceive a child born into extreme poverty? And not only did Pope Francis apparently casually reverse Catholic teaching from inside an airplane cabin, but he did so by using opaque reasoning and in a way that seemed to suggest Catholics might be sinning against the Sixth Commandment by *not* contracepting.

This might seem like a strange way to begin a book arguing for the papacy. How can airing the Church's dirty laundry demonstrate the *truth* of Catholicism and its most distinctive doctrine?

Other readers may say I haven't even scratched the surface of the Church's folly. I haven't said a word about clerical sex crimes and their cover-ups. I haven't mentioned the widespread heresy that too often goes unchallenged within Catholic dioceses, seminaries, and parishes, or the seeming indifference of some Church leaders toward banal or blasphemous liturgies. I haven't spoken of many of the other scandals that seem to suppurate by the day.

But I chose my one example for a reason.

The idea for this book started nearly a decade ago, during the pontificate of Pope Benedict XVI. On my blog *Shameless Popery*, I wrote a series of five articles on the topic of "Pope Peter," exploring the biblical basis for the idea that the papacy was established by Christ, with Simon Peter as the first pope. That seed would eventually flower into this book, but along the way, several things happened.

Pope Francis was elected in 2013, and although I admired many aspects of his apparent humility and his general down-to-earth nature, I missed the theological clarity of his predecessors' styles. From the beginning, critics accused the pope of breaking with Church tradition, and on my blog and elsewhere I battled against them and their uncharitable interpretations of his off-the-cuff remarks. But this airplane interview in 2016 was a sort of breaking point for me. I found it simply indefensible. Indeed, after those remarks, some orthodox Catholic philosophers did try to show that they could be harmonized with Catholic teaching . . . only to have their interpretation rejected by the pope's own spokesman.[8]

Part of the problem has been pastoral. Thirteen months earlier, the pope had publicly criticized a mother of seven children for being irresponsible while saying that Catholics need not "breed like rabbits."[9] Now he was suggesting that those with Zika who nevertheless follow Church teaching might be guilty of sinning against the Fifth Commandment—the commandment against *murder*. Living in a way that is faithful to the Church's sexual ethic is difficult enough in the face of a hostile world; feeling like even the pope doesn't have your back makes it almost unbearably harder.

But the deeper problem is ecclesiological. The Church cannot be right in teaching that contraception is contrary to the law of God today and then go and declare it acceptable tomorrow—not without compromising its claim to be a bastion of truth. The Zika story is really part of a broader story about a dismaying lack of clarity that has dogged this pontificate from the start. What does it mean to believe in the "teaching authority of the pope" in a world in which endless debates rage over what his words even *mean*? Many of the world's Catholics, and many on the outside looking in, are grappling with that question.

The experience hasn't caused me to become a "Francis-hater," or still worse to lose faith in Christ's promises to his Church. I still love the pope and pray for him daily. But my thoughts on the papacy have been purified. As Catholic apologists sometimes do, I once took a posture of triumphalism. To be sure, like anyone familiar with the history of the Church I knew that there *were* some bad popes, but the problem always seemed safely distant. My entire life had been spent amid the pontificates of Karol Wojtyła and Joseph Ratzinger, two of the brightest and holiest men of the twentieth century. It seemed a given that in Rome we would always have a sort of theologian-in-chief, a pope capable of articulating the nuances of Catholic doctrines with brilliant lucidity.

These past few years have been a reminder that such clarity can't be taken for granted. And *there* is the silver lining to this crisis.

St. John Henry Newman (1801–1890) observed that "it is a common occurrence for a quarrel and a lawsuit to bring out the state of the law, and then the most unexpected results often follow."[10] In the case of the papacy, "St. Peter's prerogative would remain a mere letter, till the complication of ecclesiastical matters became the cause of ascertaining it. While Christians were 'of one heart and one soul,' it would be suspended; love dispenses with laws."[11]

That is to say, when everyone is in agreement, as in the early days after Pentecost, it may not always be clear (at least to an outsider) who's in charge or what the limits to his authority may be. The true sign of obedience, as Newman rightly noted, is in the face of a "quarrel or a lawsuit." It's when we *disagree* that we see how much (or how little) respect for authority we have. And so it is precisely here that the papacy as a divinely ordained structure of authority shines through.

Perhaps there is another silver lining as well: the accumulating scandals in the Catholic Church (including some that long predate Pope Francis's pontificate) mean that many non-Catholics are sincerely asking, "Why are you still Catholic?" This book is my own answer to that question.

1

GETTING THEOLOGY RIGHT

IF YOU WANT to know whether or not you should be a Catholic, there's only one issue you need to solve: is the papacy true or not? To be sure, the papacy isn't the most *important* doctrine: the existence of God, the divinity of Christ, the Eucharist, and countless other teachings are of greater importance. But it's the most *distinctive*. Think about it this way: the existence (or non-existence) of a truck bed is the distinctive feature in determining if you're looking at a truck or a car, even though the truck's bed is a great deal less vital to the truck than is, say, the engine.

Jews believe in the existence of the God of Abraham, Protestants believe in the divinity of Christ, and the Eastern Orthodox believe in (and have) the Real Presence of Christ in the Eucharist. So none of those three doctrines, as crucially important as they are, is enough to tell me why I should be a Catholic specifically. But the papacy *does* solve this question. Quite simply, if the Catholic Church's claims about the papacy are true, then everyone should be a Catholic. If they're not true, then nobody should be a Catholic.

Within that debate, the crucial question can be understood in one of two ways. One way of approaching the question is by asking, "Who was the first pope?" If the first pope was St. Peter, then we know that the papacy is of apostolic origin. And if Peter was made the first pope by Jesus, then we know that the papacy is part of God's plan for the Church. Thus, we should be part of the Church that has the pope. On the other hand, if the first pope was someone else, then the papacy *isn't* of apostolic origin, and we should reject the Catholic Church. Of course, the person holding this latter position ought to be able to explain when and how the papacy arose and who the first pope was, and we should probably see evidence of Christian outcry over the introduction of an alien papacy.

The other way of approaching the question is by asking, "What was the role of Peter among the Twelve, and what are the implications of this for subsequent generations?" Not everything that was established with the apostles was intended to continue into future generations, but some things were. So this line of inquiry is asking *what kind of Church Christ wants.* After all, it's his Church. If Christ wanted the Church to look like a democracy, we would reasonably expect him to establish it as such. So what can we learn from Christ's words and actions related to the Church?

Getting Theology Wrong

There's a common way that we regularly do theology wrong. Let's say you want to know what to believe about infant baptism or the nature of the Eucharist. What do you do? If you're like most of us, you start investigating. You see what you can find from the Bible, do a bit of Google searching, and maybe pick up the writings of some trusted biblical exegetes or commentators or theologians. If it's really weighing on you, perhaps you sit down with your priest or pastor or a knowledgeable friend. After weighing up the evidence, you're then ready to decide your position on the doctrine at hand. If the doctrine is of great enough significance to you, your newfound position might motivate a change of denominations.

This attitude accounts for a large part of the denominational movement *within* Christianity, distinct from the problem of Christians leaving Christianity entirely. A 2014 Pew study found that most people raised as Protestants no longer identify with the denomination in which they were raised. Among those raised as Reformed Protestants, for instance, 34 percent remained Reformed, while 42 percent "now identify with a different Protestant denominational family."[12] Some of this is simply the process of coming into an adult faith (as opposed to blindly believing what your parents taught), but it also points to what *Christianity Today* calls the "tremendous amount of turbulence *inside* Protestantism."[13] A recent study following thousands of Protestants from 2010 to 2014 found that 16 percent of them changed denominational families in just that four-year stretch.[14]

But the problem here isn't simply Christian disunity or denominational instability. It's that these theological inquiries presuppose a particular theological framework: that it's the duty of every Christian to solve every theological issue to his own satisfaction, and then to find a church or denomination in which to make a home (at least for now). What's missing from this? The role of the Church as teacher and, particularly, as an *authoritative* teacher we can trust, and whose answers are more reliable than the answers I would come to on my own.

What's striking here is how unbiblical this all is. Where does Scripture suggest that we should conduct theology in this way? In contrast, Hebrews calls us to "obey your leaders and submit to them; for they are keeping watch over your souls, as men who will have to give account" (Heb. 13:17), and the leaders being referred to are "those who spoke to you the word of God" (7). God's promise to us is that "I will give you shepherds after my own heart, who will feed you with knowledge and understanding" (Jer. 3:15)—not that each of us will be left to be his own shepherd.

Think of it like a courtroom. Before a judge can decide a particular matter, he must know two things. First, does he have the proper jurisdiction over the matter at hand? Jurisdiction "is the power to hear and determine the subject matter in controversy between parties to a suit, to adjudicate or exercise any judicial power over them."[15] Should another court be hearing the issue? Has a higher court already settled the question? And second, what's the governing law? These aren't just important questions; they're the ones that have to be settled *first*, because without answering them properly, you can't move forward properly. A judge who rushed past these questions to get into the "meat" of the case would be failing to do his job. He would risk usurping another court's authority, and there would be little reason to trust his decision if he made it using the wrong legal basis.

When a theological dispute comes before the courtroom of our mind, we would do well to ask the same questions. Is the theological question at hand something each individual Christian is called to sort out for himself, or is there a higher authority that can settle these questions? And if it *does* fall to us, what is the "governing law" by which we determine the right answer? Are we to adjudicate using Scripture alone, or is there anything binding in Tradition or prior teachings of the visible Church? And yet, we typically *don't* do this—we simply assume that it's up for us to decide, using the Bible alone or whatever happens to be our preferred theological method.

Asking Better Questions

Part of the problem here is that we often start by asking the wrong questions about the Church. We begin with a set of our own theological conclusions and then judge the Church by how well it accords with our own views. If we're 100 percent convinced on every "Catholic doctrine," we'll join the Church, and if not, we won't. But even if we *are* 100 percent convinced, there's still a problem. Addressing a group of Catholics, C.S. Lewis said:

> The real reason I cannot be in communion with you is not my disagreement with this or that Roman doctrine, but to accept your Church means, not to accept a given body of doctrine, but to accept in advance any doctrine your Church hereafter produces. It is like being asked to agree not only to what a man has said, but what he's going to say.[16]

The trouble with Lewis's position is that he's asking the wrong questions. The proper question isn't, "Do I agree with the Church on this or that issue?" or, "Does that doctrine match my reading of Scripture?" or even, "What might the Church declare tomorrow?" Instead, it's, "What is the Church?"

Ironically, the best answer to Lewis's objection comes from . . . C.S. Lewis. He recognized that there are people who approach Jesus in this way, simply as someone who had some great teachings. For instance, author Kurt Vonnegut explained his religious humanism by quoting his grandfather, Clemens: "If what Jesus said was good, what can it matter whether he was God or not?"[17] Lewis recognized the folly of such a position. The right question isn't, "Do I agree with Jesus' teaching on this matter?" but, "Is Jesus really who he claims to be?" If he is, and I disagree with him on a particular topic, then I need to change. If he isn't, then it doesn't matter if I like a lot of his message, since the foundational reason why he claims we should heed anything he says in the first place is a falsehood. But we can't just treat him as a teacher whose teachings we accept when we happen to find them "good." Lewis put the matter this way:

> You must make your choice. Either this man was, and is, the Son of God, or else a madman or something worse. You can shut him up for a fool, you can spit at him and kill him as a demon or you can fall at his feet and call him Lord and God, but let us not come with any patronizing nonsense about his being a great human teacher. He has not left that open to us. He did not intend to.[18]

Indeed, "the really foolish thing that people often say about [Jesus]" is "I'm ready to accept Jesus as a great moral teacher, but I don't accept his claim to be God." But notice how similar that is to Lewis's own approach to the Catholic question. In a letter to H. Lyman Stebbins, Lewis explained his position on the Catholic Church this way:

> If there were an ancient Platonic Society still existing at Athens and claiming to be the exclusive trustees of Plato's meaning, I should approach them with great respect. But if I found that their teaching was in many ways curiously

unlike his actual text and unlike what ancient interpreters said, and in some cases could not be traced back to within 1,000 years of his time, I should reject their exclusive claims—while ready, of course, to take any particular thing they taught on its merits.[19]

But the Catholic Church's claim isn't simply that it should be listened to because it's ancient, or that it's a church that was popular throughout much of history, or even that it's right on a great many teachings that the world (and most Protestant denominations) get wrong. Rather, the Church holds itself out to be directly founded and sustained by Jesus Christ, in some mysterious way an extension of his incarnation. If that claim is false—if the Catholic Church doesn't even know what the Catholic Church is—there's no particular reason to approach it with "great respect." If the claim is true, we can trust the Church even if it contradicts our personal reading of Scripture. But what the Church certainly *isn't* is a "great moral teacher," a manmade body dedicated to the preservation of the teachings of Jesus Christ, like the "Platonic Society." It's either a great deal more or a great deal less than that. Christ has not left that option open to us. He did not intend to.

So the right question isn't whether, left to your own devices, you would come to the same conclusions on purgatory or the Immaculate Conception or regenerative baptism. It's about whether the Church *is* what it says it is. If it isn't, it's a false church, even if (like all false churches) it gets enough right to be attractive. But if the Church is what it says it is, then your objections to its teachings are wrong, even if you don't yet know *why* they're wrong...since its teachings are really the teachings of its Head. As Jesus said to some of his earliest representatives, "He who hears you hears me, and he who rejects you rejects me, and he who rejects me rejects him who sent me" (Luke 10:16). So the question we ought to be asking is not, "Can I find scriptural support for all of these Catholic teachings?" but, "Is the Catholic Church what it claims to be?"

The Question of Faith

Behind the question of both Jesus' identity and the Church's, there is a question of what it means to believe. We are not called to a blind faith, but rather (in the famous words of the eleventh-century theologian St. Anselm), "faith seeking understanding."[20] But there's a world of difference between faith seeking understanding and faith *contingent upon* understanding, which is no faith at all. If I believe where I agree and deny where I disagree, the one I believe is myself.

At the end of John 6, after Jesus has presented his radical teaching on the Eucharist, the crowd is stunned. These followers had stayed with him even when he seemed to present himself as the son and equal of God (John 5:18). But now Jesus has gone too far, in their view. At first, the crowds simply murmur against him (6:41), but with each subsequent clarification, Jesus seems to double down in increasingly graphic terms on his teaching about the Eucharist. Finally, they've had enough. Saying, "This is a hard saying; who can listen to it?" many of them abandon him (60,66). Jesus makes no effort to soften the force of his teaching to keep his number of followers, the way a modern preacher might. Instead, he challenges even the Twelve. Simon Peter, in one of his first shows of leadership, says, "Lord, to whom shall we go? You have the words of eternal life; and we have believed, and have come to know, that you are the Holy One of God" (68–69). Peter doesn't claim to understand the teaching, or to have all of his questions and confusion clarified. He simply accepts it on the basis of Jesus' identity as the Holy One of God. He'll come to understand more in time. But he doesn't wait to believe until he fully understands.

This is reinforced in the following chapter. In his ministry to Jerusalem, the people begin to debate who Jesus is. St. John identifies two groups. The first (John 7:25–27) says, "Is not this the man whom they seek to kill? And here he is, speaking openly, and they say nothing to him! Can it be that the authorities really know that this is the Christ?" But they second-guess themselves because they have an unanswered theological objection: "Yet we know where this man comes from; and when the Christ appears, no one will know where he comes from." Jesus wastes little time on such questions (even though we readers realize that he could have clarified everything). Instead, he rebuffs the questioners with such force that many of them joined those seeking to have him arrested (30). Others, however, asked a better question: "When the Christ appears, will he do more signs than this man has done?" (31). In other words, Jesus presents himself as the Messiah and performs miracles. Even if they don't have every one of their questions answered, they have enough to believe.

At a certain point, you've been given enough to trust, and conditioning your belief on getting yet more free answers or yet more free bread is a form of faithlessness or disobedience.

I've tried to compile, and answer, some of the best and most popular Protestant objections to the papacy. But there's no way I can answer every possible objection you can dream up, and a book that tried to do so would be tediously long. Instead, my goal is to give you *enough* to believe that the Catholic Church, with the papacy, was instituted by Christ, and that we should be part of it. What you do from there is up to you.

2

I WILL BUILD
MY CHURCH

BEFORE WE CAN say whether or not Jesus placed St. Peter at the head of the earthly Church, we've got to clear up what we mean by *Church*. Catholics and Protestants tend to understand this word in different ways. One of the clearest ways that we can see this is by discussing the idea of the "true Church." For Catholics, that's the Catholic Church, based on the idea that it was founded by Jesus Christ and preserved by the Holy Spirit throughout history. If you're unfamiliar with Protestantism, you might imagine that Protestants speak of their own denominations in the same way: that the "Baptist church" or "Methodist church" is the one true Church. This would make a certain amount of sense: if you think it's important enough for *you* to be a Methodist, why isn't it important for *me* to be a Methodist? But barring a few fringe elements within Protestantism, these days, few Protestants actually say anything of the sort.

Instead, most Protestants will argue that there is no true Church on earth, in the sense of any particular denomination or visible body. Matt Slick, a radio host and the main author behind the popular Calvinist website CARM (Christian Apologetics and Research Ministry), claims that people "mistakenly think that there is an earthly organization that is the one true church as if a collection of people, church structures, and 'authority' designates that it is the 'one true church' on earth."[21] J.C. Ryle, the Evangelical Anglican bishop of Liverpool at the turn of the last century, likewise argues that "no visible Church has any right to say, 'We are the only true Church'" and that "no visible Church should ever dare to say, 'We shall stand forever. The gates of hell will not overcome us.'"[22]

What both sides agree upon is this: in Matthew 16, there's a moment when Peter confesses Jesus as the Christ, and Jesus responds to him, "And I tell you, you are Peter, and on this rock I will build my church" (Matt. 16:18). We'll look at that passage much closer later on, but for now, just focus on those last five words. When Jesus says to Peter, "You are Peter, and on this rock I will build my church," we can become so fixated on understanding who or what he means by "this rock" that we can overlook his promise, "*I* will build my church."

There's a parallel here to marriage. One of the strongest arguments used by conservative Protestants against redefining the legal definition of marriage to include same-sex couples (and other proposed innovations) is that marriage isn't something for us to invent or design. Marriage, along with biological sex, is something that we instead *discover*, something ultimately designed by God rather than us. Focus on the Family's Kermit Rainman, for instance, argues that "revisionist gay theology violates God's intentional design for gender and sexuality by saying that women don't need men and men don't need women." Instead, Rainman says:

Scripture begins and ends with the picture of marriage as an institution ordained by God—designed for the union of a man and a woman in a life-long, faithful, covenantal relationship. This view is affirmed by Moses, Christ, and Paul, and has been upheld through thousands of years of Judeo Christian history and tradition.[23]

If Jesus is the one who builds the Church, then the same principle applies here. It is sinful folly to imagine that our job is to invent new forms of marriage. But God *also* designed the Church, and so our job ought not to be to create new churches or denominations, or "new ways of being church."[24] Instead, it ought to be to discover God's plan for the Church, to understand the structure of that Church, and to become fully united with that church—and, thus, the design plan for the world. So where, and what, is this Church?

To summarize, the Church is a visible community. As a community, it has some structure and basic organization, and there are specialized roles within the community. Christ himself is the ultimate head of the Church. But this visible Church is not simply on earth. The holy souls in purgatory and the saints in heaven are also a part of this Church. These are what the *Catechism* refers to as the "three states of the Church" (CCC 953). Traditionally, they are known as the *Church Militant*, *Church Suffering*, and *Church Triumphant*.[25] Things aren't always so black and white: just like any other society, there are people on the borders, related to the Church in a more complicated way than simply "in" or "out."

How Might a Protestant Respond?

Throughout this book, I will respond to some of the best Protestant arguments *against* the Catholic view of the Church, the papacy, and St. Peter's role. Since "highbrow" and "low-brow" Protestants often run in different circles, I've done my best to cultivate a mix of professors, theologians, preachers, and popular authors. It's important to recognize at the outset that there's no such thing as "the" Protestant view on virtually any topic in Christianity. Indeed, this is precisely one of the critiques of Protestantism from a Catholic perspective: there is no one capable of speaking on behalf of the whole, no presence capable of unifying and leading the various factions. As a result, it's unlikely that anyone will feel represented by all of these authors (many of whom disagree with one another), but hopefully everyone will find at least some of their likely objections presented.

If you went back in time and asked a Christian from the first 1,500 years of Church history what the Church is, there's a good chance you would get something that sounds like the answer I mentioned above. But starting in the mid-1300s, a seminary professor and priest named John Wycliffe started to preach a radically different vision of the Church. It changed the course of Church history. The alternate vision of the Church from Wycliffe was embraced by Jan Hus, and then Martin Luther, and then (with some important modifications) John Calvin. It's for this reason that Wycliffe is sometimes called the "Morning Star of the Reformation," and although there's no such thing as a "Protestant doctrine" agreed upon by all Protestants, Wycliffe's take has, historically at least, come close.

The heart of Wycliffe's claim was simple: "Those who will one day be blessed in heaven are members of holy Church, and *no one besides*."[26] That is to say, "the Church" means the ultimately saved. It solves the problem of bad Catholics (and particularly bad clergy) neatly: it turns out that they were never part of the Church. Luther puts the view succinctly:

28

"God be praised, a seven-year-old child knows what the church is: holy believers and 'the little sheep who hear the voice of their shepherd.'"[27] Elsewhere, he says you cannot tell who is and isn't a Christian because "Christianity is a spiritual assembly of souls in one faith," and "this is the way Holy Scripture speaks of the holy church and of Christendom. It cannot speak about it in any other way."[28] As for "physical, external Christendom," Luther argues that this is "manmade," and that it's an abuse of the language to apply terms like "spiritual" or "church" to it.[29]

The Reformer John Calvin takes a slightly more nuanced view, arguing that "the scriptures speak of the Church in two ways." The first is "the Church as it really is before God," comprising "the elect who have existed from the beginning of the world." This is Luther's invisible Church. The second is the visible Church, and Calvin warns that "in this Church there is a very large mixture of hypocrites, who have nothing of Christ but the name and outward appearance."[30] As Slick summarizes, "The invisible church is the church made up of true believers. The visible church consists of those who say they are Christian but may or may not be truly saved."[31]

This shift in understanding the Church is a turning point for the Protestant Reformation. As the historian Eugene Rice recounts, it's a myth that the Reformation was primarily about reform:

> The leaders of the Protestant Reformation, too, were sensitive to ecclesiastical abuses and wished to reform them. Yet the reform of abuses was not their fundamental concern. The attempt to reform an institution, after all, suggests that its abuses are temporary blemishes on a body fundamentally sound and beautiful. Luther, Zwingli, and

Calvin did not believe this. They attacked the corruption of the Renaissance papacy, but their aim was not merely to reform it; they identified the pope with Antichrist and wished to abolish the papacy altogether.[32]

As Rice explains, "The Protestant Reformation was not strictly a 'reformation' at all," because "in its relation to the Church as it existed in the second decade of the sixteenth century, it came not to reform but to destroy."[33] But you cannot simultaneously hold that Christ founded the visible Church and spend your life trying to destroy the visible Church and change its doctrines. So it's necessary that the Reformers hold that the church that everyone could see isn't the *true* Church. Instead, the true Church is invisible, and no one knows who's part of it, and we need to implement the Reformers' ideas to bring the visible church closer to this invisible Church.

One Church or Two?

So what does this view of the Church get wrong? For starters, Wycliffe and Luther can't be right that the Church is just the invisible church of the saved, since there are far too many biblical references to the earthly structure and governance of the Church. And Calvin can't be right to separate the visible from the invisible Church, since it creates two separate churches. That's not an acceptable solution. It's not just that the New Testament consistently speaks of "the church" in the singular (cf. Matt. 18:17; Acts 8:3, 12:1, 12:5; etc.). It's also because St. Paul describes the Church as the body of Christ and the Bride of Christ (cf. Eph. 5:23–32), and it runs directly counter to the meaning of these expressions to suggest that Christ has multiple brides or multiple bodies. In Christ's own words, he promises to build "my Church." Where are these other churches coming from?

I should quickly note that Protestant theologians are divided over whether or not their view requires two separate churches. For instance, the biblical scholar (and Presbyterian minister) John Bright is quite explicit that he believes that "the visible churches are not the Church. At best they are shot through with sin and pride and are but the palest approximation of the body of Christ," and that "over these frail weak churches there towers this other Church, the Church invisible."[34] John MacArthur likewise says that "although the visible and invisible church were initially the same, the picture changed as false believers associated with the church."[35]

Such a view raises huge theological problems. How can Christ have multiple brides, or multiple bodies? And why doesn't Scripture ever mention this second, invisible, truer Church? Why are there so many passages about the oneness of the Church and absolutely none about the "twoness"? Even many of the "invisible Church" advocates recognize this difficulty and seek to find ways around it. For instance, the Scottish theologian James Bannerman (1807–1868) insists that it's really just "the same Church under two different characters."

> We do not assert that Christ has founded two Churches on earth, but only one; and we affirm that that *one* Church is to be regarded under two distinct aspects. As the Church invisible, it consists of the whole number of the elect, who are vitally united to Christ the Head, and of none other. As the Church visible, it consists of all those who profess the faith of Christ, together with their children.[36]

It's true that both Catholics and Protestants would say there are visible and invisible aspects of the true Church. Bannerman describes the visible Church as "an outward and visible society, embracing and encompassing the invisible and spiritual one; in other words, an outward Church, within which the invisible Church of real believers is embosomed, protected, perfected."[37] The image seems to be something like Russian nesting dolls: on the outside is the visible Church, but the true Church is somewhere inside this. But if that's true, then we're not actually talking about two churches, one visible and one invisible. Moreover, he says that "the proper party with whom the covenant of grace is made, and to whom its promises and privileges belong, is the invisible Church of real believers. It is this Church for which Christ died."[38] So Christ died not for the visible Church, but for the invisible Church. Does this still sound as though we're talking about one and the same Church?

It may be that the only real difference between Bright's views and Bannerman's is that Bright is being straightforward about the implications of his beliefs. The Westminster Confession of Faith (1647), one of the most important Reformed confessions, decrees that "the catholic or universal church, which is invisible, consists of the whole number of the elect, that have been, are, or shall be gathered into one, under Christ the Head thereof; and is the spouse, the body, the fullness of him that filleth all in all." In addition, there is "the visible Church, which is also catholic or universal under the gospel," but of this second universal Church, even "the purest churches under heaven are subject both to mixture and error; and some have so degenerated, as to become no churches of Christ, but synagogues of Satan."[39] This is an important detail, because it means that *even if there were a single visible Church over the whole world*, it would still (a) be subject to error and (b) not be the same as the invisible Church.

Despite the protestations of some Protestant theologians, what's being described can't be reduced to simply two aspects of the same church. Instead, these theologians and confessions are clearly describing two distinct churches: a holy invisible one and a less holy visible one. Only one of these, according to these theologians, is a part of the New Covenant. What's more, these two churches have different membership. The Second Helvetic Confession, composed by the Swiss Reformer Heinrich Bullinger, says that "the Church of God may be termed invisible; not that the men whereof it consists are invisible, but because, being hidden from our sight, and known only unto God, it cannot be discerned by the judgment of man."[40] We can know who's a member of the visible Church, but we can't know who's a member of the invisible Church.

The problem here is not that there are visible and invisible dimensions to the Church, or even that there are those who might be connected to the Church in ways known only to God. Rather, it's in creating two realities: a visible Church and an invisible Church, that are not only separate, but even at times pitted against each other. To approach the problem from a slightly different angle, if the "visible Church" *isn't* the Church headed (and saved) by Christ, then we shouldn't give it the name "Church" at all, and we're back to the Lutheran position that the only Church is the invisible one.

The Judas Problem

Whether we consider the theories of the Church advanced by Hus, Wycliffe, Luther, Calvin, or most of their successors, they share the same strength and weakness. Part of the appeal of the "invisible Church" theories is that they let us explain away the bad behavior of Christians. Focus on the Family's Robert Velarde explains that it's important for us to distinguish the visible and invisible Church "so that we do not confuse what we sometimes see fallible churches doing with the reality of the universal church. Not only do visible and local churches often host nonbelievers, but also the believers themselves are imperfect, resulting in challenges and tensions in every visible church."[41] That's the advantage: if the invisible Church is hidden somewhere within the visible Church, and no one can say quite where, then there's no risk of responsibility for the bad behavior of Christians.

But it's not at all clear that Jesus wants us to approach the Church the way a dishonest company uses shell corporations. Indeed, it's worth looking at how differently Jesus and the Reformers approach perhaps the biggest personnel scandal in the Church's history, Judas Iscariot. Wycliffe argued that "Judas was a thief and no member of Christ, nor part of holy Church, though he ministered the order of bishop."[42] Likewise, Calvin conceded that Judas was an apostle, since he possessed "apostolical office," but denied that he was ever in any way a part of the body of Christ, since "not one of those whom Christ has once ingrafted into his body will he ever permit to perish."[43]

Wycliffe's and Calvin's distinction—that Judas could somehow be a bishop and an apostle without being a part of the Church—beggars belief. The idea that apostles are part of the body of Christ isn't just implicit in Scripture. St. Paul says it explicitly (1 Cor. 12:27–28):

Now you are the body of Christ and individually members of it. And God has appointed in the church first apostles, second prophets, third teachers, then workers of miracles, then healers, helpers, administrators, speakers in various kinds of tongues.

An apostle is *by definition* a part of the body of Christ, the Church. If Calvin can't harmonize that with his vision of the Church and his understanding of predestination, then those are the ideas that need amending. Moreover, Judas isn't a false apostle, like the men Paul seems to have encountered in Corinth. Jesus called him by name, as we see in the Gospel of Matthew, which says that Jesus "called to him his twelve disciples and gave them authority over unclean spirits, to cast them out, and to heal every disease and every infirmity. The names of the twelve apostles are these: . . . and Judas Iscariot, who betrayed him" (Matt. 10:1–4). Indeed, Jesus seems to make a point of this when he says, "Did I not choose you, the twelve, and one of you is a devil?" (John 6:70).

Lest there be any confusion, St. John adds that Jesus "spoke of Judas the son of Simon Iscariot, for he, one of the twelve, was to betray him" (71). So the shortcoming of this view is that it contradicts the way Jesus describes his own Church. There's no room for Judas in Luther's church, but there is in Jesus' Church. (That doesn't mean that Judas is saved: the whole point is that, *contra* the Reformers, there are at least some unsaved people in the Church.) So it's clear that Jesus' Church and Luther's aren't the same.

Ecclesial Deism

A second problem with this view is the role it gives to the visible Church and to the question of denomination. I experienced this personally while evangelizing on a secular campus, when a Baptist faculty member said to my friend and me that "God doesn't care what church you're in, as long as you're a believer!" In the past, when I encountered claims like this one, it was usually in opposition to Catholicism. But here, the woman clearly meant it as an olive branch of sorts, to let us know she considered us fellow Christians, despite our being Catholic. This made it all the stranger, as if you were to comfort someone going through marital difficulties by telling him that his struggles don't matter to God, as long as he has faith. It's a claim much more at home in a religious system like deism (in which God winds the universe up like a clock and then lets it go) than Christianity, in which God has entered history. Indeed, my friend Bryan Cross coined the term "ecclesial deism" for this belief, which he defines as follows:

> Ecclesial deism is the notion that Christ founded his Church, but then withdrew, not protecting his Church's Magisterium (i.e., the apostles and/or their successors in the teaching office of the Church) from falling into heresy or apostasy. Ecclesial deism is not the belief that individual members of the Magisterium could fall into heresy or apostasy. It is the belief that the Magisterium itself could lose or corrupt some essential of the deposit of faith, or add something to the deposit of faith, as, according to Protestants, allegedly occurred in the fifth, sixth, and seventh ecumenical councils.[44]

In other words, the problem here isn't just that Protestants are separating the visible Church from the invisible Church. It's that they're suggesting that God let the entire visible Church actually fall into doctrinal error, or even apostasy. After all, there's no way that all of the competing denominations of Christianity, or even all of the competing denominations of Protestantism, could be right. So that leaves us with three possibilities. The first is that God doesn't care about these doctrinal issues. If that's the case, it hardly makes sense for us to divide into camps as Christians. As St. Paul would say, "I appeal to you, brethren, by the name of our Lord Jesus Christ, that all of you agree and that there be no dissensions among you, but that you be united in the same mind and the same judgment" (1 Cor. 1:10). The second is that God does care about these doctrinal issues, but none of the visible churches on earth get it right. That's the "ecclesial deism" position—*everyone* is in error, and God hasn't protected anyone. The third is that God does care about these doctrinal issues, and one Church is right. And it can be only one, since two disagreeing churches can't both be right.

The Unassembled Body

The "invisible Church" of Protestantism isn't united in any visible, meaningful way. In fact, as proponents of this theory will tell you, its members exist in a variety of denominations preaching contradictory creeds. But the result of this is that the "church" becomes reduced to the number of believers— that the Church is, as one "Bible handbook" puts it, "people who believe."[45] In this ecclesiology, "Church" becomes just a stand-in for the total number of believers. In other words, it's *atomistic*, reducing the whole to the sum of the parts. It's the same mistake that the astronomer Carl Sagan makes about his body when he says, "I am a collection of water, calcium, and organic molecules called Carl Sagan. You are a collection of almost identical molecules with a different collective label."[46] But every minute, millions of neutrophilic white blood cells are dying and being replaced in a process known as apoptosis.[47] If "you" are just the sum total of your cells, and that precise sum total only exists for a fraction of a second, then you don't functionally exist. To put it another way, if Sagan is right, a different person began reading this sentence from the one who finished reading it. Plus, as Sagan notes, you and I are each made up of water, calcium, and organic molecules—so what makes one collection you and another collection me?

The difference is what philosophers call the *form*. The difference between a chunk of marble and Michelangelo's *David* is not a quality of the molecules of the marble, but the form or arrangement of the matter. In human beings, the "principle by which we primarily understand, whether it be called the intellect or the intellectual soul, is the form of the body."[48] In other words, there's a unifying design to each human body, arranging the constituent molecular parts. Once we die, that plan goes away, and the parts decompose and go their separate ways.

That's what Sagan is missing about the human body, and it's what many Protestant authors are missing about the body of Christ. If the Church is just a cross-section of believers, then it exists only as a concept or a measurement, like "the set of left-handed people" or the temperature outside. It's a mere "collective label," to use Sagan's term. The result is that you're left with nothing, which is how you get a Church that can't do anything and "is at no time more than a few years old"—as the minister Albert Torbet claimed back in 1917.[49] In fact, this atomistic "Church" is much younger than Torbet lets on. Like Sagan's body, the body of Christ is in constant flux, as members come to faith and are baptized on the one hand and physically or spiritually die on the other. If Torbet is right, the Church is perhaps never more than a few seconds old. That doesn't sound like the Church established by Christ two thousand years ago, over which he promised that the gates of hell wouldn't prevail. Rather, the church Torbet is describing is wiped out by the gates of hell every few moments.

The corrective, in both cases, is the same. Just as Sagan errs by missing the form of the human body, these Protestant authors err by missing the form of the Church. "As it is," St. Paul says, "there are many parts, yet one body" (1 Cor. 12:20). We're not just molecules or organs, but a body that's formed, assembled together by Christ. We're not just the sum total of a collection of stones, but "living stones" being "built into a spiritual house" (1 Pet. 2:5). Paul puts it this way (Eph. 4:19–22):

> So then you are no longer strangers and sojourners, but you are fellow citizens with the saints and members of the household of God, built upon the foundation of the apostles and prophets, Christ Jesus himself being the cornerstone, in whom the whole structure is joined together and grows into a holy temple in the Lord; in whom you also are built into it for a dwelling place of God in the Spirit.

Torbet and others who think like him are good at seeing the stones and bad at seeing the "whole structure." They're right to see that the Church is made up of people, but they're wrong to reduce the Church to the total number of people, just as Sagan was right to see that the body is made up of molecules but wrong to reduce the body to the sum total of those molecules. They've missed the crucial and unmistakable difference between a collection of rocks and a house.

An Invisible Assembly?

One of the most devastating critiques of these invisible Church theories comes from the Norwegian Lutheran theologian Harald Hegstad, who argues that "it is the concrete, visible church that is the only real church."[50] Hegstad points out that these invisible Church theories run directly contrary to both the way the Church is spoken of in the New Testament and even the meaning of the word itself:

> The word we usually translate as church comes from the Greek word *ekklesia*. In secular usage the Greek word simply means a political gathering of citizens. In the New Testament, however, *ekklesia* also alludes to the Hebrew *kahal*, which is used in the Old Testament to refer to the people of Israel gathered in the presence of God (Deut. 23:2–8; 1 Chr. 28:8; Mic. 2:5). . . . *Ekklesia* is both *the act of coming together* (to fellowship/to commune) and the *group that comes together* (the fellowship/the community). The church is not only present in the worship service, but continues to be the church beyond the formal gathering.[51]

The important detail to note here is that "both the term itself, and its use in the New Testament presuppose not only a group of people, but a group of people that *gathers together*."[52] This is impossible for the "invisible Church." As Bannerman explains, "The form of the invisible Church cannot be distinguished by the eye of man, for the features and lineaments of it are known only to God."[53]

Since there are no known members of the invisible Church (save for Christ himself), and no visible structures, or buildings, or locations, that can be identified with the invisible Church, there's nowhere to assemble, and no one to do the assembling. We've already seen that Bannerman's "visible Church" isn't a church because he says it isn't the one headed by Christ, or party to the New Covenant; but now it turns out that his "invisible Church" isn't a church either, as it is not an *ekklesia*.

A Disembodied Incarnation

The problem with viewing the body of Christ as an "invisible assembly" isn't just that it can't assemble. It's that it's no longer a "body" in any meaningful sense of the term. Most Christians know that St. Paul refers to the Church as the "body of Christ" (1 Cor. 12:27), but fewer think about the meaning of these words. Consider why the Second Person of the Holy Trinity took on a body in the first place. As St. Athanasius (296–373) explains, God saw that "men, having rejected the contemplation of God, and with their eyes downward, as though sunk in the deep, were seeking about for God in nature and in the world of sense, feigning gods for themselves of mortal men and demons," and he responded lovingly, by taking "a body, and as man walks among men and meets the senses of all men half-way."[54] In other words, Christ rescues us from idolatry by becoming "the image of the invisible God" (Col. 1:14), so that he might, in Athanasius's words, "persuade them by the works he did that he is not man only, but also God, and the Word and Wisdom of the true God."[55]

Indeed, this is the lynchpin of the Incarnation: that God became visible, that "the Word became flesh and dwelt among us" (John 1:14). For the Word to take on a body is for the Word to become visible. The grittiness of the Incarnation is a scandal from the start of Christianity, with the Gnostics fighting it hard. St. John seems to have them in view when he warns that "many deceivers have gone out into the world, men who will not acknowledge the coming of Jesus Christ in the flesh; such a one is the deceiver and the Antichrist" (2 John 1:7). So those within the Church who deny the physical reality of the body of Christ are liars and antichrists.

What should we make of those who deny the physical reality of the body of Christ, the Church, then? After all, Paul describes the Church as Christ's "body, the fullness of him who fills all in all" (Eph. 1:23). It's not just that the Church is the body of Christ; it's that you don't have the fullness of Christ without the Church. In other words, there's a certain real sense in which the Church is the body of Christ because it's a continuation of his Incarnation. After all, the whole "body" imagery suggests and supposes visibility. So what can be said of those who reduce the body of Christ that is the Church from something visible and tangible to an invisible thing known only to God? Gottfried Locher, president of the Protestant Church in Switzerland (PCS),[56] asks the critical questions:

> What exactly is to be understood by an invisible body? How can the Church of the Creed be the body of *Christ*, if visible churchdom is not identical with this body? What does one mean if one calls the true Church the *body* of Christ, and yet this body lacks physical ("bodily") qualities, such as being visibly realized in time and space?[57]

So the Protestant view can't account for how the "body of Christ" is both a "body" and "of Christ." Given his position, you might imagine that Locher raises these questions rhetorically, to show why this understanding of the invisible Church actually makes sense. But he doesn't. Instead, he concludes that "calling the Church a mixed body ultimately goes along with maintaining a logical distinction between the historical church and the body of Christ," but that "the price to be paid for such two-dimensionality is a congregation which remains ontologically deprived of its inmost essence: to be the visible body of Christ."[58] In other words, the Reformers did what they needed to do to justify breaking away from the visible Church, but what they did (creating an unbiblical separation between the visible Church and the invisible Church) ended up gutting the Church's inmost essence as the visible body of Christ.

Three Other Visions of the Church

For a variety of reasons, even many Protestant thinkers are dissatisfied with the general Protestant vision of the Church. There are three major alternate views worth mentioning at least briefly.

Baptists often apply the biblical passages about the Church exclusively to the "visible, local congregation" while denying the existence of any "invisible, universal Church."[59] The difficulty with this view is that it conflates the *universal* Church and the *invisible* Church. These Baptists are right to reject the invisible view of the Church but wrong to conclude that this leaves us with only the local congregation. St. Paul, who isn't a member of the local church of Corinth, can nevertheless say to them that "by one Spirit we were all baptized into one body—Jews or Greeks, slaves or free—and all were made to drink of one Spirit" (1 Cor. 12:13). So there is a universal Church to which all the baptized are connected; it just isn't the kind of invisible Church theorized by the Reformers.[60]

Anglicans have historically been associated with what's called the *branch theory*. Charles Lemuel Dibble explains in the *Anglican Theological Review* that "the Anglican is convinced that the Church is a living, organic thing and hence visible."

He agrees with the Eastern that the visible Church must have unity of orders and doctrine. These he feels sure he has. Yet he finds himself excluded, for different reasons, by both Roman and Eastern. To meet this situation, he develops the "branch" theory of the Church. According to this theory, the Catholic Church exists in three branches: Roman, Eastern, and Anglican.[61]

Dibble notes that this view of the Church avoids what Anglicans regard as the errors of Orthodoxy and Catholicism, but it does so "only by throwing logic to the winds . . . it is somewhat amusing that the Anglican church should claim to be one with two others, one of which repudiates it bitterly and the other of which holds out the left hand."[62]

That leaves one final view, the idea that "the Church" is just any gathering of two or three in Christ's name. It's based on Christ's promise that "where two or three are gathered in my name, there am I in the midst of them" (Matt. 18:20). Miroslav Volf argues that *where two or three are gathered in Christ's name, not only is Christ present among them, but a Christian church is there as well*, perhaps a bad church, a church that may well transgress against love and truth, but a church nonetheless."[63] But it's enough to look at the context of Jesus' words to see that this conclusion doesn't follow. Immediately before this, Jesus says that "if your brother sins against you, go and tell him his fault, between you and him alone." If this doesn't work, "take one or two others along with you, that every word may be confirmed by the evidence of two or three witnesses." And if even this doesn't work, "tell it to the church; and if he refuses to listen even to the church, let him be to you as a Gentile and a tax collector" (15–17). But this process only makes sense if there's a difference between the "two or three" in the second step and "the church" in the third step.

So if the proper understanding of the Church isn't the one articulated by Luther and Calvin, and it's not any of these three other views, what's the correct view?

3

A CITY ON A HILL

IF THE MAJOR Protestant theories about the Church are wrong, where does that leave us? We need to return to the words of Jesus. In the Sermon on the Mount, he says (Matt. 5:14–16):

> You are the light of the world. A city set on a hill cannot be hid. Nor do men light a lamp and put it under a bushel, but on a stand, and it gives light to all in the house. Let your light so shine before men, that they may see your good works and give glory to your Father who is in heaven.

This passage was famously used by the Puritan John Winthrop to describe the Massachusetts Bay Colony, and was later applied (by figures as diverse as John F. Kennedy, Ronald Reagan, and Sarah Palin) to describe *America* as the city on a hill.[64]

But of course, that's not what the text actually means. Jesus wasn't giving a sermon about America. The Reformed theologian Richard Gamble traces the history of how this passage has been interpreted and concludes that the early

Church Fathers, continuing on down to the time of Aquinas in the thirteenth century, "understood the city's visibility as expressing the same meaning as Jesus' point in the following verse about a lamp's visibility on a stand and its power from that height to illuminate the whole house."[65] For about the first thirteen hundred years of Christianity, Gamble says, these authors interpret Jesus' words in a variety of ways, "but always within a fairly narrow range and always in reference to the church. . . . It was Jesus' metaphor for his Church as his own body, for its ongoing teaching ministry, and for the conspicuous doctrine and life of his disciples and the teachers of the Word who followed after them."[66] As Gamble points out, the early Protestants agreed with Catholics that the passage was about the Church, not about godly or exceptional nations.

Washington University's Abram Van Engen points out an important difference, however. Whereas seventeenth-century Protestants (like Winthrop) applied the "city on a hill" to "the gathering of the godly in particular places," for Catholics, the passage was about the Church, as a "permanent, visible, universal institution: Jesus' true followers were 'set on a hill' to be seen by all."[67] The Catholic argument is simple: Jesus appears to be promising *perpetual visibility* to his Church, and Protestant communities cannot plausibly apply that to themselves. After all, "since Protestants first appeared in the 1500s—since they had been effectively nonexistent, invisible, unknown, or unseen for over a millennium—how could they argue that they were descended from the life and teachings of Christ?"[68]

Some seventeenth-century Puritans and some modern Baptists argue that there *is* an unbroken line of visible Protestant (or even specifically Baptist) churches throughout the last two thousand years, but that argument doesn't stand up to historical scrutiny. We'll leave those claims for chapter 12. By far the more common response to the problem of Matthew 5:14 is to just reinterpret Jesus' meaning about the city on a hill. Catholics say the Catholic Church *is* the city on a hill of which Jesus speaks. Protestants have instead suggested "that this church or that town, this people or that place, had become, for a time, 'like unto' a city on a hill."[69] It was this watering down of the meaning of the passage that let "city on a hill" go from being about the Catholic Church to being about the United States of America, since a nation as well as a parish could claim to be "like" a city on a hill.[70] But clearly, Jesus had something more in mind when he told that first generation of Christians that "you are the light of the world" and "a city set on a hill cannot be hid."

Reclaiming the meaning of Jesus' words should be our starting point. The Church that Jesus founded is both a light and a city. The visibility of the Church isn't incidental to these descriptions—the entire point is that the light shines "before men," and the city on a hill "cannot be hid." As the light of the world, the Church is an extension of Christ its head, who elsewhere says, "I am the light of the world; he who follows me will not walk in darkness, but will have the light of life" (John 8:12). The Church's task is to proclaim "the light of the gospel of the glory of Christ" (2 Cor. 4:4). As a city, the Church is a visible, structured society. These two images are meant to go together: the visibility of the Church is key to the effectiveness of its proclamation of the gospel, "that they may see your good works and give glory to your Father who is in heaven." But as John MacArthur notes, this is impossible with an invisible Church: "People in the world cannot detect the invisible church of real Christians. They see only the visible church of those who profess to be Christians."[71] So Jesus' words can't be directed at this imaginary, invisible Church, somewhere out there in the noumenon. Rather, the city on a hill that he's speaking of is by definition of the visible Church.

The Visible Society

So what does the society of this city look like? One of the clearest writers to take up this question is St. Robert Bellarmine (1542–1621), a strong opponent of any theories of the Church that made the "true Church" invisible or cut too sharp a divide between the invisible and the visible. Bellarmine points out that any theory of the Church that requires "internal virtues to constitute a man 'within' the Church" thereby makes "the true Church invisible," leading to the numerous problems we looked at in the prior chapter.[72] As God reminds the prophet Samuel, "man looks on the outward appearance, but the Lord looks on the heart" (1 Sam. 16:7). Bellarmine offered this understanding of the Church instead:

> But it is our teaching that there is only one *ecclesia* [Church], and not two, and that this one and true Church is the assembly of men bound together by the profession of the same Christian faith and the communion of the same sacraments, under the rule of the legitimate pastors, and especially that of the Roman pontiff, the one vicar of Christ on earth.[73]

Given these three things, Bellarmine argued that "it is easy to infer which men belong to the Church and which do not belong to it. . . . For the Church is an assembly of men, as visible and palpable as the assembly of the Roman people, or the Kingdom of France, or the Republic of the Venetians."[74]

This description of the Church has proven extremely controversial, even among modern Catholics. The French theologian Christian Salenson writes that "the Church no longer recognizes itself in the definition of Robert Bellarmine, who thought that the Church was like the Republic of Venice, an organized and hierarchical society."[75] The heterodox[76] Catholic priest Hans Küng goes farther, claiming that "no Catholic today who believes in the real Church would bluntly take the line of that champion of Counter-Reformation theology, Cardinal Bellarmine, and consider the Church to be as visible as the Republic of Venice."[77] Instead, Küng argues that "the believer who holds no office is a Christian and member of the Church of Christ; a man who holds office without faith is no Christian and not a member of the Church."[78] Küng's first point is uncontroversial. Even Bellarmine's description (that a true Christian is "under the rule of the legitimate pastors") presupposes a layman, not a pastor. As for his second point, Küng has fallen back into the error of John Wycliffe, trying to exclude Judas from the Church that Jesus includes him in.

Both of these critics badly misunderstand Bellarmine's argument.[79] Building on the theology of St. Augustine, Bellarmine argues that "the Church is a living body, in which there is a soul and a body. And the internal gifts of the Holy Ghost, faith, hope, charity, and the rest are the soul. The external profession of the faith and the communication of the sacraments are the body."[80] He freely admits that "some are of the body and not of the soul"—that is, faithless members of the Church. These, Bellarmine compares to "hairs or fingernails or evil liquids in a human body." In other words, yes, they are members of the body of Christ, but no, they're not *living* members of the body. His point is not that they are saved, but that they are members of the Church. Bellarmine is defining the *body* of Christ but acknowledging that membership in the body is worthless without also sharing in the *soul* of Christ. On this point, Scripture clearly sides with Bellarmine, not Küng. Jesus gives the following parable:

> Again, the kingdom of heaven is like a net which was thrown into the sea and gathered fish of every kind; when it was full, men drew it ashore and sat down and sorted the good into vessels but threw away the bad. So it will be at the close of the age. The angels will come out and separate the evil from the righteous, and throw them into the furnace of fire; there men will weep and gnash their teeth (Matt. 13:47–50).

In other words, the Church on earth contains both good fish and bad, both the saved and some measure of the unsaved. We will not be able to fully sort out who is who here on earth—that's the place of the Final Judgment. Such a vision of the Church is a direct refutation of any theology that says everyone in the Church will be saved or that the Church is just the cross-section of the saved. No, this visible society clearly includes some who are Christians on the level "of the body and not of the soul."

Bellarmine also readily acknowledges that there are some (he mentions catechumens and even excommunicates!) who might be in the opposite situation, connected to the Church at the level of the soul but not the body. Here, too, Scripture is on his side. As St. Paul says, "If the foot should say, 'Because I am not a hand, I do not belong to the body,' that would not make it any less a part of the body" (1 Cor. 12:15). The plain suggestion is that the body of Christ includes even some people who think of themselves as on the outside.[81] In other words, it's easy to say where the *fullness* of Christ's

Church is, but it's impossible to find the outer boundaries. It's better to be united to the Church in soul than in body. That is, it's better to be a devout believer outside the visible bounds of the Church than a faithless member within it. But it's better still to be a full member, body and soul.

Contrary to a popular myth,[82] such an idea is not new in Catholic thought. When the crowds on Pentecost were "cut to the heart" by St. Peter's preaching, they asked, "Brethren, what shall we do?" and Peter answered, "Repent, and be baptized every one of you in the name of Jesus Christ for the forgiveness of your sins; and you shall receive the gift of the Holy Spirit" (Acts 2:37–39). At this, "those who received his word were baptized, and there were added that day about three thousand souls" (41). From this, we can see both that baptism is important for salvation and that it's the normal doorway into the Church. Those who are baptized are saved (invisibly) and brought into union with the Church (visibly). But this gets complicated when Christians break off from the visible Church and continue to baptize new members. Are those new members somehow part of the Church that the schismatics broke off from? The Catholic Church has repeatedly said "yes." More than 400 years before Bellarmine, the Fourth Lateran Council said that "the sacrament of baptism is consecrated in water at the invocation of the undivided Trinity—namely Father, Son, and Holy Spirit—and brings salvation to both children and adults when it is correctly carried out by anyone in the form laid down by the church."[83] The Council of Trent, rather than denying this Church teaching, elaborated on it, to make it perfectly clear that all trinitarian baptisms are valid, even if administered by heretics.[84]

This means that even though the Church is a visible body, there are still some who are connected to it invisibly.

And indeed, that is completely consistent with Bellarmine's description of the Church as a visible society like the Republic of Venice. At any given moment, a society will have members outside its visible boundaries and foreigners and visitors within. For three years, I studied theology in Rome. Bodily, I was in Italy, but I was still an American at heart and in a very real sense. I was, if you will, invisibly connected to a visible society, the United States. Likewise, we can coherently talk about people behaving in an "un-American" way, just as we can talk about Christians behaving in an un-Christian way. But it doesn't follow from this that there is one visible America and another invisible America, or that the "true America" just lives in our hearts or in the mind of God.[85]

As a visible society, the Church is also an *orderly* society, not simply a spiritual anarchy. This is another critique some modern Catholics have levied against Bellarmine's view of the Church. For instance, Loyola Marymount's Jeffrey VanderWilt accuses Bellarmine of placing undue emphasis "upon the hierarchy, the domination of the clergy over the laity, and legalistic understandings of grace and reconciliation."[86] Anyone who reads Bellarmine can see that nothing of the sort is true. He describes the Church as a visible society, and although the idea of a society includes government, it isn't reducible to it. Nor is the government the most important, or vital, part of a society. And these same charges could be levied (equally unjustly) against Paul, who writes to Timothy about qualifications for bishops (1 Tim. 3:1–7) and deacons (8–13), and then explains that "I am writing these instructions to you so that, if I am delayed, you may know how one ought to behave in the household of God, which is the church of the living God, the pillar and bulwark of the truth" (14–15). To Paul, and to Bellarmine, the true Church is at once the household of God, the pillar and foundation of the truth, and a place in which household governance is handled by clergy.

Israel and the Church

It may be helpful to think of the Church not in analogy to the Kingdom of France or the Republic of Venice, but in its relationship with the Kingdom of Israel. After all, if we want to know what it looks like for God to organize a people, this is an undeniable example of it. God establishes Israel as a visible society with its own land, with borders and boundaries (Num. 34), and subdivided into tribes (Gen. 49). It has a class of ordained priests (Num. 1:47–54) and a governing authority provided by God (cf. Judg. 2:16–19, 3:9; 2 Sam. 2). God even orders Moses to take a census to number the inhabitants of Israel (Num. 1:1–46). Israel was not just every bit as visible and structured as France or Venice, but visible and structured in precisely the same ways.

Yet there is more to Israel than its visibility or structure lets on. To understand Israel, consider God's opening words to Abraham, the father of the Jewish people: "Go from your country and your kindred and your father's house to the land that I will show you. And I will make of you a great nation, and I will bless you, and make your name great, so that you will be a blessing. I will bless those who bless you, and him who curses you I will curse; and by you all the families of the earth shall bless themselves" (Gen. 12:1–3). This is the entire history of the Jewish people in three verses. This is the promise that gives the "promised land" its name, and connected to this land is the promise of making a "great nation," Israel. The mission *ad gentes*, to the nations, to all "the families of the earth," begins here.

This is the paradox of Israel. On the one hand, the Hebrew word *qadash* means, "to set aside, to consecrate, or to make holy."[87] The strict dietary code, for instance, exists precisely to set the Israelites aside from the other nations, that they may be holy. The Psalmist even laments that "they did not destroy the peoples, as the Lord commanded them, but they mingled with the nations and learned to do as they did" (Ps. 106:34–35). And yet, God simultaneously is calling Israel to play a role in bringing those nations back to him. Rahab is converted and saved; Jonah goes to preach to the Assyrian Ninevites, and they repent; and "Ruth the Moabitess" (Ruth 1:22) gets an entire book of the Old Testament. Something of this paradox is captured brilliantly in Psalm 87. It begins with an ode to Zion, Jerusalem, as might be expected. But then the psalm takes a stark twist (4–6):

> Among those who know me I mention Rahab and Babylon; behold, Philistia and Tyre, with Ethiopia—"This one was born there," they say. And of Zion it shall be said, "This one and that one were born in her"; for the Most High himself will establish her. The Lord records as he registers the peoples, "This one was born there."

In the midst of praising Zion, the inspired Psalmist numbers as native sons the faithful of some of Israel's historic oppressors and fiercest enemies. The idea seems to be that God sees even them as what St. Paul would later call Jews "inwardly" (Rom. 2:29).

Christians sometimes think there was no evangelism among the Jews of the Old Testament, but that isn't entirely right. When Paul and Barnabas arrive in Antioch of Pisidia, they encounter "many Jews and devout converts to Judaism" (Acts 13:43). Throughout the Old Testament, there's an ever-growing sense that something new is about to happen that will somehow relate to the Gentiles. The prophet Jeremiah reveals that "the days are coming, says the Lord, when I will make a new covenant with the house of Israel and the house of Judah" (Jer. 31:31), and the prophet Isaiah makes it clear that this new covenant will incorporate the Gentiles in a radically new way. Through Isaiah, God promises, "I am coming to gather all nations and tongues; and they shall come and shall see my glory" (Isa. 66:18). And so faithful Israelites knew that more was to come, and that God's arrival would involve the gathering in of the nations.

When Jesus arrives as Israel's long-awaited Messiah, he applies the beginning of Isaiah 61, the messianic prophecy beginning "The Spirit of the Lord is upon me," to himself (Luke 4:18–22).[88] As if to point them toward the need for the Messiah to gather together the nations, he interprets Isaiah 61 "by reference to 1 Kings 17 and 2 Kings 5. In both these passages, God's messengers or prophets showed that God was the God of foreigners as well as of Israel. In 1 Kings 17 Elijah is saved by the sacrifice of a Sidonese widow, and in 2 Kings 5 Elisha heals an enemy army general."[89] Immediately, the congregation turns on him and wants to kill him. But Jesus is simply pointing out that the Messiah prophesied by Isaiah is the Savior of the Gentiles as well as the Jews. It's time to gather in the nations.

Israel as the Church

With Israel, then, God created a visible, structured people of God. But what does that have to do with the Church? How we understand Jesus' relationship with the Old Testament will color how we understand the Church's relationship with Israel. This has been a source of confusion from early on in the history of the Church. One of the earliest heresies was that of Marcion of Sinope (A.D. 85–160), who claimed that the God of the Old Testament and the God of the New Testament were different gods.[90] This heresy has perhaps never entirely disappeared: we hear echoes of it when Richard Dawkins claims that "the God of the Old Testament is arguably the most unpleasant character in all fiction"[91] or when Friedrich Nietzsche complains that the New Testament spoiled the spirit of the Old.[92] Even among today's Christians, it's not uncommon to hear some version of this contrast, which is why *The West Wing*'s fictional President Josiah Bartlett (presented as a Catholic on the show) answers a senator's struggles with believing in the God of the Old Testament by saying, "I'm more of a New Testament man, myself."[93] But Marcion was at least more intellectually consistent than these "neo-Marcionites." His Bible had no Old Testament, and even the New Testament was so gutted that St. Epiphanius of Salamis (c. 310–403) called it a gospel "without beginning, middle, or end," a "cloak full of moth holes."[94] Why? Because you cannot read far into the New Testament without hearing about how the Old is being fulfilled.

A second way we can misunderstand the relationship between the Old Covenant and the New Covenant is dispensationalism, a "novel method of biblical interpretation" invented by an ex-Anglican priest named John Nelson Darby in the nineteenth century.[95] If you're familiar with the best-selling *Left Behind* series or the idea of the "Rapture" (as an event apart from the Second Coming of Christ, in which believers are collectively taken up into heaven), then you've encountered dispensationalism. By the mid-twentieth entury, "dispensationalism was overwhelmingly the most dominant and influential system of biblical interpretation among conservative Protestant churches and groups."[96]

The crux of dispensationalist theology is the idea that "God had two completely different plans operating in history: one for an earthly people, Israel, and the other for a heavenly people, the church."[97] C.I. Scofield (1843–1921), who popularized dispensationalism in America, began his most famous book (tellingly titled *Rightly Dividing the Word of Truth*) by explaining that "whoever reads the Bible with any attention cannot fail to perceive that more than half of its contents relate to one nation: the Israelites," while there is "another distinct body, which is called the church. This body also has a peculiar relation to God and, like Israel, has received from him specific promises. But similarity ends there, and the most striking contrast begins. . . . Comparing, then, what is said in Scripture concerning Israel and the Church, he finds that in origin, calling, promise, worship, principles of conduct, and future destiny that all is contrast."[98]

It is hard to overstate just how radical was the break Scofield saw between Israel and the Church. He went so far as to say that Christians need not worry about the moral law of the Old Testament, including the Ten Commandments, arguing that "it is not, then, a question of dividing what God spoke from Sinai into moral law and ceremonial law—the believer does not come to that mount at all."[99] James Borland, former president of the Evangelical Theological Society, argues that "the church is not found in the Old Testament. Rather, the Old Testament anticipates [the] Messiah's kingdom. . . . But when the Jewish leaders and people rejected Christ's offer of the kingdom, especially as seen in Matthew 11–12, Jesus announced something new—the church."[100]

In this view, the Church isn't the fulfillment of God's plan for Israel so much as his back-up plan. But while God's plan for the Church was a radical break from his plan for Israel, the plan for Israel remains in place.[101] Liberty

University's Thomas Ice argues that "the church is unique in the plan of God and separate from his plan for Israel. The church partakes of the spiritual promises of the Abrahamic covenant as fulfilled through Christ, but Israel—and not the church—will fulfill its national destiny as a separate entity." As a result, these dispensationalists believe in a "church age" running from Pentecost until the Rapture, after which point "the church has no earthly prophetic destiny."[102] This poor ecclesiology partially accounts for the overwhelming support for the modern state of Israel among (particularly older) American Evangelicals.[103] The core problem here is that it treats Christ and the Church not as the fulfillment of God's promises to Israel, but as something radically distinct, two completely different religions duct-taped together, or running independently, alongside one another.

This is a sharp contrast from the way the Bible speaks of the New Covenant fulfilling the Old, or the way Jesus speaks of the gathering-in of the Gentiles, or the way St. Paul speaks of the *ingrafting* of the Gentiles. Paul describes Israel as an olive tree and says that "some of the branches were broken off," while these Gentile converts "were grafted in their place to share the richness of the olive tree" (Rom. 11:17). He reminds his Gentile readers, "They were broken off because of their unbelief, but you stand fast only through faith. So do not become proud, but stand in awe. For if God did not spare the natural branches, neither will he spare you" (20–21). Paul is clearly not describing the wholesale replacement of one covenant people with another, nor is he describing two separate plants, one Jewish and one Gentile (it's hard to understand how anyone could read the epistle to the Romans and come away with that message). Instead, he's saying he continues to prune and maintain the olive tree, the People of God that began with Israel. With the arrival of Christ and the formation of the Church, you have not the disregarding of Israel, but the pruning: those Jews who reject Christ are cast off, and those Gentiles who accept him are grafted in.

This understanding of ingrafting is critical for understanding the Church. It's for this reason that Church Fathers like St. Augustine can speak of the body of Christ as existing "from Abel the just right up to the end of the world."[104] And this is what Jesus means when he warns the chief priests and Pharisees that "the kingdom of God will be taken away from you and given to a nation producing the fruits of it" (Matt. 21:43). He means nearly the antithesis of the popular dispensationalist view that "the kingdom of God does not exist at all during the church age because it has been removed from Israel and will be reestablished on earth at Christ's second coming."[105] Rather, the hardhearted Pharisees and chief priests are broken off the olive tree that is the kingdom, while faithful Gentiles will be grafted in.

Jesus isn't throwing out Israel; he's just evicting some of the faithless tenants and inviting in new ones. This means that the Church is still Israel, simply reorganized. After all, the New Covenant is made between God and "the house of Israel" (Heb. 8:8–12). This is why Paul can say that "he is a Jew who is one inwardly, and real circumcision is a matter of the heart, spiritual and not literal" (Rom. 2:29) and can end his letter to the Christians of Galatia by saying, "Peace and mercy be upon all who walk by this rule, upon the Israel of God" (Gal. 6:16). The Church isn't God's "plan B" after (some of) the Jews rejected Jesus.[106] It's the full expression of the New Covenant that he'd been promising all along.

This informs how we approach the question of the Church as a visible society. As we've seen, Israel has always been a visible society, and throughout this process of ingrafting, as

Israel fulfills its destiny in becoming the Church, opening its doors to the Gentiles, there's no transition in which it suddenly turns invisible. Quite the contrary: Jesus says, "I have other sheep, that are not of this fold; I must bring them also, and they will heed my voice. So there shall be one flock, one shepherd" (John 10:16). In other words, the ingrafting occurs by *gathering the Gentiles together.* If he merely meant that there would continue to be God-fearing Gentiles and God-fearing Jews, but that their identities would be known only to him, that was already true. For his promise to be meaningful, there must be some way in which the Gentiles and Jews are *visibly* gathered together in one place: the flock of Christ.

Not only is this New Covenant community visible, but it's structured as well. In a sermon preached against the Catholic priesthood, John MacArthur claims:

> We don't need any priests. Revelation 1, "You are a kingdom of priests." We only need one high priest and it's not the pope. We have one mediator, the man Christ Jesus. The veil is torn. We go right into the Holy of Holies. You are a priest and I am a priest unto God.[107]

It's clear that MacArthur is comfortable affirming that there are no priests, that we're all priests, and that only Christ is a priest. The one position he rejects is that *some* of us are priests, because "the reformers rejected completely the idea of a special priesthood." But this is exactly what God promises about the New Covenant, when he says of the faithful Gentiles, "*Some of them* also I will take for priests and for Levites" (Isa. 66:21).

The Israel in the Old Testament was "a kingdom of priests and a holy nation" (Exod. 19:6) that still had a sacrificial priesthood consisting of some of the members of the tribe of Levi. One of the Levites, Korah, turns against this special priesthood, saying, "All the congregation are holy, every one of them, and the Lord is among them; why then do you exalt yourselves above the assembly of the Lord?" (Num. 16:3). Korah and his followers are then swallowed into the earth in a literal schism when they attempt to offer sacrifice on their own (32). Likewise, the "Israel of God," the Church, is "a royal priesthood, a holy nation" (1 Pet. 2:9), that nevertheless has a sacerdotal priesthood. This priesthood fulfills the prophecy through Malachi that "in every place incense is offered to my name, and a pure offering; for my name is great among the nations, says the Lord of hosts" (Mal. 1:11). St. Jude warns against those in the Church who "reject authority" and "perish in Korah's rebellion" (Jude 1:8, 11).

In the last chapter, we saw how treating the Church as the invisible collection of the saved is both untenable and contrary to Scripture. In this chapter, we looked at some of the evidence pointing to the Church being a visible, structured society, a city on a hill, and the fuller blossoming of Israel. The question that remains for the rest of this book is this: if this is true, what role (if any) does Jesus entrust to Pope St. Peter and his successors?

4

SERVANT OF THE SERVANTS OF GOD

PERHAPS THE CLEAREST teaching on the papacy is at the Last Supper. That may surprise some readers. After all, there's an all too common misconception that the Catholic claim for the papacy boils down entirely to Jesus' words to Peter in Matthew 16:18 ("upon this rock, I will build my church") and the identification of the rock with Peter himself. To be sure, we'll cover that ground later in this book, but it's more important to start with the Last Supper. It's there, after all, that we find the Twelve arguing (once again) over which of them is the greatest. Here Jesus spends a great deal of time imparting final words of wisdom to the Twelve before his passion and death. In other words, given the context, this is precisely where we would *expect* to find Jesus talking about structures of authority within the Church.

Some Protestants find the fact that Jesus is still having to answer these questions as a sort of argument from silence against the papacy. One author objected, "Why did the disciples even ask the question if Jesus had already established Peter as the authority? Obviously, they did not understand

Jesus' statement about the rock, as recorded in Matthew 16, as referring to Peter as the head of the church."[108] This much is surely true. At this point, the Twelve still don't have a full and clear understanding of the papacy. But this is hardly an argument against the papacy. After Jesus prophesied his death and resurrection, we find the Twelve quietly "questioning what the rising from the dead meant" (Mark 9:10), so the confusion of the Twelve is no indication that Jesus had been silent on this point. And this isn't even the first time that Jesus has had to answer the question about which of them is the greatest (cf. Luke 9:46–48). So the mere fact that the Twelve are asking which of them is the greatest is hardly evidence that Jesus hasn't already answered the question.

A related objection is that if the papacy is true, we might expect to hear about it from Jesus here. In the words of a nineteenth-century Protestant poet:

> When the twelve had a strife, who should greatest be
>   made,
> And this on the night when their Lord was betrayed,
> Why did not Christ tell them, to quiet the strife
> "I've made Peter Prince, I've crowned him for life;
> And when I depart, he my vicar shall be,
> And you all must submit unto him as to me."[109]

What the poem gets right is that we *should* expect to see something related to the papacy in Jesus' response. What it gets wrong, as with the other Protestant critiques, is that it's imagining a funhouse distortion of what Catholics believe about the papacy. In other words, it's *not* the Catholic belief that the pope is to be a tyrant king viewed as equal to Christ. As we'll see, Jesus *does* "crown" Peter, but with a different sort of leadership.

The Kingship of the Apostles

Before we get to what Jesus said to Peter, it's important to understand the setting. The Twelve are debating over greatness once again, and Jesus responds in a new way. In the past, Jesus called their attention to the heights of holiness by placing a child in their midst and saying, "Whoever humbles himself like this child, he is the greatest in the kingdom of heaven" (Matt. 18:4). But here at the Last Supper, he will speak of a different sort of greatness: authority. "The kings of the Gentiles exercise lordship over them; and those in authority over them are called benefactors. But not so with you; rather let the greatest among you become as the youngest, and the leader as one who serves" (Luke 22:25–26).

In contrasting the authority of the Twelve with that of the "kings of the Gentiles," Jesus' comparison presupposes that the Twelve have some kind of royal authority, but of a different kind from what they were accustomed to among the Gentiles. Indeed, the word he uses that's translated here as "leader" is *hēgeomai*, the same word used to describe the "*ruler* who will govern my people Israel" (Matt. 2:6) and the same word St. Stephen uses to describe Joseph as "*governor* over Egypt" (Acts 7:10). A few verses later, the implicit kingship being promised the Twelve is made explicit: "As my Father appointed a kingdom for me, so do I appoint for you that you may eat and drink at my table in my kingdom, and sit on thrones judging the twelve tribes of Israel" (Luke 22:29–30). Craig A. Evans is probably correct that "judging" here is not punitive (like condemning), but "administrative and judicial."[110] It is remarkable that this promise has received so little commentary, and has gone so little-noticed among Christians, because it ought to revolutionize the way in which we revere the apostles.

There is a view popular among some Protestants that God is jealous of his glory, such that he would never share it with Mary or the saints. Such objections are regularly raised against the Catholic practice of venerating the saints. Some of this distorted view of God arose from a misreading of a single Bible verse, stripped of context: in this case, Isaiah 42:8, which says "I am the Lord, that is my name; my glory I give to no other, nor my praise to graven images." The context there is pretty clearly that God doesn't share his glory with any other *gods.*

Whatever the origin, we find this distorted view of God and glory put forth by several prominent Evangelicals, including former megachurch pastor James MacDonald, who claims, "God won't share his glory, and it's folly to seek it."[111] Jesus says *the exact opposite.* In a prayer to the Father at the end of the Last Supper, he says, "The glory which thou hast given me I have given to them, that they may be one even as we are one" (John 17:22). Indeed, he criticizes those who *don't* seek this glory that comes from God: "How can you believe, who receive glory from one another and do not seek the glory that comes from the only God?" (5:44). St. Paul promises "glory and honor and peace for every one who does good," and that "to those who by patience in well-doing seek for glory and honor and immortality, he will give eternal life" (Rom. 2:10,7). So seeking God's glory isn't folly; it's *salvific.*

It's for this reason that Paul can say to the Corinthians that "we all, with unveiled face, beholding the glory of the Lord, are being changed into his likeness from one degree of glory to another" (2 Cor. 3:18), and why he can challenge them, "And would that you did reign, so that we might share the rule with you!" (1 Cor. 4:8). To St. Timothy, he promises that "if we endure, we shall also reign with him" (2 Tim.

2:12), just as the book of Revelation proclaims that Christ has made the ransomed Christians into "a kingdom and priests to our God, and they shall reign on earth" (Rev. 5:10). Christ promises that "he who conquers and who keeps my works until the end, I will give him power over the nations, and he shall rule them with a rod of iron" (2:26–27). This is a sharing in *Christ's own divine governance*, as Revelation 12:5 and 19:15 make clear. And although there is a sense in which every Christian is called to share in this, a special place is foretold for the Twelve and for the mother of God (cf. Rev. 12).

There are two starkly contrasting visions of glory being put forward here. The first, a view found within various forms of Protestantism, is one in which God jealously guards his glory, refusing to share it with us. In the words of one megachurch pastor, "Salvation is a work of God and only God. There is glory to be given for this incredible work. It is not going to be a glory given to man in any way, shape, or form because all things are ultimately for the glory of God."[112] This view of glory is *zero-sum*, meaning that if God gives us glory, he has a little less. But the other view, the one preached by Jesus Christ and the apostles (and with a special emphasis by Paul) is that God calls us to pursue heavenly glory and to *share in it*. It's why Paul considers present afflictions merely as "preparing for us an eternal weight of glory beyond all comparison" (2 Cor. 4:17). The problem with the binary view is that it imagines us as rivals to God rather than his children. A parent is glorified when his son excels. It's why we can honor our father and mother, and praise the well lived lives of the saints, without offending or diminishing God's supreme honor. Ultimately, as one nineteenth-century priest pointed out, "all honor redounds to God, because without his grace the greatest saint that ever lived might have been the greatest sinner."[113]

This is true of the honor of office as well as the honor of sanctity. Understanding this is key to making sense of an apparent biblical contradiction. Jesus tells us to "render to Caesar the things that are Caesar's, and to God the things that are God's" (Luke 20:25), yet *everything* belongs to God. Plus, doesn't he warn us that "no one can serve two masters; for either he will hate the one and love the other, or he will be devoted to the one and despise the other" (Matt. 6:24)? How can we harmonize these two sayings? Jesus does it for us before Pilate, when he says, "You would have no power over me unless it had been given you from above" (John 19:11). Paul likewise teaches that everyone should "be subject to the governing authorities," for "there is no authority except from God, and those that exist have been instituted by God," such that "he who resists the authorities resists what God has appointed" (Rom. 13:1–2; Peter says something similar in 1 Pet. 2:13–14).

What does this have to do with the papacy? A great deal. Many of the arguments against the papacy are rooted in this binary view—that Jesus *or* Peter is the rock, and that if Peter has any authority, honor, or glory, it must come at Christ's expense. But if we are to have any chance of understanding Jesus' words at the Last Supper, to recognize the kingship of the Twelve generally and Peter specifically in the plan of Christ, then we need to be free from the blinders of the binary view.

The Eternal Role of the Church

Another aspect of Christ's words worth noting is the eternal perseverance of the Church. Certain Protestant theologians, particularly those influenced by dispensationalism, will sometimes speak (as *Grace to You*'s John MacArthur does) of "the time between the first and second comings of Christ" as "the church age."[114]

We see this view rebutted in Christ's words to the Twelve. To the Twelve, a small band of faithful Jewish believers, he says, "You are those who have continued with me in my trials; as my Father appointed a kingdom for me, so do I appoint for you that you may eat and drink at my table in my kingdom, and sit on thrones judging the twelve tribes of Israel" (Luke 22:28–30). It's a witness to the fact that the Church isn't an instrument in the hands of God fit to be disposed and replaced, or an unintended "parenthesis" or divine plan B. Rather, St. Paul speaks of the Church as the body of Christ and the Bride of Christ, mystically united to Christ (Eph. 5:23–32), and most shockingly as his "body, the fullness of him who fills all in all" (1:23).

This is important context for understanding the papacy in the plan of Christ. Many Protestants approach the question as if, after centuries of carefully preparing Israel, creating particular offices and commanding specific structures, and generally cultivating a specific model of leadership, God suddenly became indifferent to the nature and structure of the Church, leaving it up to us to decide for ourselves. This runs directly contrary to both the letter and spirit of Christ's promise: "*I* will build my church" (Matt. 16:18). A good test is this: what would Christianity look like if Christ *didn't* establish the Church? After all, if Christ hadn't established the Church, we would still expect to see Christians organizing (just as the followers of many of the world's great religious and moral figures have formed schools of thought during their leaders' lifetimes or after their deaths). The difference is that we wouldn't expect those manmade organizations, well-meaning though they may be, to be unified or to interpret their leader in the same way. Peter Kreeft poses the question well:

Suppose he had not established a single, visible church with authority to teach in his name. Suppose he had left it up to us. Suppose the Church was our invention instead of his, only human and not divine. Suppose *we* had to figure out the right doctrine of the Trinity, the two natures of Christ, the sacraments, Mary, and controversial moral issues like contraception and homosexuality and euthanasia. Who then could ever know with certainty the mind and will of God? How could there then be one Church?[115]

Instead, Kreeft argues, we would expect in such a world to find numerous Christian denominations teaching contrary doctrines. The implication is clear: Protestantism looks as though it's not established by Christ. That is, it *looks* and *acts* like a group of people creating their own church as a way of honoring Christ, rather than what we would expect to see if Christ had built his own church. If the Church is manmade, then we shouldn't spend much time debating its organization or structure. On the other hand, if we understand the Church to be something that (a) has been part of the plan of Christ from the beginning, (b) is mystically united to Christ as his body and Bride, and (c) will exist forever, even in heaven, then we should care a great deal about the Church's nature and structure.

Strengthen Thy Brethren

Our Lord now turns his attention from the Twelve to St. Peter, saying: "Simon, Simon, behold, Satan demanded to have you, that he might sift you like wheat, but I have prayed for you that your faith may not fail; and when you have turned again, strengthen your brethren" (Luke 22:31–32). In and of itself, this is a remarkable passage, although much is lost in translation. The *Enduring Word* biblical commentary remarks on this verse that "Satan wanted to completely crush and defeat Peter."[116] But this fundamentally misunderstands the verse. It's about Satan's plan to crush and defeat not Peter, but all of them...or all of us.

The error here is simple. Unlike Hebrew and Greek, today's English lacks a formal "you-plural." As a result, we miss an important shift in Jesus' words from you-plural to you-singular in this passage. Fortunately, there are still plenty of regional or slangy options: depending on where you're from, you might use *y'all, youse, yinz, you guys, you lot*, or something else. The passage is clearer if we plug in a you-plural so we can understand what's going on. Now it reads, "Simon, Simon, behold, Satan demanded to have you all, that he might sift all of you like wheat, but I have prayed for *you* that your faith may not fail; and when you have turned again, strengthen your brethren." Now we can see the important shift that's obvious in the Greek but lost in the English—that Satan is out for *all twelve* (and, more broadly, all of Jesus' followers), and that Jesus responds by praying for *one of them*, Peter, and then commissioning *him* to strengthen the others.

How Might a Protestant Respond?

What might Protestants say in response to this passage? Keith Mathison, in *The Shape of Sola Scriptura*, writes that Peter

> overestimates his own faith despite Jesus' warning. That is an especially dangerous place for any believer to be, and therefore Jesus, because of his love for Peter, prays especially for him. . . . This text in Luke 22 is a beautiful picture of our Lord's love and concern for Peter. It has absolutely no bearing on the question of the papacy.[117]

To be sure, part of what's going on here is that Peter's going to deny Christ three times. But that doesn't really explain the phrase "strengthen your brethren." This isn't as much exegesis as a hand-waving dismissal. The problem with Mathison's read is clear from John Calvin's commentary on the passage, in which he notes that *all* of the Twelve are described as making similar boasts, and all are described as falling away. "Peter said to him, 'Even if I must die with you, I will not deny you.' *And so said all the disciples*" (Matt. 26:35). Calvin rightly notes that the fact that they should do this even "after Peter had been reproved" shows "how little they knew themselves."[118] And Jesus warns that *all* of the Twelve, not just Peter, are about to fall away: "You will all fall away because of me this night" (31). Sure enough, after Jesus' arrest, "*all the disciples* forsook him and fled" (56).

So why do we focus on Peter's denial? Two reasons. One is simply that Peter doubles back and "followed him at a distance" (Matt. 26:58), while most of the Twelve are nowhere to be found. Only he allows himself to be put into harm's way again, either out of love of Christ or an overestimation of his own strength, or both. The second is that Peter is consistently held to a higher standard throughout the Gospels. When all of the Twelve fall asleep in the Garden, it's only one who gets rebuked: Peter (Matt. 26:40; Mark 14:37). Jesus explains this principle expressly: "Every one to whom much is given, of him will much be required; and of him to whom men commit much they will demand the more" (Luke 12:48). Why is more expected of Peter? Because more has been entrusted to him.

By itself, then, Luke 22:31–32 is a remarkable passage, and it seems to say Peter has a unique commission among the apostles. All of the Twelve are boasting of their fidelity to Christ, Satan plans to sift all of them like wheat, and they will all fall away. Jesus' response is to fortify *one of them*, St. Peter, by praying for him specifically, and commissioning him to "strengthen your brethren." He gives this commission to Peter alone, in front of the other apostles. Now connect it to the broader scriptural context. The Twelve have just been arguing about who the greatest is, and Christ has explained to them that the leader is to be "as one who serves" (Luke 22:26), giving himself as the perfect model: "For which is the greater, one who sits at table, or one who serves? Is it not the one who sits at table? But I am among you as one who serves" (27). He then calls Peter to serve the other apostles.

Understood within this context, Jesus is calling Peter to leadership, but of a specific kind: what we might call *servant leadership*. This is an important counter to many of the arguments against the papacy. Broadly speaking, there are two categories of "disproofs" of the papacy—when popes seem to act arrogantly and when they don't. In the first category, the objection is simple: if Peter and subsequent popes are called to be servant-leaders, to strengthen their brothers, what do we make of popes who *don't* live like this (at least by our own assessment)? We'll look at this problem more closely in the chapter on "bad popes," but for now, perhaps it will suffice to say this: Jesus is saying how Church leadership *ought* to look. He says to "let the greatest among you become as the youngest, and the leader as one who serves" (Luke 22:26) while giving himself as the model leader, but he never says, "The leader loses his authority if he fails to live up to my example." St. Paul likewise calls husbands to "love your wives, as Christ loved the church and gave himself up for her" (Eph. 5:25), but it doesn't invalidate the marriage when husbands fail to meet this standard.

St. Peter, Fellow Presbyter

A stranger objection is at the opposite extreme. Some Christians (both Catholics and Protestants) have a sort of distorted mental image of the papacy, in which the pope is supposed to decide *everything* and supposed to throw his authority around. This is never what biblical headship looks like, whether we're talking about a family, a nation, or a church. But nevertheless, we find certain Protestant authors who will object (in essence) that because Peter was humble, he couldn't have been pope. A key passage in this debate is 1 Peter 5:1, in which Peter says, "I exhort the elders among you, as your fellow elder and witness of the sufferings of Christ." Peter's humility here parallels St. Paul's usage of terms like "my fellow prisoner" (Philem. 1:23), "our beloved fellow worker" (1), "my brother and fellow worker and fellow soldier" (Phil. 2:25), "my kinsmen and my fellow prisoners" (Rom. 16:7), and "my partner and fellow worker in your service" (2 Cor. 8:23), and his self-description as a "servant of Christ" (1 Cor. 3:5; 2 Cor. 11:23).

After all, Peter could cite his authority but doesn't. There's no question that apostles and elders are distinct: the two orders are distinguished no fewer than five times within Acts 15 alone. And there's no question that Peter is an apostle (Matt. 10:2), not merely an elder. But just as Paul forwent some of his rights as an apostle (cf. 1 Cor. 9), we see Peter declining to explicitly invoke his apostolic authority. In approaching his readers in this way, Peter can be read as leading with humility and rooting his spiritual counsel in shared experience rather than the authority of his office.[119] The Baptist theologians Michael S. Wilder and Timothy Paul Jones rightly note that Peter "is not denying the importance of his apostolic role when he refers to himself as a fellow elder. If anything, he is deepening our understanding of what it meant to be an apostle. We should understand that the apostolic office included the work of an elder."[120]

But some Protestant apologists view this servant leadership as somehow debunking Peter's role as the first pope. For instance, CARM's Matt Slick objects that "if Peter was supreme among the apostles, why does he state that he is a fellow elder instead of asserting his supremacy?"[121] The English Methodist John Benson (1749–1821) likewise argues:

> So Peter, the first, and one of the chief, though not the head, of the apostles, appositely and modestly styles himself. Commentators justly observe, that if Peter had been the prince of the apostles, as the Papists affirm, he would in this place, and in the inscription of his two epistles, certainly have assumed to himself that high prerogative.[122]

So if Peter is an apostle, but doesn't insist upon his office, that's apposite and modest, and helps us to better understand the servant leadership to which apostles are called. But if Peter is a pope, but doesn't insist upon his office, that somehow disproves the papacy. It should be clear that this double standard is rooted in a false vision of the papacy, one incompatible with humble leadership. In this view, any time that Peter or his successors act in the way that Christ called them to act, they're repudiating their office. One might just as well ask why Jesus washed the feet of the Twelve at the Last Supper, instead of "assum[ing] to himself that high prerogative." The simple answer is that the papacy doesn't, and shouldn't, look like an overbearing boss, or a Gentile emperor, or whatever strawman vision of the papacy these critics are assuming.

Strikingly, the early Christians understood what Slick and Benson fail to grasp: that "fellow presbyter" is a *great* way of understanding the pope's role as a servant of the servants of God and a co-laborer in the vineyard. In the year 397, a local council of North African bishops assembled to discuss the canon of Scripture—that is, which books belong in the Bible. The canon that they agreed upon is the same one used today by the Catholic Church (and, strangely, is often cited favorably by Protestants who seem unaware that their own Bible lacks seven of the books included by Carthage).[123] In 419, a copy of this biblical canon was sent to Pope Boniface with the inscription: "Let this be made known to our brother and fellow-priest Boniface, or to other bishops of those parts, for the purpose of confirming that canon, because we have received from our fathers that those books must be read in the Church. . . . Let it also be allowed that the Passions of Martyrs be read when their festivals are kept."[124] Referring to Pope Boniface as "fellow-priest" should be read as intentionally evoking Peter's self-description as "fellow presbyter."[125]

This is the meaning behind Jesus' words to Peter at the Last Supper. Yes, he is to be a leader of sorts for the apostles, but he's to be a *servant leader*, who leads in order to strengthen his brother bishops and fellow priests. It's the clearest of many biblical indications that the Petrine office exists not for the pope, but for the good of the Church.

5

THE GOOD SHEPHERD CALLS A SHEPHERD

WHAT DOES IT take to become a pastor? According to the popular Protestant site 9Marks,[126] "There seems to be no biblical indication that the New Testament office of elder or pastor requires a special 'calling.'"[127] Such a view is controversial even within Protestantism. A better biblical interpretation comes from Erwin Lutzer, pastor emeritus of the nondenominational Moody Church in Chicago,[128] who says, "God's call is an inner conviction given by the Holy Spirit and confirmed by the word of God and the body of Christ."[129] In other words, the question is whether being a pastor is an *occupation* ("a being employed in something") or a *vocation* (a "spiritual calling," from the Latin *vocare*, "to call").[130]

The biblical evidence is clear that pastoral leadership within the Church is a vocation to which one must be called by God, not simply an occupation to be pursued. This is the clear model of leadership throughout Scripture, from God's calling of Abraham as the first patriarch (Gen. 12:1; Isa. 51:2) down to the Jewish priesthood. As the epistle to the Hebrews notes, "Every high priest chosen from among men is appointed to act on behalf of men in relation to God, to offer gifts and sacrifices for sins," and "one does not take the honor upon himself, but he is called by God, just as Aaron was" (Heb. 5:1, 4). This was also the case for the prophets. As the Lord says to Jeremiah, "Before I formed you in the womb I knew you, and before you were born I consecrated you; I appointed you a prophet to the nations" (Jer. 1:5). Even in the selection of kings, we find a need for God's calling. Part of the reason seems to be, as the Lord said through Samuel in choosing King David, that "the Lord sees not as man sees; man looks on the outward appearance, but the Lord looks on the heart" (1 Sam. 16:7).[131]

Does God quit calling leaders in the New Testament? Not at all. Through Jeremiah, God had also promised, "I will give you shepherds after my own heart, who will feed you with knowledge and understanding" (Jer. 3:15). In other words, New Testament shepherds (which is what the word "pastors" means, after all) are given by God, not simply by their own ambition or by popular acclaim. This is illustrated throughout the New Testament. After spending the night in prayer, Jesus "called his disciples, and chose from them twelve, whom he named apostles" (Luke 6:13). Or as St. Mark puts it, Jesus "went up into the hills, and called to him those whom he desired; and they came to him. And he appointed twelve, to be with him, and to be sent out to preach and have authority to cast out demons" (Mark 3:13–15).

After Judas's death, St. Peter quoted Psalm 108 ("His office let another take," cf. Acts 1:20) to announce that one of the men "who have accompanied us during all the time that the Lord Jesus went in and out among us, beginning from the baptism of John until the day when he was taken up from us—one of these men must become with us a witness to his resurrection" (Acts 1:21–22). The assembled brethren then choose two men who meet these qualifications: "Joseph called Barsabbas, who was surnamed Justus, and Matthias" (23). But the acclaim of the people is not enough. They all then turned to prayer, and the casting of lots, to let the Lord have the final say (24–26).

This need for a calling isn't limited to the apostles in the New Testament Church. According to Jesus, one of the critical distinctions between a true pastor and a "thief and robber" is whether or not the man has a calling from Christ (John 10:1–5):

> Truly, truly, I say to you, he who does not enter the sheepfold by the door but climbs in by another way, that man is a thief and a robber; but he who enters by the door is the shepherd of the sheep. To him the gatekeeper opens; the sheep hear his voice, and he calls his own sheep by name and leads them out. When he has brought out all his own, he goes before them, and the sheep follow him, for they know his voice. A stranger they will not follow, but they will flee from him, for they do not know the voice of strangers.

Lest there be any confusion, he adds, "I am the door of the sheep" (John 10:7). So the man who simply declares himself to be a pastor, then, is no true shepherd. He is merely a "thief and a robber," stealing sheep from the flock of Christ. The true shepherd must be called by Christ himself.

How do we know if a man is called by Christ, instead of being a robber or a thief? Erwin Lutzer proposes three criteria: first, "an inner conviction," which he distinguishes from "feelings and hunches" which can come and go; second, scriptural confirmation of the call, ensuring that "a person has the qualifications listed in 1 Timothy 3"; and finally, "the body of Christ helps us understand where we fit within the local church framework."[132] Although 9Marks is leery of a "special, supernatural, subjective call from God," the site also points to the attributes listed in 1 Timothy 3 as the qualifications needed and affirms that the man "should also have a local church's affirmation of his gifts and character." Neither Lutzer nor 9Marks goes so far as to say the Church can refuse ordination to an objectively qualified candidate who desires to become a pastor. That's a contrast from the Church of the New Testament. By all accounts, Barsabbas was objectively qualified to replace Judas as an apostle. Nothing in Scripture gives us any reason to doubt either his "gifts" or "character." Indeed, there were likely a great many of the 120 assembled brethren who met the criteria laid out by Peter in Acts 1:21–22. But only one man, St. Matthias, was chosen.

A better understanding of pastoral calling comes from St. Francis de Sales (1567–1622), who points out that whenever the Lord sends anyone, he does so in one of two ways. The first way, which he called "immediate" or "extraordinary" mission, is "when God himself commands and gives a charge, without the interposition of the ordinary authority which he has placed in the prelates and pastors of the Church."[133] He gives the examples of Jesus sending the apostles (Matt. 28:19) and God sending Moses to Pharaoh (Exod. 3:10) and points out that anyone claiming to be sent directly from God should be able to "prove it by miracles: for I pray you, where should we be if this pretext of extraordinary mission was to be accepted without proof?"[134]

But the ordinary way that God sends people isn't through this kind of miraculous revelation. It's through the body of Christ, the Church. More specifically, it's a top-down process. Although qualified candidates might be suggested by the Christian people, they must ultimately be ordained by the laying on of hands. In selecting the first deacons, Peter urged the brethren to "pick out from among you seven men of good repute, full of the Spirit and of wisdom, whom we may appoint to this duty" (Acts 6:3). But although seven qualified candidates were put forward by the brethren, it was still left to the apostles to do the actual appointing and ordaining: "These [men] they set before the apostles, and they prayed and laid their hands upon them" (6). And this laying on of hands isn't automatic or a mere formality. St. Paul, who reminds St. Timothy "to rekindle the gift of God that is within you through the laying on of my hands" (2 Tim. 1:6) also warns him, "Do not be hasty in the laying on of hands," but "keep yourself pure" (1 Tim. 5:22). Paul likewise tells St. Titus that the reason "I left you in Crete" was "that you might amend what was defective, and appoint elders in every town as I directed you" (Titus 1:5).

Besides direct divine revelation (extraordinary sending) and ordination through the leadership of the Church (ordinary sending), there's no third option. Nothing in Christianity permits you to simply go and start your own church because you're a gifted speaker or preacher. Indeed, so thoroughly does the Bible (in both the New and Old Testament) reject such an approach that when Paul speaks of the need for evangelization, he asks, "But how are men to call upon him in whom they have not believed? And how are they to believe in him of whom they have never heard? And how are they to hear without a preacher? *And how can men preach unless they are sent?*" (Rom. 10:14–15). It's unthinkable, in his mind, that a man would just go to preach because he felt as though the job needed doing, or because he felt personally qualified. That's not enough. Instead, the preacher must first be *sent*.

This is a different Paul from the caricature one sometimes hears of a rogue apostle, operating entirely independently of the Twelve and the visible structure of the Church. The Paul of the Bible presents himself as one who had an extraordinary sending by Jesus Christ (Gal. 1:11–17), which he nevertheless confirmed with Peter (1:18) and then the other apostles (1–10). Ultimately, it was the Holy Spirit who said through the church at Antioch, "Set apart for me Barnabas and Saul for the work to which I have called them" (Acts 13:2; cf. 13:9). And so we find Paul being sent by Christ, by the Church, and by the Spirit speaking through the Church.

We see this relationship with the Church on full display when Paul and Barnabas run into a group of men teaching a contrary doctrine. In Acts 15:1, Paul encounters these so-called "Judaizers." By the next verse, we read that "when Paul and Barnabas had no small dissension and debate with them, Paul and Barnabas and some of the others were appointed to go up to Jerusalem to the apostles and the elders about this question" (Acts 15:2). It turns out, it was these other men who were preaching without authorization, and the resultant Council of Jerusalem laments "that some persons from us have troubled you with words, unsettling your minds, *although we gave them no instructions*," and remedies the situation by sending Paul, Barnabas, and two other men (24–27).

In other words, part of the problem that the Church recognized wasn't just that there were men preaching false doctrines. It was that these were men who tried to *send themselves* to preach, and to disastrous effect. The solution was therefore not merely a theological one, correcting the doctrine. It was also an ecclesial one, sending Church-commissioned orthodox preachers to replace the self-appointed heretical ones. Paul would later identify these two distinct problems in his description of the Judaizers as "insubordinate men" as well as "empty talkers and deceivers" (Titus 1:10). Their insubordination was rejecting the authority of the visible Church by assuming for themselves the mantle of preacher.

This biblical view, that a pastor or preacher must be sent either miraculously or through the leadership of the visible Church, is ultimately fatal to the Protestant position. Amazingly, Martin Luther seemed to recognize this. In a homily on John 10, in which Jesus contrasts the shepherds called by Christ from robbers and thieves, Luther explained:

> No one should step into the office and preach from his own presumption and without a commission from those having the authority. But under present conditions, if we should wait until we received a commission to preach and to administer the sacraments, we would never perform those offices as long as we live.[135]

In other words, Luther recognized that what he was doing was the sort of presumptuous behavior condemned by Christ in the gospel he was preaching. But he reasoned that just this once, the evil was necessary, since otherwise, he wouldn't ever get to perform the office. But that's the whole point: Christ leaves the Church with the ability to refuse pastoral office to those whom the Church chooses. To say the other party's consent is important unless it keeps you from getting what you want is merely another way of saying that you don't really care about consent.

Moreover, it's never just this once. Once you decide it's okay to ignore the order set up by Christ when it won't get you what you want, you'll find more and more reasons to do so. After all, it would be absurd to require the second generation of Protestants to obey the commandments that the first generation of Protestants disregarded. Moreover, how could those who were never sent in the first place be tasked with passing on the ministry to the next generation? If the first generation of Reformers were "thieves and robbers," the mere passage of time doesn't turn them into proper gatekeepers. And it's precisely in this way that we end up today with a situation in which neither Lutzer nor 9Marks has much of a role for the Church other than to confirm an aspiring pastor's gifts and talents and to help him understand where he fits "within the local church framework." It's a sheepfold without a gate, because so many successive generations of pastors have grown accustomed to climbing in "by another way" (John 10:1).

Contrast this with the call of Peter. We know that Peter, as one of the apostles, was called to be a shepherd over the People of God. This is clear from Matthew's account:

> When [Jesus] saw the crowds, he had compassion for them, because they were harassed and helpless, like sheep without a shepherd. Then he said to his disciples, "The harvest is plentiful, but the laborers are few; pray therefore the Lord of the harvest to send out laborers into his harvest." And he called to him his twelve disciples and gave them authority over unclean spirits, to cast them out, and to heal every disease and every infirmity. The names of the twelve apostles are these: first, Simon, who is called Peter (Matt. 9:36–10:2).

Jesus' language of "sheep without a shepherd" is an Old Testament allusion. When Moses neared death, he prayed for a successor "that the congregation of the Lord may not be as sheep which have no shepherd" (Num. 27:17), and it was in response to this prayer that Joshua was chosen to succeed Moses. Compare that with what happens in the New Testament. Peter and the other disciples are "successors" of Jesus in a different way from how Joshua was a successor of Moses. Moses wasn't going to be there to assist Joshua, whereas Christ (being God as well as man) promised, "I am with you always, to the close of the age" (Matt. 28:20). So the apostles don't replace Christ in this way, but there is nevertheless a sense in which they are called to continue the mission of Christ in shepherding his people.

In addition to Peter's calling simply as one of the Twelve, there's also biblical evidence for a particular calling to be shepherd over the flock of Christ. As we'll see in greater depth in chapter 7, these pastoral images are connected to fishing images. When Simon Peter expressed astonishment at Jesus performing a miraculous catch of fish through him, Jesus replied to him, "Do not be afraid; henceforth you will be catching men" (Luke 5:10). We'll explore the deeper meaning of this calling in the next chapter, but for now, suffice it to say that it connects with Jesus' image of the kingdom of God as a net of good and bad fish (Matt. 13:47–50), and that the risen Jesus deliberately recalls this image via a second miracle in John 21:6. When the disciples made it back to Jesus on the shore, they discovered "a charcoal fire there, with fish lying on it, and bread" (John 21:9). Each element of the breakfast is significant and evocative. We then find this exchange between Jesus and Peter:

When they had finished breakfast, Jesus said to Simon Peter, "Simon, son of John, do you love me more than these?" He said to him, "Yes, Lord; you know that I love you." He said to him, "Feed my lambs." A second time he said to him, "Simon, son of John, do you love me?" He said to him, "Yes, Lord; you know that I love you." He said to him, "Tend my sheep." He said to him the third time, "Simon, son of John, do you love me?" Peter was grieved because he said to him the third time, "Do you love me?" And he said to him, "Lord, you know everything; you know that I love you." Jesus said to him, "Feed my sheep" (15–17),

This doesn't appear to be simply a generic apostolic mission. During his public ministry, Jesus had already "called to him his twelve disciples and gave them authority over unclean spirits, to cast them out, and to heal every disease and every infirmity." It's in this sending that Matthew goes from calling them "disciples," which means *students*, to "apostles," which means *messengers* (e.g., Matt. 10:1–2). In this apostolic mission, the Twelve were sent to proclaim that "the kingdom of heaven is at hand" and to "heal the sick, raise the dead, cleanse lepers, cast out demons" (Matt. 10:7–8).

Something different is happening here, something specific to Peter. How do we know that? Because Jesus has finished breakfast with several of the Twelve (John 21:2 records that "Simon Peter, Thomas called the Twin, Nathanael of Cana in Galilee, the sons of Zebedee, and two others of his disciples were together") and then singled out one of them, Simon Peter. He then addresses Simon by his family name, as it were: "Simon, son of John." And he doesn't simply ask Peter, "Do you love me?" He asks, "Do you love me *more than these*?" That is, he's quite explicitly asking something from Peter that he wouldn't and couldn't ask from any of the others (since it would be impossible for each of the disciples to love Jesus more than the others do).

If Jesus had meant to call the Twelve in this way, or even to call the seven disciples gathered for breakfast, he could easily have done so. But instead, he draws Peter apart from the rest, asks him for more than the rest, and then tells him (and only him), "Feed my sheep." Understood against the backdrop of the Old Testament, this is a clear call to headship and leadership over the whole people. Recall the Lord's call to David, upon his royal anointing: "You shall be shepherd of my people Israel, and you shall be prince over Israel" (2 Sam. 5). Like Moses before him, this call to lead the people of God came while David was tending sheep (1 Sam. 16:11; cf. Exod. 3:1–2). As the Psalmist would later recount, the Lord "chose David his servant, and took him from the sheepfolds; from tending the ewes that had young he brought him to be the shepherd of Jacob his people, of Israel his inheritance" (Ps. 78:70–71).

The early Christians in both the East and the West understood the significance of this calling. Pope St. Gregory the Great, in a letter to the Emperor Mauricius Augustus, explained, "For to all who know the gospel it is apparent that by the Lord's voice the care of the whole Church was committed to the holy apostle and prince of all the apostles, Peter. For to him it is said, 'Peter lovest thou me?' 'Feed my sheep.'"[136] St. Augustine likewise explained that "to Peter did Christ commend his lambs to be fed, who fed even Peter himself."[137] This distinction neatly captures the difference between Peter, as shepherd over the whole flock, and Jesus, the Good Shepherd who pastors even Peter himself. St. John Chrysostom, one of the most important Church Fathers in the East, likewise explained that Christ shed his blood "that he might win these sheep which he entrusted to Peter and his successors."[138]

How Might a Protestant Respond?

Whether you approach John 21 via a straightforward reading, or through the lens of the Old Testament, or by listening to what the early Christians had to say about it, the conclusion is the same: Jesus is calling St. Peter uniquely to shepherd the entire flock of Christ, the Church. Or to put it another way, Jesus entrusts his entire flock to be fed by Peter.

How might a Protestant respond to this? The most popular way is what's called the *reinstatement theory*.[139] According to this theory, "there can be little doubt but that the whole scene is meant to show us Peter as completely restored to his position of leadership."[140] Or as D.A. Carson puts it, "These verses deal with Peter's reinstatement to service, not with his elevation to primacy."[141] John Calvin argues that this passage exists to show how "Peter was restored to that rank of honor from which he had fallen."

> That treacherous denial, which has been formerly described, had, undoubtedly, rendered him unworthy of the apostleship; for how could he be capable of instructing others in the faith, who had basely revolted from it? He had been made an apostle, but it was along with Judas, and from the time when he had abandoned his post, he had likewise been deprived of the honor of apostleship. Now, therefore, the liberty, as well as the authority, of teaching is restored to him, both of which he had lost through his own fault.[142]

According to Calvin, this also explains why Jesus' words are addressed exclusively to Peter:

> Namely, that being free from every disgraceful stain, he might boldly preach the gospel; and the reason why

Christ thrice appoints him to be a pastor is, that the three denials, by which Peter had brought on himself everlasting shame, may be set aside, and thus may form no barrier to his apostleship, as has been judiciously observed by Chrysostom, Augustine, and Cyril, and most of the other commentators. Besides, nothing was given to Peter by these words, that is not also given to all the ministers of the gospel.[143]

Give this explanation the credit that it deserves. Protestants are right to see parallels between Peter's threefold denial of Christ and his threefold affirmation of Christ. Simon Peter had declared his superior love for Christ by boasting, "Even though they all fall away, I will not" (Mark 14:29). Jesus responds by warning him, "Before the cock crows, you will deny me three times" (26:75). That night, he does just that, denying Christ in response to three different people's questions, while warming himself by a "charcoal fire" (John 18:18). So now Jesus has prepared a charcoal fire (21:9, in the only other time Scripture mentions charcoal fires), and has asked Peter three times to affirm his love for him. And it's true that St. Cyril of Alexandria comments that this is Christ's way of succoring the erring disciple, giving Peter a change to provide "compensation, as it were, to counterbalance his error and set things right. Anyone would grant that a verbal transgression forms the basis of a merely verbal accusation against him, and it can be wiped out in the same way."[144]

But there are important differences between the Church Fathers' views and the reinstatement view. Calvin invokes St. John Chrysostom, St. Augustine, and St. Cyril of Alexandria. The first two of those, as we've just seen, read this passage very differently from how Calvin does. So does Cyril. At the moment of Peter's threefold denial, Calvin speaks of Peter having "brought on himself everlasting shame," while Cyril describes the "incomparable fervor and admirable zeal of his love toward Christ" that Peter showed even in swimming out to Christ before the others (John 21:7). One reason for these contrasting views of Peter is that the Fathers believed that Peter was already forgiven by this point. Augustine speaks of his being "elated by his presumption, prostrated by his denial, *cleansed by his weeping*, approved by his confession," and finally "crowned by his suffering," as Jesus predicted (18).[145]

Cyril sees the forgiveness coming even earlier. At the Last Supper, when Jesus says to Peter, "When you have turned again, strengthen your brethren," Cyril comments that Peter "had not yet sickened with the malady of faithlessness, and already he has received the medicine of forgiveness: not yet had the sin been committed, and he receives pardon: not yet had he fallen, and the saving hand is held out: not yet had he faltered, and he is confirmed."[146] But whether Peter was forgiven pre-emptively or not until his repentant tears (Matt. 26:75), the point is that the Church Fathers aren't actually arguing for the reinstatement view.

That's because the *reinstatement* view cannot sustain a careful reading of Scripture. Peter was not the only one who declared, "Even if I must die with you, I will not deny you," after all. St. Matthew points out that "so said all the disciples." And it wasn't only Peter who failed to live up to these presumptuous claims: "All the disciples forsook him and fled" (Matt. 26:35,56). If Calvin is right that Peter's betrayal of Christ means he is no longer an apostle, it would seem to follow that *none* of the Twelve remains an apostle. Fortunately, Scripture teaches otherwise. When the women return from the empty tomb, they go and proclaim the Resurrection to "the eleven" (Luke 24:9), a numbering that includes Peter (but not Judas) among the disciples on Easter morning. When they heard this, "Peter then came out with the other disciple, and they went toward the tomb" (John 20:3). But how could John be "the other disciple" if Peter's not also a disciple?

Between this moment and the appearance to the disciples that evening, Jesus appears just to Peter (1 Cor. 15:5). St. John Chrysostom explains this by saying that Christ appeared first to "the leader of the whole company and the most faithful: since indeed there was great need of a most faithful soul to be first to receive this sight," so that "he that first confessed him to be Christ was justly also counted worthy first to behold his resurrection."[147] And so, when the two disciples who encounter Christ on the road to Emmaus return to Jerusalem, "they found the eleven gathered together and those who were with them, who said, 'The Lord has risen indeed, and has appeared to Simon!'" (Luke 24:33–34). As they are saying this, Jesus appears to the disciples, calls them his "witnesses," and says, "Behold, I send the promise of my Father upon you; but stay in the city, until you are clothed with power from on high" (48–49). This is a significant moment, because by Calvin's telling, Peter has not yet been "reinstated," which Calvin claims he needs to be in order to "boldly preach the gospel."[148]

John describes what seems to be the same Easter evening resurrection appearance and tells how Jesus appeared to "the disciples" and said, "Peace be with you. As the Father has sent me, even so I send you" and then breathes on them, saying, "Receive the Holy Spirit. If you forgive the sins of any, they are forgiven; if you retain the sins of any, they are retained" (John 20:19–23). An "apostle" is one who is sent (from the Greek *apostolos*, meaning "messenger" or "one who is sent on a mission"). And here Jesus is, explicitly sending them on mission. Are we to believe that at this point Jesus still hasn't forgiven Peter and is unwilling to send him as an apostle?

Finally, look at John 21 itself. The chapter begins: "Jesus revealed himself again to *the disciples* by the Sea of Tiberias" and that "Simon Peter, Thomas called the Twin, Nathanael of Cana in Galilee, the sons of Zebedee, and two others of his disciples were together" (John 21:1–2). Based on the chronology of John 20, we know that the events of John 21 happened at least a week after Easter (perhaps much later—the Evangelist's transition is simply "after this" in John 21:1). For the reinstatement theory to be correct, Peter must not be a disciple or an apostle between his threefold betrayal of Christ on Holy Thursday and his alleged restoration. Yet we find Peter repeatedly numbered among the apostles, repeatedly described as a disciple, and given (along with the others) an apostolic mission to be a witness to Jesus Christ. All of this happens before his alleged restoration to ministry.

D.A. Carson is right to see the two possibilities in this passage as either "Peter's reinstatement to service" or else "his elevation to primacy."[149] But since Peter's apostolic "reinstatement" isn't chronologically or theologically tenable, and since Scripture repeatedly speaks of him as an apostle and a disciple in the period in which Protestant exegetes claim that he wasn't, it's clear that it's not the first of these two interpretations. That leaves the second. If Peter is already an apostle when Jesus is talking to him, then it's clear that Calvin is wrong in saying that "nothing was given to Peter by these words, that is not also given to all the ministers of the gospel."[150] Peter is addressed by name amid a group of seven disciples and given the task of caring for the entire flock of Christ. It's reasonable to conclude that Jesus meant to address these words not to each of the seven disciples gathered, or each of the eleven remaining disciples, or all ministers everywhere, but specifically to "Simon, son of John" (John 21:15–17).

6

JESUS TETHERS PETER TO HIMSELF

ONE OF THE most remarkable interactions between God and man, and one of the most revealing, happens in a small, strange Gospel passage that we typically overlook. It's a short scene from the life of Jesus, six verses in total, and found only in the Gospel of Matthew. In fact, it's fitting that St. Matthew should be the only one to record the event, both because of his interest in showing Jesus' Jewishness and because Matthew was himself a tax collector. Understanding the meaning of this miracle will involve our understanding something about the twelve tribes of Israel and about the way the tax system worked in those days. The passage in question is from Matthew 17 and begins this way (22–25a):

> As they were gathering in Galilee, Jesus said to them, "The Son of man is to be delivered into the hands of men, and they will kill him, and he will be raised on the third day." And they were greatly distressed. When they came to Capernaum, the collectors of the half-shekel tax

[*didrachma*] went up to Peter and said, "Does not your teacher pay the tax?" He said, "Yes."

Jesus is with some or all of the disciples (see Matt. 17:19). They have returned to Capernaum, where Jesus lived (4:13), and it is here that they—or more specifically, St. Peter—are approached about the temple tax.[151] The tax was known in Hebrew as "the half-shekel" or "half-shekel tax" and comes from Exod. 30:13, which says that "each who is numbered in the census shall give this: half a shekel according to the shekel of the sanctuary (the shekel is twenty gerahs), half a shekel as an offering to the Lord."[152]

It is worth noting that the tax collectors go to Peter to find out Christ's opinion, and it is striking that Peter feels comfortable answering on Christ's behalf in this way. Given this, we might expect that Christ would be annoyed with Peter for his impudence, but that's not what we find at all (Matt. 17:25b–27):

And when he [Peter] came home, Jesus spoke to him first, saying, "What do you think, Simon? From whom do kings of the earth take toll or tribute? From their sons or from others?" And when he said, "From others," Jesus said to him, "Then the sons are free. However, not to give offense to them, go to the sea and cast a hook, and take the first fish that comes up, and when you open its mouth you will find a shekel; take that and give it to them for me and for yourself."

The Scandals of Jesus and Peter

Jesus' miracles aren't magic tricks. His supernatural feats always have a pedagogical component—that is, they're always revealing something about God's power, not just reminding us that he has power. In the miracle of the multiplication of loaves (John 6:1–14), for example, we see God's providence for us and his attentiveness to our daily needs, empowering us to pray, "Give us this day our daily bread" (Matt. 6:11). It also draws the crowds to connect Jesus with Moses, who provided the manna in the desert (John 6:31). Further, it shows the crowd that Jesus has the authority to miraculously go beyond the natural physical limitations of ordinary bread, vital context for Jesus' teaching on the Eucharist the next day (25–71).

So what is the significance of this miracle with the coin in the fish's mouth? Jesus explains that it is so as "not to give offense to them" by not paying the tax. This translation obscures something shocking in the Greek: the verb there, (*skandalisōmen*), is in the first-person plural, so a better translation is "lest *we* offend." What's so shocking about that? Try to recall another time where Jesus uses "we" like this. Jesus repeatedly speaks of himself as radically distinct from those around him. There are dozens of instances in which Jesus refers to "my Father" or "your Father," but no instances of him referring to "our Father." John 20:17 is the most blatant example. While speaking to Mary Magdalene, Jesus calls the Father "my Father and your Father," and "my God and your God," notably avoiding saying "our Father" or "our God." Even in the "Our Father" prayer, the "our" is not "Jesus and us." Jesus specifies that the prayer is for "when *you* pray" (Matt. 6:5–9; Luke 11:1–2). There are no instances of him praying it with the disciples, simply teaching it to them.

This would be clearer in a language with *clusivity*. If you tell me, "We're having dinner at six," does that mean I'm invited? It's unclear in English (and Hebrew and Greek) without further context. This is in contrast to languages (such as Chechen) that have clusivity—meaning a different "we" for "us and you" and "us, but not you."[153] So pay attention any time you see Jesus using a "we," and you'll see he consistently uses the "exclusive we," meaning *not you*. Jesus repeatedly takes pains to distinguish himself from his listeners. To the Samaritan woman, he says, "You worship what you do not know; we worship what we know, for salvation is from the Jews" (John 4:22). It's "we" language, but clearly excluding her. It's okay if the Samaritan woman (rightly) associates him with the Jews, but before a Jewish audience, Jesus will remind them that Jesus' distinction still exists. And so, to Nicodemus he says, "We speak of what we know, and bear witness to what we have seen; but you do not receive our testimony" (3:11).[154] The "we" here clearly excludes Nicodemus and seems to include only himself and the Holy Spirit. He immediately adds that he is revealing heavenly things, and that "no one has ascended into heaven but he who descended from heaven, the Son of man" (3:13).

Why is this? Because Jesus shares our human nature, but he is radically unlike us, and his relationship with the Father is different in kind, not just degree, from our relationship with the Father. These carefully worded expressions from his lips don't allow us to forget his humanity in the face of his divinity, or his divinity in the face of his humanity. So it's shocking that Jesus should break from his own apparently deliberate pattern in such a dramatic way in this one instance, explaining to Peter that the miracle is done "lest *we* offend." Who is this "we"? Just Jesus and Peter. Jesus doesn't extend this even to the other disciples. Notice that the miracle provides only a shekel so that Peter can "take that and give it to them for me and for yourself" (Matt. 17:27). Certainly, Jesus *could* have miraculously filled the fish's mouth with enough shekels to cover all of the disciples or the crowds or all Capernaum. But no, the miracle gives just enough coinage "for me and for yourself."

It is no coincidence that this miracle requires Peter to catch a fish. Jesus could have caused the coins to materialize out of thin air or chosen any number of more predictable ways of miraculously producing money. But he chooses to send Peter fishing for a miraculous catch yet again. As we shall see in the next chapter, this is a recurring image that Jesus uses to show Peter his unique role as a "fisher of men" (Matt. 4:29; Mark 1:17; Luke 5:10). So not only is the miraculous *amount* specific to Peter, but so is the personalized *mode* of the miracle. Is there any way to read this and *not* conclude that Peter has a special relationship as the vicar of Christ? The term *vicar* comes from the Latin *vicarius*, meaning "a substitute, deputy, or proxy." It's someone who is authorized to speak or act on another's behalf. In this instance, we see Peter doing just this for Christ, representing him in relation to the payment of the tax. Rather than rebuking him or reminding him of the infinite chasm between God and man, Jesus draws Peter to himself, tethering him, if you will, by speaking of them as a "we."

The passage is yet richer in the Greek. We'll take a closer look at this verbiage in chapters 8 and 9, but for now, recognize that there is some multilayered wordplay occurring here in Matthew 16–17. Jesus renames Simon "Peter"— *Petros*, the masculine form of the Greek word for rock (*petra*). He then says, "Upon this rock (*petra*), I will build my church" (Matt. 16:18). A few verses later, when Peter rebukes Jesus, Jesus calls him a *skandalon* (23). The word *skandalon* (the root of our English word *scandal*) literally means something that you trip over, like a "trap-stick" or a "stumbling stone."

The pun is a prophecy for the sometimes scandalous nature of the papacy, as Cardinal Ratzinger (the future Pope Benedict XVI) acknowledged: "Has it not remained this way throughout all church history, that the pope, the successor of Peter, has been *petra* and *skandalon*, rock of God and stumbling stone all in one?"[155] Peter later uses this same wordplay back toward Jesus, describing him as "a stone that will make men stumble [*lithos proskommatos*], a rock that will make them fall [*petra skandalou*]" (1 Pet. 2:8). So there are only two men referred to in the New Testament as *petra* and *skandalon*: Jesus and Peter. And Jesus recalls this wordplay in Matthew 17 by saying the miracle is being performed "lest we offend" (*skandalisōmen*)—that is, lest others should stumble over the rock of Jesus and the rock of Peter.

The Priestly Tax Exemption

Just what would be the cause of scandal? Jesus' claim that he and Peter are exempt from the temple tax. He claims that the two of them are exempt because "the sons are free" not to pay the tax. The common mistake is to think this means "sons *of Israel*." But that isn't right. The sons of Israel weren't exempt from the temple tax. Quite the opposite. The tax was introduced in Exodus in this way: "When you take the census of the people of Israel, then each shall give a ransom for himself to the Lord when you number them, that there be no plague among them when you number them" (Exod. 30:12). So it is nearly *only* the sons of Israel who are paying the tax (along with converts and freed slaves). We also know that Jesus isn't exempt on account of being God. This would explain his own tax exemption, but it wouldn't explain Peter's. So what exemption is Jesus claiming? That he and Peter are sons *of the temple*—that is, priests. The Jerusalem Talmud[156] illuminates the four groups exempted from the temple tax:

> From whom did they demand collateral? Levites, Israel-ites, converts, and freed slaves. But not from women and slaves and minors. And any minor whose father had be-gun to donate the half-shekel on his behalf—he may not stop paying. They did not demand collateral from priests, for the sake of peace.[157]

There were rabbinical disputes over whether or not the priests should also be required to pay the tax, but it is clear that they were at least sometimes exempted, and for good reason (beyond simply keeping the peace). Both the priests and Levites lived off of the tithes of the people (Heb. 7:5), but the priests collected "a tithe of the tithe" even from other Levites (Num. 18:21,26).[158] This tithing exemption at least extended to a priestly exemption from paying the temple tax, which "was meant to support the operation of the Jerusalem temple" and is therefore distinct from a strict tithe.[159] This seems to be Jesus' point in Matthew 17, and it is the only clear exemption that would apply to him (as he is certainly not a woman, slave, or minor). So if he is exempt (as he claims), it must be because of his priestly status. How can Jesus Christ claim such an exemption? As the epistle to the Hebrews explains, it is because he is "a merciful and faithful high priest in the service of God," "the apostle and high priest of our confession," and a priest of a higher order than that of the Levitical priests of old (Heb. 2:17, 3:1, 7:11).

If *this* is what he is claiming, it is no surprise that he should quickly add that the temple tax would nevertheless be mi-raculously paid, so as "not to give offense to them" (Matt. 17:27). Christ, being free from the strictures of the Law, nevertheless freely submits rather than claiming his rightful tax exemption. There's even a precedent for this from his infancy. The Virgin Mary paid the "sin offering" upon the birth of Jesus (Luke 2:22–24; Lev. 12:1–8), despite his sinlessness and virginal conception.[160] But what is remarkable is that he claims this exemption not for himself alone, but for Peter as well. Neither Peter nor Jesus is a son of Aaron, or even Levi. And so either Jesus is wrong to claim himself and Peter as exempt from the temple tax, or else he's presenting himself as the "high priest of the good things that have come" (Heb. 9:11), and claiming that Peter somehow participates in this priesthood.

How Might a Protestant Respond?

John Calvin, in his exegesis of Matthew 17:24–27, makes several claims. First, rather than viewing Peter as serving as Christ's vicar, speaking on his behalf, he claims that he's making *"une excuse bien modeste et honneste,"* that is, "a very modest and civil excuse" on Christ's behalf.[161] In other words, instead of Peter speaking on behalf of Christ, Calvin depicts him as covering for Christ, as if the Lord were a deadbeat with outstanding debts.

Calvin next speculates: "That they address him [Peter] rather than the other disciples was, as I conjecture, because Christ lived with him; for if all had occupied the same habitation, the demand would have been made on all alike."[162] This is pure conjecture, as he admits, although it is likely true that Jesus lived with Peter. (Surely, the fact that Jesus chose to live with Peter points *more* to Peter's unique role rather than less.) Ultimately, Calvin is treating the miracle as if it were simply happenstance. Jesus pays for himself and Peter, because the two of them happened to be together when the taxmen came calling. But even if the two men lived together, Jesus could have easily paid the tax for each of his disciples. The text shows that Jesus is explicit that the miracle covers only Jesus and Peter. It's not some oversight because the others didn't happen to be there.

Besides this, it is not clear that Peter *was* alone. A few verses earlier, we read that "the disciples came to Jesus privately" (Matt. 17:19). Afterward, "they were gathering in Galilee" (22). Between these two events, when "they came to Capernaum, the collectors of the half-shekel tax went up to Peter" (23). The text suggests that the group went to Capernaum, whereupon Peter is approached. If Peter *is* the only one present when the taxmen call, it is only because Jesus wanted it that way, just as earlier in the chapter we hear how "Jesus took with him Peter and James and John his brother, and led them up a high mountain apart" (1).

Calvin's explanation for Christ's exemption from the tax is that, "as he is the only Son of God, he is also the heir of the whole world, so that all things ought to be subject to him, and to acknowledge his authority."[163] Therefore, Calvin opposes both the Catholic and the Anabaptist interpretations of the passage:

> The pope has not less foolishly than successfully abused this passage to exempt his clergy from the laws; as if the shaving of the head made them sons of God, and exempted them from tributes and taxes. But nothing else was intended by Christ than to claim for himself the honor of a king's son, so as to have at least a home privileged and exempted from the common law.
>
> And therefore it is also highly foolish in the Anabaptists to torture these words for overturning political order, since it is more than certain, that Christ does not

say any thing about a privilege common to believers, but only draws a comparison from the sons of kings, who, together with their domestics, are exempted. [164]

Calvin is right that Jesus is the Son of God and the king of kings, but he is wrong to view this as the basis Jesus is claiming. That would only explain Jesus' tax exemption, not Peter's. As Calvin says, Jesus "is the *only* Son of God" in the order of nature (our adopted sonship is of a different order). Yet Jesus says that "the sons," plural, are exempt (Matt. 17:26), and singles out himself and Peter. So that leaves only the Catholic interpretation (that this is the priestly exemption) or else the "tortured" Anabaptist position that would view *all* Christians as exempt. Neither Calvin nor the Anabaptists seem familiar with the particulars of the temple tax, under which the sons of Israel (the predecessors of Christians) were *not* exempt, but only the priestly sons of the temple.

From his own series of unfounded conjectures, Calvin concludes that "it is therefore very ridiculous in the Papists, on so frivolous a pretense, to make Peter a partner in the dignity of Christ." But this partnership (not equality) is provided by Jesus himself, in making the two unlike men a single "we." Calvin claims it would be equally logical to "make all swine-herds vicars of Christ, for they paid as much as he did." But of course, the Catholic claim isn't that Peter is the vicar of Christ simply because he paid the temple tax. If Jesus spoke of a swineherd as a "we" with him, if he miraculously paid for just his and that swineherd's tax, and if he paid for it by having the coins appear in the mouth of a pig after declaring, "You will be a swineherd of men," Christians would logically conclude that that swineherd was being deputized in a special way by Jesus. But he didn't tap a swineherd as his shepherd; he chose a fisherman.

To recap, then, we see Jesus treating Peter as his vicar in this passage. We see him performing a miracle just for himself and Peter, tethering the two together in a special way. We see him—in a remarkable departure from his normal speaking style—using the "inclusionary we" to describe himself and Peter. Where else does God Incarnate speak of himself and a sinful man as "we"? All of this is in the context of Jesus both sending Peter out to catch fish, representing his evangelical role, and being a priestly son of the temple.

7

THE FISHER POPE

WHAT IS A MIRACLE, and how does it differ from magic? Both "miracle" and "magic" are notoriously hard concepts to define, and differing religions demarcate their respective limits differently. The closest we get to a biblical answer is in Moses' and Aaron's encounter with "the wise men and the sorcerers" of Pharaoh (Exod. 7:8–13). At the Lord's instruction, Aaron "cast down his rod before Pharaoh and his servants, and it became a serpent." The "magicians of Egypt" then did likewise, but "by their secret arts," rather than by obedience to God (10–11). This suggests that the chief distinction between miracle and magic, within the framework of Scripture, is that "magic is manipulative; miracle, which is an aspect of religion, is supplicative."[165] That is, miracles rely on God, whereas magic seeks an occult means of getting around him.

But there is another, more subtle, dimension to biblical miracles. In the New Testament, Jesus' miracles are "living parables," illustrating and animating his teachings. This is a stark contrast from the way that Jesus is sometimes depicted in false gospels. For instance, in the so-called "Infancy Gospel of Thomas," the young Jesus is presented as striking another child dead in a fit of irritation after the running child bumped into his shoulder.[166] It's raw power, with no meaning beyond "I can do this." The biblical miracles, in contrast, have more to them. It's for this reason that we see the Jesus of the Bible exercising his divine power, not by killing people, but by healing and even raising them from the dead. Commenting on the three instances in which the New Testament records Jesus raising people from the dead, St. Augustine notes that "surely the Lord's deeds are not merely deeds, but signs. And if they are signs, besides their wonderful character, they have some real significance." In these cases, he suggests, the deeper meaning is that "every one that believes rises again."[167]

The scriptural way of describing this dimension of miracles is calling them "signs" or "signs and wonders" (cf. Deut. 6:22; John 2:11; Acts 6:8; etc.). With any of the biblical miracles, we should ask, "What was the *meaning* of this miracle?"[168] For instance, although Jesus doesn't kill an innocent boy in the New Testament, he does cause a fig tree to shrivel up and die (Matt. 21:18–22). In *Why I Am Not a Christian*, The British philosopher Bertrand Russell said that the "curious story" had "always rather puzzled me." Indeed, he cited this as a "moral problem" within Christianity that showed Christ's inferiority to teachers like the Buddha and Socrates.[169] But Jesus isn't behaving in an insensible or ill-tempered way. Recall that John the Baptist had prepared the way for Christ by calling his listeners to "bear fruit that befits repentance," since "every tree therefore that does not bear good fruit is cut down and thrown into the fire" (3:8,10). Jesus continued with this imagery, comparing the spiritual fruitlessness of Israel to a barren fig tree (Luke 13:6–9), drawing upon the prophetic language of Isaiah 5. When Christ causes the fruitless fig tree to shrivel, he's not having an emotional outburst or "punishing" the tree as if it were a moral agent capable of knowing right from wrong. Instead, it's as if Jesus is enacting the parable of the fig tree.

What, then, are the three miracles involving a miraculous catch of fish, and why is St. Peter closely involved in all three? Part of the meaning is that the miraculous catches remind us of the need to trust in God, a lesson that fishing itself teaches. Building upon the theology of St. Athanasius and other Church Fathers, C.S. Lewis describes miracles as "a retelling in small letters of the very same story which is written across the whole world in letters too large for some of us to see."[170] The supernatural events in the Bible tend to build upon, and in some way resemble, natural events. And as the nineteenth-century Baptist preacher Charles Spurgeon observed, "a fisher is a person who is *very dependent, and needs to be trustful*." Since he cannot see the fish, every act of fishing "is an act of faith."[171] The Reformed theologian and pastor Tim Challies likewise suggests five ways that evangelization resembles fishing: both require going; expertise; diligence; dependence upon providence; and confidence.[172]

All of this is true, but we shouldn't miss the obvious: these miracles are also personalized for Simon, who was a fisherman by trade (Matt. 4:18; John 21:3). They're also, as we shall see, closely connected with Jesus' description of the kingdom of God on earth (Matt. 13:47). In other words, these are the sort of miracles we shouldn't be surprised to find, if Jesus intended to entrust the Church to the care of the "fisher pope," Peter.

The First Miraculous Catch of Fish

With that in mind, consider the first miraculous catch of fish, recounted in Luke 5:1–11. This miracle occurs prior to Christ's calling of the apostles in general (Luke 6:13), and Simon Peter in particular (John 21:15–17), which we considered back in chapter 4. But it's another instance in which we find Jesus calling Simon Peter in a personal way, and the setting for it is remarkable. As Jesus was teaching by the "lake of Gennesaret" (that is, the Sea of Galilee), "the people pressed upon him to hear the word of God." Seeing two fishing boats docked on the shore while their owners washed the fishing nets, Jesus climbed "into one of the boats, which was Simon's," and "asked him to put out a little from the land. And he sat down and taught the people from the boat" (Luke 5:1–3).

On the surface, this seems like a chance encounter, as if Jesus chose the boat at random, but the broader context shows otherwise. Simon appears to be already familiar with Jesus and refers to him as "master," and (depending on which Gospel chronology you're following), it may have happened after the healing of Simon Peter's mother-in-law.[173]

With Jesus is a large crowd, "pressed upon him to hear the word of God" (Luke 5:1). With Simon are Andrew, James, and John, each of whom will also be called as disciples (Luke 5:10; Mark 1:16). But Jesus speaks directly to Simon Peter, telling him to "put out into the deep and let down your nets for a catch" (Luke 5:4–5). Obeying, "they enclosed a great shoal of fish," a catch so large that "their nets were breaking," and they needed to enlist the help of their fishing partners (6–7). Upon seeing the miraculous catch of fish, Simon Peter falls down before Jesus, crying out, "Depart from me, for I am a sinful man, O Lord," and both he and "all that were with him" are described as being "astonished" (8–9).

The meaning of this miracle is spelled out for us by Christ. As St. Luke recounts, "Jesus said to Simon, 'Do not be afraid; henceforth you will be catching men'" (Luke 5:10). It would be no exaggeration to say this miracle is for Simon Peter.

These words are not addressed to the crowds, or even to the other future apostles. Rather, they are addressed "to Simon." In some unique way, different from the general way he calls all believers, or the specific way that he calls the other apostles, Christ is calling Simon Peter to be the fisher of men.

The Second Miraculous Catch of Fish

The second miraculous catch of fish, the one recounted in Matt. 17:24–27, is also intended specifically for Simon Peter. As we saw in the last chapter, Jesus has Simon Peter miraculously catch a fish that suffices to pay the temple tax for Jesus and Simon, and no others. The particularity of the miracle is unavoidable.

Recall C.S. Lewis's earlier point that miracles build upon the natural world in some way, which Lewis calls the "family *style*" of the Father and the Son. To illustrate this, he points to the feeding of the five thousand and observes that "bread is not made there of nothing. Bread is not made of stones, as the devil once suggested to our Lord in vain." Instead, "a little bread is made into much bread," just as "every year God makes a little corn into much corn."[174] John Calvin's suggestion of applying the miraculous catch of fish to a swineherd, the Infancy Gospel of Thomas's idea of Jesus using his divine power to kill a running boy, and even the devil's idea to turn stones into bread all reveal the same blindness. Each misses the idea of a miracle as living *parable*, treating it only as a show of *power*.

The Third Miraculous Catch of Fish

The third miracle involving a miraculous catch of fish comes after the Resurrection (John 21:1–14). By this point, the apostles and other disciples know of the resurrection of Christ. Seven of them, led by Simon Peter, are out on the Sea of Tiberius—that is, the Lake of Galilee. As before, they spend all night fishing and catch nothing. Jesus appears to them on the shore, although they don't originally know it's he. In the first miracle, he found them on the shore and told Peter to cast out into the deep. This time, he finds them already on the water, and he tells them to "cast the net on the right side of the boat, and you will find some" (6). At this point, the Beloved Disciple realizes that the man on the shore is "the Lord," and he informs Peter, who dresses, jumps into the water, and swims to Jesus (7–8).

Arriving on shore, Peter and the others discover "a charcoal fire there, with fish lying on it, and bread" (John 21:9). We might already suspect that this miracle is going to involve Peter, given that he is named five times in John's brief telling, and that it's a miraculous catch of fish. The mention of a "charcoal fire" confirms this. The one other mention of a "charcoal fire" in all of Scripture is earlier in the Gospel of John. After Jesus' arrest, "the servants and officers had made a charcoal fire, because it was cold, and they were standing and warming themselves; Peter also was with them, standing and warming himself" (18:18). That is, it was beside a charcoal fire that Peter denied Jesus three times. And so now Jesus has prepared another "charcoal fire," and upon it he already has fish.

These are clearly not the fish that the apostles just miraculously caught, because "they were not able to haul it in, for the quantity of fish," and had opted to simply drag the nets behind the boats toward shore after Peter jumped ship (John 21:6,8). No, these fish are there when they arrive. If the apostles' initial failure to catch fish was a reminder that apart from Christ, they can do nothing, this would seem to drive home the inverse: that Christ can do everything, with or without them (or us). And yet he sends them to fish anyway. Jesus says to them, "Bring some of the fish that you have just caught" (10). That is, Christ chooses to work through these human intermediaries, even though he need not. This point applies to the apostles generally and also to one of them in particular. It's Simon Peter alone whom we see responding to Christ's calling, as he "went aboard and hauled the net ashore, full of large fish, a hundred and fifty-three of them; and although there were so many, the net was not torn" (11).[175]

There seem to be three aspects to this third miraculous catch: the first, the catch itself; the second, that the net was not torn; and the third, that at the Lord's command, Peter was able to singlehandedly bring the catch in. After all, recall that all of the others were incapable of doing so, even working together. The detail about the net is a striking contrast to the first miraculous catch of fish, in which the "nets were breaking" because of the size of the catch (Luke 5:6). So why don't the nets tear this time?

To understand these details, it's important to recognize what this miracle *signifies*, in what way it's a living parable. Both early Christians and modern scholars have treated this scene (and indeed, the entire final chapter of John) as about the Church. One reason to believe this is the broader structure of John's narrative. There are two chapters in the Gospel of John dedicated to appearances of the risen Christ. The first of these, John 20, tells about the disciples' initial encounter with Jesus, and their coming to believe in him. John tells us that whereas "Jesus did many other signs in the presence of the disciples" that remain unwritten, these signs "are written that you may believe that Jesus is the Christ, the Son of God, and that believing you may have life in his name" (John 20:30–31). As St. Augustine noted, this passage "indicates, as it were, the end of the book; but there is afterward related how the Lord manifested himself at the Sea of Tiberias."[176]

In other words, John 21 reads as a sort of epilogue to the Gospel. And the miraculous catch of fish it describes *isn't* for the purpose of bringing the disciples or us to faith in Christ, or in the Resurrection.[177] By this point, the disciples know Jesus has risen from the dead. John tells us that this "was now the third time that Jesus was revealed to the disciples after he was raised from the dead" (John 21:14), so the purpose doesn't seem to be to convince any doubting Thomases. Instead, this chapter "expresses a strong and continuing interest in disciples of the second generation."[178] Just as Luke writes both his Gospel (describing the life, death, and resurrection of Christ) and the Acts of the Apostles (describing what comes next), the final chapter of John's Gospel begins to point to what comes next. Augustine sees in the miraculous catch of fish "special reference to the mystery of the Church," particularly as it will stand at the Last Judgment.[179]

As Pope St. Gregory the Great (540–604) explained, the ship of the Church passes along on the sea of this "present world, which is in a constant state of upheaval, through the tumultuousness of its affairs and the passing waves of this transitory life," journeying toward Christ, who has "now passed beyond the transience of fleshly life," and who stands on the shore, signifying "the enduring state of eternal rest."[180] Now that he has risen, he is no longer in the boat in the same manner that he once was, but through his miraculous power, he shows his ongoing presence in the Church. Read in this light, the nets and fish in this "living parable" are all about evangelization and the Church. The miraculous catch is a sign, as St. Cyril of Alexandria (378–444) says, of "the work of Christ, who gathers the multitude of the saved by his own power into the apostolic net, as it were, the church on earth."[181] And this is exactly what we hear from Christ elsewhere, when he describes the kingdom of God on earth as "a net which was thrown into the sea and gathered fish of every kind," until the good and bad fish (the saved and the damned) are separated by angels at the close of the age (Matt. 13:47–50).

If this is a miracle about the Church, what does it have to say about Peter? At the outset, it is Peter who says, "I am going fishing," to which the other disciples reply, "We will go with you" (John 21:2–3). Peter is called to be a fisher of men; the others are called to be fishers of men *with Peter*. When Christ sends them to bring in the catch, Peter acts alone, but on behalf of the whole. He is capable, at Christ's urging, of doing what the other apostles were incapable of doing: bringing the catch home to the eternal shores without tearing the net. If we are the fish, and the kingdom is the net, Peter is given a unique role in leading that net toward the shore, to ensure that it doesn't tear. The Greek word used here for "torn" is from *schisma*, where we get our word *schism*. Peter's role is to bring the Church to the eternal shore without letting it rupture through schism.

The last piece necessary to understand this third miracle is what comes right after it. The late British Evangelical F.F. Bruce notes that "there is more in it than meets the eye" in the third miraculous catch, and "something of its inner significance is unfolded in the discourse that follows."[182] The discourse in question is the one we discussed back in chapter 5, in which Jesus thrice asks Peter, "Do you love me?" Just as the meaning of the first miraculous catch was made clear by Jesus' invitation to Peter, "Do not be afraid; henceforth you will be catching men" (Luke 5:10), so in this final catch, the meaning is made clear by Jesus' instructions to Peter: "feed my lambs," "tend my sheep," and "feed my sheep"

(John 21:15–17). As a fisher of men, he is called to reach those who are not yet evangelized, and in this, he is joined by all those who can say with the apostles, "We will go with you" (2–3). As shepherd, Peter is called to care for both the lambs and the sheep, both those new to the faith and those more advanced.[183]

How Might a Protestant Respond?

Broadly speaking, there are three types of Protestant exegetes: first, those who understood that something is being said in these miracles about Christ's plan for the Church; second, those who understand that something is being said about Christ's plan but miss any connection to the Church; and finally, those who miss any deeper significance, treating it only as Jesus once again proving to the disciples that he is risen.[184] Thankfully, most Protestants recognize that at least the first and third of these miraculous catches of fish are telling us something about the Church. The first miracle is almost too plain to miss. You can scarcely see Christ causing a miraculous catch of fish, hear the call for Peter to become a "fisher of men," and fail to connect the two. And so, when we see the two similar miracles, it's only logical to ask if these are picking up where the first left off. Indeed, with a few outliers, "most interpreters agree that symbolism pervades the description" of the third miracle, with "the act of fishing, the role of Peter, and the drawing of the unbroken net" being "relatively easy to interpret."[185]

To be sure, there are a handful of commentators who don't get even this much. John MacArthur, for instance, is the pastor of a Southern California megachurch and host of the popular *Grace to You* radio program, and he was named the fourth most influential Protestant pastor in America by a sample of more than 1,000 other Protestant pastors.[186] In MacArthur's commentary on John 21, he seems capable of seeing nothing more than meets the eye. D.A. Carson, the Reformed theologian upon whom MacArthur relies, has said that in the image of the untorn net, "it is hard not to see an allusion to Luke 5:1–11, where the nets were torn."[187] MacArthur, in contrast, finds it "surprising" that the nets are untorn but thinks it nothing more than "the type of detail that an eyewitness would note, especially a fisherman like John." MacArthur fails to connect this to the tearing of the net in Luke 5:6 (a Gospel written by not a fisherman, but a physician) or to see any deeper meaning suggested. In the catch where John says there were exactly 153 fish, MacArthur finds only evidence of the veracity of the recording (the "simple, obvious explanation" is that "this was the actual number of fish they had caught") and finds explanations seeing significance in the number "fanciful."[188] He understands that the passage has something to say about "self-effort" and "spiritual power" but fails to mention the Church even once in his chapter analyzing the passage.

Most Protestant exegetes fare better. Martin Luther, for instance, recognized the boats and net in the first miracle as a symbol of the Church, with the two boats in Luke 5 representing the Jews and Gentiles; with no sense of self-awareness, he suggested that the tearing of the nets represented those "who establish sects and factions of their own," who "may not and cannot continue with the true band of God's people in the assembly of the Church."[189] Charles Spurgeon likewise understood the net in both Luke 5 and John 21 to be connected to Church unity and schism. Noting that some lamented that "in the visible Church the net breaks," he said, "I do not at all grieve over it." Indeed, his own Metropolitan Tabernacle broke away from the Baptist Union, becoming the largest church in the world to be unaffiliated with any denomination. Spurgeon justified this attitude by claiming that it was really just "the invisible Church—the Church within the Church" that was one. The important thing was not to avoid external schism, but to "take care that you are not a schismatic in your heart."[190]

Unfortunately, even those Protestant commentators who recognize that this passage is about the Church typically pay little attention to the special role that Peter is playing in these miraculous catches. Some exegetes eliminate Peter's individuality entirely. Martin Luther treats Peter's role as a mere stand-in for conscience, a "figure of those who should believe in the eternal possessions" in the first miraculous catch, while more modern exegetes suggest that Peter simply "represents the disciples as a character group" in the third miraculous catch.[191] But Peter is mentioned by name repeatedly, and in ways that single him out from the other disciples.[192] This suggests that he is neither just another apostle nor just another person with a conscience, even if he is meant to be a model for others.

In understanding the third miraculous catch, two questions are worth considering. First, how is it that Peter alone brings in the catch of fish in John 21:11, when the rest of the apostles had been incapable of doing so in John 21:8? John Calvin offers no answer. He comments on verses 10 and 12 but passes over 11.[193] John MacArthur does comment on it, saying there was "a book and a movie when I was a little kid called *The Big Fisherman*, and I used to ask, 'Why does everybody think Peter is big?' This is it right here, because six guys have been dragging this thing in, the other disciples in verse 8."[194] Carson likewise views this simply as evidence that Peter is "a physically strong man," apparently stronger than the other six apostles combined.[195] Charles Spurgeon fares slightly better in using Peter's strength here to argue that "in the invisible Church, God will make his servants just strong enough—just strong enough to drag their fish to shore."[196] Spurgeon's explanation has the advantage that it recognizes something out of the ordinary here, without turning Peter into the Incredible Hulk, or totally ignoring the passage. But he still fails to answer the question. If Peter's strength is miraculous, what's the meaning of the miracle?

Second, how should we understand the relationship between the miraculous catch of fish in John 21:1–14 and the conversation between Jesus and Peter in John 21:15–19? The two events seem to be obviously connected (cf. John 21:15), but many Protestants read vv. 15–19 in ways that seem to contradict their own readings of vv. 1–14. For instance, MacArthur sees the description of Peter at the start of John 21 as "indicating his general leadership of the apostles," as does Carson.[197] Spurgeon, as we've seen, sees his actions as indicative of a miraculous, supernatural strength. Yet immediately after describing Peter as the leader of the apostles in John 21:1–14, each of these Protestant exegetes claims that Peter *isn't even one of the apostles* by John 21:15–19. Carson views Christ's special commissioning of Peter as dealing "with Peter's reinstatement to service, not with his elevation to primacy."[198] MacArthur likewise reads this as a "restoration" so Peter can share in "the same responsibility given to every pastor."[199] Spurgeon claims that "Peter was in peculiar need of a reordination,"[200] a nonsensical proposition if "the gifts and the call of God are irrevocable," as St. Paul says in Romans 11:29. In their attempt to avoid the plain, "papal" reading of the text, these exegetes contort themselves into self-contradiction—first singling Peter out as a leader of the apostles and then denying his leadership and even his apostleship.

Contrast this with how early Christians read the passage. Pope St. Gregory the Great (540–604) recognized the interconnectedness of the miraculous catch of fish and Jesus' three questions to Peter, saying, "Why was Peter the one who brought the net to land? Our holy church had been entrusted to him. It was to him individually that it was said, 'Simon, son of John, do you love me? Feed my sheep.' What was afterward disclosed to him in words was now indicated to him by an action."[201] Immediately, we can see why Peter would be at the heart of Jesus' three miracles involving multiplication of fish; why he is depicted as leading the other apostles at the start of John 21; why he is the one depicted as bringing the net to land; and why Jesus' words to him are not a "reinstatement" to the office he was already exercising, but a special calling to him as the leader of the apostles.

8

PETER AND THE ELEVEN

THERE'S A DETAIL, perhaps so small that you didn't notice it, in some of the biblical passages that we've looked at: Peter has a literal primacy. For instance, in St. John's account of the third miraculous catch of fish, he says, "Simon Peter, Thomas called the Twin, Nathanael of Cana in Galilee, the sons of Zebedee, and two others of his disciples were together" (John 21:2). Is it significant that Peter is listed first?

It turns out that this is something of a pattern. Each of the synoptic Gospels gives us a list of the twelve apostles (Matt. 10:2–4, Mark 3:16–19, and Luke 6:13–16). There's also a list of the Twelve, minus Judas, given in Acts 1:13. Comparing these four lists reveals some remarkable similarities and dissimilarities. Each of these lists begins with Peter, and each list ends with Judas. By itself, this might be unsurprising: perhaps the Evangelists were copying an earlier list, some "Q source" now lost to history?[202] The difficulty with such a theory is that between Peter and Judas, there is less of a clear pattern. John MacArthur (whose exegesis I criticized in the last chapter) does an excellent job of summarizing these four lists:

In all four biblical lists, the same twelve men are named, and the order in which they are given is strikingly similar. The first name in all four lists is Peter. He thus stands out as the leader and spokesman for the whole company of twelve. The Twelve are then arranged in three groups of four. Group one always has Peter at the head of the list, and that group always includes Andrew, James, and John. Group two always features Philip first and includes Bartholomew, Matthew, and Thomas. Group three is always led by James the son of Alphaeus, and it includes Simon the Zealot; Judas son of James (called "Thaddaeus" in Mark and "Lebbaeus, whose surname was Thaddaeus" in Matthew); and finally, Judas Iscariot. (Judas Iscariot is omitted from the list in Acts 1 because he was already dead by then. In the three lists where Judas's name is included, it always appears last, along with a remark identifying him as the traitor.)[203]

Within these groups, the ordering appears to matter little. After Peter, Mark names Andrew. Matthew and Luke name John. Acts (written by Luke) names John. Who was in the spots between Peter and Judas apparently mattered so little to Luke that he lists them in different orders between his Gospel and the book of Acts.

In terms of biographical details, we find something similar. Certain details are included, apparently at the whim of the Evangelist. St. Matthew refers to himself as "Matthew the tax collector," whereas the others just say "Matthew." St. Mark tells us Jesus nicknamed James and John *Boanerges* or "Sons of Thunder," a detail not found in the others. St. Luke tells us (both in his Gospel and in Acts) that Simon was called "the Zealot," whereas the other two refer to him simply as "Simon the Cananaean."[204] There's no discernible pattern.

But when it comes to Peter and Judas, the synoptic lists are remarkably similar. Matthew's list begins with "Simon, who is called Peter," and ends with "Judas Iscariot, who betrayed him" (Matt. 10:2–4). Mark's list begins with "Simon whom he surnamed Peter" and ends with "Judas Iscariot, who betrayed him" (Mark 3:16–19). Luke's list begins with "Simon, whom he named Peter" and ends with "Judas Iscariot, who became a traitor" (Luke 6:13–16).[205] In other words, it's not only that the lists begin and end with the same two people each time. It's that the same explanations are given for *why* they're listed where they are: Simon is first, because he's Peter, the rock; and Judas is last, because he's the traitor who betrayed Christ.

Peter and the Pillars

MacArthur mentions that Peter is the head not only of the Twelve, but of a cluster of four apostles that he labels "group one." The second, third, and fourth spots on every biblical list of the Twelve are filled by James, John, and Andrew, albeit in no particular order. In the case of Andrew, the reasoning seems to be that he is "Andrew, Simon Peter's brother" (John 1:40, 6:8). But in the case of James and John, it's that they, alongside Peter, are the three apostles whom St. Paul describes as the ones "reputed to be pillars" (Gal. 2:9). In other words, Peter, James, and John appear to have a special place within the Twelve.

One of the ways we see this is that Jesus repeatedly separates them from the rest of the apostles. For instance, when Jesus went into the house of Jairus to raise his daughter from the dead, he "allowed no one to follow him except Peter and James and John the brother of James" (Mark 5:37). Likewise, at the Transfiguration, "Jesus took with him Peter and James and John, and led them up a high mountain apart by themselves" (Mark 9:2; cf. Matt. 17:1, Luke 9:28). They weren't simply apart from the crowds; they were apart from the other apostles. And it's Peter and John who are tasked by Jesus with instructions for preparing the Last Supper (Luke 22:8).

These three "pillars," along with Peter's brother Andrew, are the ones who approach Jesus to speak with him "privately" about the destruction of the temple and the end of the world (Mark 13:3–4). Jesus appears to open up to these men more than he does to even the rest of the Twelve. All of this is physically on display on Holy Thursday, in the garden of Gethsemane. Upon arriving, he said to his disciples, "Sit here, while I pray" (Mark 14:32). But then he "took with him Peter and James and John, and began to be greatly distressed and troubled. And he said to them, 'My soul is very sorrowful, even to death; remain here, and watch'" (Mark 14:33–34). Once more, the other disciples are left outside, whereas the "pillars" are drawn farther in.

Two things are notable about this. The first is that Peter and the other pillars were not simply, as some Protestant exegetes suggest, the "natural leaders" of the apostles.[206] That is, they did not just naturally rise to the top based on their innate personality traits. Instead, we find Jesus repeatedly drawing them aside, to the exclusion of the rest of the apostles. To approach the question from the opposite angle, the exclusion of the other eight apostles is not simply due to a lack of ambition on their part, but because Jesus does things like forbid them to enter the house of Jairus with him and tells them things like "sit here" while he takes the pillars with him deeper into the garden of Gethsemane. This is significant, since it undermines many of the Protestant arguments against the papacy. For instance, the nineteenth-century Anglican William Dexter Wilson argued that the authority given to St. Peter first was given "afterward to all the apostles equally and alike" and that St. Matthias (who replaced Judas) and Paul "seem to have had, and exercised, equal authority with the original twelve."[207] But the idea that all of the Twelve were all called to the identical and equal office is rebutted by the existence of these three "pillars," evidence of a sort of call within the call, an inner circle of apostles handpicked by Jesus Christ.

The second notable detail is that, even among the three "pillars" or the four members of "group one," Peter is clearly the leader. In describing the Transfiguration, St. Luke refers to the three pillars as "Peter and those who were with him" (Luke 9:32). And after Jesus goes to pray in the garden of Gethsemane, "he came and found them sleeping, and he said to Peter, 'Simon, are you asleep? Could you not watch one hour?'" (Mark 14:37). After separating the pillars from the rest of the Twelve, Jesus has singled one of the pillars out, apart from the others. Peter is held to a higher standard than the others, since "everyone to whom much is given, of him will much be required; and of him to whom men commit much they will demand the more" (Luke 12:48). This should be understood as part of a broader pattern: Jesus "withdrew with his disciples" from the crowds, although "a great multitude from Galilee followed" (Mark 3:7). From within this group of disciples, "he appointed twelve" (14). From the multitudes, he draws the disciples; from the disciples, he draws the apostles; from the apostles, he draws the pillars; and from the pillars, he calls Peter.

The Protestant theologian James B. Jordan makes a fascinating connection between the pillars and the Old Testament.[208] Back in the book of Exodus, God called "Moses and Aaron, Nadab, and Abihu, and seventy of the elders of Israel" to come to the mountain, where "they saw the God

of Israel" (Exod. 24:9–10). This prefigured the Transfiguration, in which Jesus both leads the pillars up the mountain
to see God and is the God that they see. But Moses went
with the priests, represented there by three men: the high
priest Aaron and his sons Nadab and Abihu. Jesus went with
Peter, James, and John. If this analogy holds, Peter is in the
role of "high priest" to Jesus. Indeed, Jordan sees this in other places in the New Testament. When Peter denies Christ,
he is in "the courtyard of the high priest" (Matt. 26:58),
at the moment that Christ is before the Jewish high priest,
Caiaphas. Indeed, John makes a point of sharing that "Peter
stood outside at the door. So the other disciple, who was
known to the high priest, went out and spoke to the maid
who kept the door, and brought Peter in" (John 18:16). This
seemingly trivial detail is the only place in John's Gospel
that we see a fulfillment of Christ's words, that "he who
enters by the door is the shepherd of the sheep," and "to him
the gatekeeper opens" (10:2–3). After the death and resurrection of Christ, when Peter and John arrived at the empty
tomb, John "reached the tomb first" but "did not go in"
(20:4–5). Why? Because, Jordan argues, "it makes sense to
see the tomb as a holy of holies, which only the high priest
might enter. John instinctively holds back."[209] But then "Simon Peter came, following him, and went into the tomb"
(6). It's only at this point that John, "who reached the tomb
first, also went in, and he saw and believed" (8).

The Spotlight and the Shadow

When Luke is telling in Acts how "many signs and wonders
were done among the people by the hands of the apostles,"
he explains that "more than ever believers were added to
the Lord, multitudes both of men and women, so that they

even carried out the sick into the streets, and laid them on beds and pallets, that as Peter came by at least his shadow might fall on some of them" (Acts 5:12,14–15). It's a telling remark. All of the apostles are working miracles, "and they were all together in Solomon's Portico" (12), yet the people are striving to place themselves where Peter's shadow will fall upon them. Does this sound as though the early believers considered the apostles to have held authority "equally and alike"?

At this point, "the high priest rose up and all who were with him," and they arrest the apostles (Acts 5:17–18). After their arrest, they are brought before the high priest, who orders them to cease preaching in the name of Jesus. In response, "Peter and the apostles answered, 'We must obey God rather than men'" (29). It's not simply that Peter spoke on behalf of the other apostles, as happened so many other times. Instead, apparently, all of the apostles gave a defense, but this defense is described as coming from "Peter and the apostles," in language perhaps reminiscent of "the high priest" and "all who were with him." Strikingly, Luke doesn't say Peter and the *other* apostles. He goes beyond this and says "Peter and the apostles," as if Peter is something more than simply an apostle.

"Peter and the Eleven"

The "Peter and the apostles" language of Acts 5, treating Peter as something beyond an apostle, is common in the New Testament. At the empty tomb, the angel tells Mary Magdalene to "tell his disciples and Peter that he is going before you to Galilee; there you will see him, as he told you" (Mark 16:7). John Calvin argued that this distinction of Peter from the others was "not because he was at that time higher in rank than the others, but because his crime, which was so disgraceful, needed peculiar consolation to assure him that Christ had not cast him off, though he had basely and wickedly fallen."[210]

In other words, Calvin's view is that the "apostles and Peter" language is to show that Peter is not above, but below (or believes himself to be below) the apostleship. But this explanation fails to account for Pentecost, where "Peter, standing with the eleven, lifted up his voice" and preached to the crowds (Acts 2:14). Are we to assume that Peter, after having organized the other apostles to choose a successor to Judas (1:12–26), was unsure whether or not he was an apostle, even as he was filled with the Holy Spirit and preaching to the crowds?[211]

Indeed, Calvin's exegesis doesn't even account for Easter Sunday. When the women arrived to share this story with the apostles, "these words seemed to them an idle tale, and they did not believe them. But Peter rose and ran to the tomb" (Luke 24:11–12). Rather than Peter shamefully avoiding the empty tomb, Luke describes him as the first to believe the women's account. Luke goes on to say that "stooping and looking in, he saw the linen cloths by themselves; and he went home wondering at what had happened." Where the Evangelist sees wonder, Calvin sees something more cynical, claiming that "the great insensibility under which [Peter] still labored is evident from the fact that he again fled trembling to conceal himself, as if he had seen nothing, while Mary sat down to weep at the grave."[212] Where the Bible depicts Peter as running *toward* the tomb, Calvin describes him as running *away from* it. There's not a word of how Peter "fled trembling" anywhere in the Gospels. John's Gospel says only that "the disciples went back to their homes" (John 20:10).

These exegetical (or eisegetical) backflips are in service of Calvin's false reinstatement theory—the idea that Peter was no longer an apostle by Easter morning. The thinness of his argument is clear from the lengths to which he has to exaggerate or distort the Gospel accounts of the Resurrection. For instance, he argues that "God denied [Peter] the honor, which he shortly afterward conferred on the women, of hearing from the lips of the angel that Christ *was risen*."[213] But this is straining out gnats and swallowing camels. St. Paul tells us Jesus "appeared to Cephas, then to the Twelve" (Acts 15:5). *Cephas* is the Aramaic name for Peter, and Paul is saying Christ's first appearance, even before he presented himself to the Twelve, was to St. Peter. Note here, too, that Paul speaks of both "Cephas" and "the Twelve," recognizing Peter both as part of the apostles and as somehow distinct from the others.

Paul makes a similar distinction elsewhere, referring to "the other apostles and the brethren of the Lord and Cephas" (1 Cor. 9:5). Here, Calvin's commentary is quite different, saying, "We confess that Peter was acknowledged as first among the apostles, as it is necessary that in every society there should always be some one to preside over the others."[214] This concedes the point Calvin strained so hard to deny in his Easter morning exegesis: that Peter is both "first among the apostles," but even "preside[s] over the others," like the ruler of a society.

9

UPON THIS ROCK

"**NOW WHEN JESUS** came into the district of Caesarea Philippi, he asked his disciples, 'Who do men say that the Son of man is?'" (Matt. 16:13). So begins the most famous biblical passage related to St. Peter and the papacy. The oddness of St. Matthew's narration is lost on modern readers, because we are ignorant of the geography being described. As one scholar has noted, "If we can judge by the place designations in [Mark's] Gospel, most of Jesus' ministry was done in a ten-mile stretch along the Sea of Galilee's western shore and extending about five miles inland."[215] When Jesus does leave the area around Capernaum in Galilee, it's usually to journey to Jerusalem in the south, perhaps via Samaria. But here, for some reason, he's taken his disciples some 55 miles *north* of Galilee, completely in what we would consider the "wrong direction."

Something has drawn Jesus and the Twelve this far away from their normal ministry, and it seems to be wrapped up in the question Jesus asks: "Who do men say that the Son of man is?" (Matt. 16:13). In the ensuing conversation, Jesus will say to Peter, "You are Peter, and on this rock I will build my church" (18). Jesus then makes three promises to

Peter: that the Church he's about to found "upon this rock" will not be overcome by the gates of hell; that he will give Peter the "keys of the kingdom of heaven"; and that "whatever you bind on earth shall be bound in heaven, and whatever you loose on earth shall be loosed in heaven" (18–19). To all appearances, this passage seems to be Jesus promising Peter that Jesus going to build the Church upon Peter, with Peter in a special way at the forefront.

You might wonder why I've saved this most famous passage for last. I have four reasons. The first is precisely that it's the most famous, therefore it's the area in which I'm least likely to say anything useful. The second is that there's one particular part of the passage that's confusing: who or what does Jesus mean by the "rock" when he says, "On this rock I will build my church"? The Church Fathers read the meaning of this phrase in several different ways, and "many Fathers (e.g., Origen, Hilary, Jerome, Gregory of Nyssa, Augustine) happily employed more than one throughout their careers."[216] St. Augustine acknowledges that in an earlier book, "I said about the apostle Peter: 'On him as on a rock the Church was built,'" but that later, he argues that it should be "understood as built upon him whom Peter confessed." Ultimately, he concludes by inviting the reader to "decide which of these two opinions is the more probable."[217]

The third reason I delayed in addressing this passage is that there's a caricature of the Catholic position in which it's claimed that everything comes down to this one passage, and specifically down to the question of the identity of the rock. Evangelical critics of Catholicism often promote this strawman version of the Catholic position: the late theologian Norman Geisler called this passage the "chief biblical text used to support" the doctrine of the papacy and shared an essay on his site claiming that the Catholic Church "interprets everything about the Church through the lens of the above verse."[218] Dave Hunt likewise claims that "the pope's authority today and the Catholic religion over which he presides stand or fall" upon the "assertion" that Christ's statement to Peter made him the rock."[219] Keith Mathison is slightly more guarded but still calls it the "primary proof-text for the doctrine of Roman supremacy."[220] Yet Mathison also argues that before the Reformation, "this passage was very rarely used to support papal claims," without considering how both of these claims could be true, given that the papacy existed before the Reformation.[221]

The final reason is that the passage has a lot of imagery that needs unpacking: besides the questions "Who is the 'rock'?" and "What's the meaning of Simon's new name?" there are also the questions "What does Jesus mean by the 'keys of the kingdom'" and "What does Jesus mean by 'binding and loosing'"? For this reason, I've decided to break an examination of this passage up over two chapters. In this chapter, we'll look at the first two questions. When Jesus says, "You are Peter, and on this rock I will build my church," is he promising to build the Church on Peter, on Peter's confession, on himself, or on something else? In the next chapter, we'll unpack the other promises he makes, with the keys and the binding and loosing.

Abram and Simon, Abraham and Peter

To begin unpacking what happened at Caesarea Philippi, it's important to set the scene against its Jewish background. Jesus asks who the crowds think he is, and the answers are contradictory and unsatisfactory. Then he asks the Twelve, "But who do you say that I am?" Only one of them, Simon Peter, answers. This in itself is notable. In response to Jesus' first question about popular opinion, Matthew shares what "they said" in response. But here, there's no apostolic "they" speaking. When it comes to giving the right answer, they fall silent, and only Peter speaks. What he says is inspired: "You are the Christ, the Son of the living God" (Matt. 16:16). Jesus' response is "Blessed are you, Simon bar-Jona! For flesh and blood has not revealed this to you, but my Father who is in heaven. And I tell you, you are Peter" (Matt. 16:17–18).

In other words, after Simon correctly confesses Jesus' identity, Jesus reveals Simon's own identity to him. Jesus is the Christ, and throughout Scripture, the names "Jesus," "Jesus Christ," and "Christ" are used interchangeably for the same person. Simon is Peter (the rock), and throughout Scripture, the names "Simon," "Simon Peter," and "Peter" are used interchangeably for the same person. Both "Christ" and "Peter" are sometimes used as titles, and sometimes used as if they were proper names. Throughout this book, I've used all three names for Peter (since that's what we know him as today), but it's important to recognize that he was just Simon prior to this point. Jesus is giving him a new name.

Anyone familiar with Scripture is aware of how crucial the changing of names is.[222] Adam's responsibility in the Garden of Eden is to name the animals (Gen. 2:19), and in doing so, he enters into a new kind of relationship with them. When there's a change in God's relationship with man (for instance, in the creation of a covenant), we often see a change in names. Perhaps the most famous of these is the change in Abram's name to Abraham, which occurs after God tells Abram, "I will make my covenant between me and you, and will multiply you exceedingly" (17:2). Abram falls on his face, and God declares:

Behold, my covenant is with you, and you shall be the father of a multitude of nations. No longer shall your name be Abram, but your name shall be Abraham; for I have made you the father of a multitude of nations. I will make you exceedingly fruitful; and I will make nations of you, and kings shall come forth from you. And I will establish my covenant between me and you and your descendants after you throughout their generations for an everlasting covenant, to be God to you and to your descendants after you. And I will give to you, and to your descendants after you, the land of your sojournings, all the land of Canaan, for an everlasting possession; and I will be their God (4–8).

The pattern is the same as at Caesarea Philippi: God draws his people to himself in a new way, through one man, by changing that man's name, and by bestowing certain promises upon both him and those who will come after him. And the new name isn't given randomly. In Abram's case, the new name is "Abraham," a name meaning "father of a multitude of nations," which is precisely what God promises to make him. The "explanation for the new name of Abraham defines his destiny."[223] That is, the name change doesn't just mark the covenant. The promises of the covenant are a sort of revealing of the meaning of the name, of what it would mean to become an "Abraham."

In Matthew 16, Jesus is revealing the new way that God will draw his people to himself, and he reveals it through a personal blessing on Simon, by changing his name, and bestowing certain promises upon him. The new name, *Petros* (meaning "rock"), is intentional, the promises in the rest of the passage are a way of revealing the meaning of this name change. D.H. Williams notes the argument that "Peter was too unstable to be regarded as a 'rock,'"[224] but it's worth recognizing that at the time God changes Abram's name to Abraham, Isaac hasn't even been born. The name change is a promise, not simply a description of present realities.

Reading the Caesarea Philippi passage in this way offers three advantages: first, it's consistent with God's behavior in the Old Testament. Second, it offers a greater consistency to the passage. Read in this light, all of Matt. 16:13–23 is a way of answering the twofold questions "Who is Jesus?" and "Who is Simon?"

Recognizing this dimension of the passage reveals the folly of what can be called the "impersonal" interpretations. By this, I mean the interpretations that treat Peter as merely a symbol, a sort of stand-in for us, and not as a person, or at least not as a particularly important person. There's a certain type of Protestant exegete who interprets virtually everything in the New Testament as a sort of platitude about how believers need to have faith. For instance, MacArthur's explanation of this passage is that "Jesus' words here are best interpreted as a simple play on words in that a boulder-like truth came from the mouth of one who was called a small stone."[225] When Christ gives Peter the keys of the kingdom, MacArthur contends that "these represent authority, and here Christ gives Peter (and by extension all other believers) authority to declare what was bound or loosed in heaven."[226] This interpretation reduces the binding and the loosing, the keys of the kingdom, and even the name change of Simon to Peter as essentially three different opaque ways of saying, "Believe in Jesus." Such a denuded interpretation would be like reading God's promises to Abraham as a simple expression of the joys of fatherhood or faithfulness without recognizing that actual promises are being made to an individual man.

The Personal Nature of the Blessing

The problem with interpreting Peter out of this passage is that he is at the center of Jesus' words. The Anglican R.T. France concluded that the "rock" in Matthew 16:18 is Peter, because "the word-play, and the whole structure of the passage, demands that this verse is every bit as much Jesus' declaration about Peter as v. 16 was Peter's declaration about Jesus."[227] A careful examination will reveal that France is correct. Jesus begins the blessing by saying "blessed are you," and the "are you" is the second-person singular Greek. John Calvin claims that "this was not spoken in a peculiar manner to Peter alone," but it quite explicitly was, with Jesus blessing Simon in the singular, in the presence of the others.[228] He then addresses Simon by his birth name. He adds to this address the title "bar-Jona," which literally means "son of Jonah," and normally serves as something like a family name.

However, there are a few reasons to believe that something different is occurring here. First, from John's Gospel, we know that Simon's father is actually named John ("YHWH is a gracious giver"), not Jonah ("dove"). Jesus refers to him as "Simon, son of John" some four times (John 1:42, 21:15,16,17).[229] Second, the title "son of" (*bar*) is often used in non-literal contexts within Judaism: most famously, the Jewish *bar mitzvah* ceremony literally means that one becomes a "son of the commandment,"[230] and Jesus refers to James and John as "sons of thunder" (Mark 3:17). Finally, Jesus has just spoken a few verses earlier about how "an evil and adulterous generation seeks for a sign, but no sign shall be given to it except *the sign of Jonah*" (Mt. 16:4).

If the two references to Jonah in Matthew 16 belong together, then we cannot understand why Peter is "bar-Jona" unless we understand what Jesus means by the "sign of Jonah." There seem to be three dimensions to this sign, two of which Jesus suggests. First, Jonah spent "three days and three nights in the belly of the whale," just as Jesus would spend "three days and three nights in the heart of the earth" in his passion, death and resurrection (Matt. 12:40). Second, Jonah preached, "Yet forty days, and Nineveh shall be overthrown!" causing the Ninevites to repent (Jon. 3:4–5). Jerusalem does not follow Nineveh's example and is destroyed by the Romans forty years thence. Thus, "the men of Nineveh will arise at the judgment with this generation and condemn [this generation]; for they repented at the preaching of Jonah, and behold, something greater than Jonah is here" (Luke 11:32). But there's a third dimension as well. Nineveh was the capital of the hated Assyrian Empire, and God was sending Jonah to preach salvation to the Gentiles. Thus, Jonah fled from Nineveh not because he was afraid that they would reject his preaching, but because he was afraid that they would accept it and be saved. He explains to God that he tried to flee to Tarshish, "for I knew that thou art a gracious God and merciful, slow to anger, and abounding in steadfast love, and repentest of evil" (Jon. 4:2).

Understood in this light, we can see why Peter would be a "son of Jonah" in the Christological sense. After all, he is the first public preacher of the passion, death, and resurrection of Christ (Acts 2:14–41), and he does so by entreating the people, "Save yourselves from this crooked generation" (40). And it is through Peter that God definitively opens the door of salvation to the Gentiles (10–11). In the household of Cornelius, Peter proclaims that "God shows no partiality, but in every nation any one who fears him and does what is right is acceptable to him" (10:34). As he preached, the Holy Spirit came upon even the Gentiles, to the shock of Peter's companions (44–45), leading to the baptism of the first Gentile converts. As Peter would later remind the Council of

Jerusalem, "Brethren, you know that in the early days God made choice among you, that by my mouth the Gentiles should hear the word of the gospel and believe" (15:7).

The Anglican C.S.C. Williams is one of only a handful of scholars to notice that "the commission of Peter to go to Cornelius, his initial reluctance to do so but his subsequent obedience, leading to the gift of the Holy Spirit being conferred on the Gentiles, had its counterpart in the commission of Jonah to the heathen at Nineveh."[231] In promising that the "evil and adulterous generation" will receive the "sign of Jonah," Jesus is foretelling his death and resurrection, his rejection by Israel, and his acceptance by the Gentiles. And in calling Peter "Simon bar-Jona," he's foretelling the particular role that Simon Peter will play in all of that, by being the first to proclaim Christ to Jerusalem and the Jewish pilgrims on Pentecost, and then being the first to preach salvation even to the Gentiles.

After invoking Simon as "bar-Jona," Jesus commends his confession of faith and tells him God the Father "revealed this to you" (Matt. 16:17). Here again, we find Peter being addressed in the second-person singular, this time with the dative. This is the same word used a verse later, when Jesus says, "I tell you" (or "I say to you"). And what does Jesus then say to Peter, singularly, in the presence of the Twelve? That "you [*singular*] are Peter."[232] So personal is this address that both Peter (1 Pet. 1:1) and others (Mark 5:37, Acts 1:13, etc.) use it as if it were Peter's personal name. All of the existing historical evidence suggests that the name Peter was coined by Jesus Christ specifically for Simon Peter.[233] This new name means "rock," and Jesus immediately adds, "And on this rock I will build my church" (Matt. 16:18), which he promises will not be overcome by the gates of hell. It looks very much like when God invented the name Abraham and then immediately explained what it meant (Gen. 17:5).

Jesus then makes three promises to Peter, each of which is again in the second-person singular: (1) "I will give you the keys of the kingdom of heaven," (2) "Whatever you bind on earth shall be bound in heaven," and (3) "Whatever you loose on earth shall be loosed in heaven" (Matt. 16:19). In case you've lost count, this marks at least ten distinct times that Jesus specifically addressed Simon Peter individually, using the second-person singular, in the span of three verses. And he did so deliberately, in the presence of the rest of the Twelve. This hasn't stopped Protestant scholars like Baylor's D.H. Williams from arguing that Peter merely "exemplifies every believer who has moments of great perception as well as a tendency toward self-centeredness and loss of divine understanding."[234] This is a recurring theme among those who don't want Peter to be the rock: they tend to interpret the passage in ways that make Peter entirely extraneous or merely one believer whom Jesus happens to be addressing in a passage meant for us all. At some point, it's reasonable to ask what more Jesus could have said to emphasize the personal nature of the blessing, or if any amount of explicit evidence would be enough to change the opinion of these exegetes.[235]

How Might a Protestant Respond?

A distinction should be made between what's believed by Protestant scholars who have studied Matthew 16 and what's held at a popular level by preachers and the lay faithful. Among scholars, there is actually a great deal of consensus (cutting across confessional lines) that the "rock" (*petra*) is Peter. Lund University's Chrys C. Caragounis (who personally disagrees with the scholarly consensus) summarizes the state of scholarship by saying that "after centuries of disagreement it would appear that Protestant and Catholic are at last united in referring the rock upon which the Church according to Mt. 16:18 is to be built, to the apostle Peter," although he adds that "most Protestant exegetes who refer [*petra*] to Peter do so under the assumption that the passage is inauthentic," the work of some later redactor trying to score theological points by putting these words in the mouth of Jesus.[236] In other words, Protestant scholars are now concluding that the rock is Peter, but rather than accepting Peter, many are rejecting the scriptural text.

There's a different debate going on at the popular level. The popular Protestant interpretation of Matthew 16:17–19 is, in essence, "anything but that" exegesis. In other words, Protestants will come to all sorts of contrary conclusions about the meaning of Matthew 16:17–19, or simply conclude that they don't know what it means, but they'll all agree that it just can't mean the straightforward Catholic interpretation. For example, Southern Baptist preacher A.T. Robinson (1863–1934) explains the passage away thusly:

> Jesus makes a play upon the name Peter (Rock). It is not perfectly clear how Jesus means the figure to be applied. He could mean himself (Christ) by "this rock," if he pointed to himself. . . . Jesus could mean Peter himself by "this rock," as representative of the twelve and as confessing his faith in Christ. . . . Or Jesus could mean the *confession* of trust made by Peter as the rock on which, in truth, the kingdom is built. The matter can never be settled for all minds.[237]

According to Robinson, it's not clear *what* Jesus means, but he obviously doesn't mean what he appears to be saying—namely, that Peter is the rock upon which the Church is going to be built.

I saw this sort of "anything but that" exegesis on display in an online forum once. Two Catholics presented the standard Catholic interpretation of Matthew 16, that Jesus is speaking of building the Church upon Peter the rock. They were quickly banned from the forum, and three different Protestants jumped in to correct them. The only problem was, none of them agreed with each other! The first said that "it is clear Christ was referring to the foundation of his Church, which is what Peter means, i.e. rock. He wasn't building his Church on Peter, but on the meaning of Peter's name, rock." The second Protestant then corrected her, saying, rather, "The rock upon which the Church was (is) built . . . is Peter's confession of faith, not the man Peter." A third Protestant then corrected them both to say: "It was not Peter or his confession upon which Christ built the church. Christ is the cornerstone rejected by the Jewish leaders. He is the rock of refuge and the firm foundation of everything that will pass through the fires of judgment."

My immediate thought was how well these feuding Protestants proved Christ's point in Matthew 16, the passage they were all attempting to interpret. Like the confused believers Jesus asked about, some were saying John the Baptist, others Elijah, and others Jeremiah or one of the prophets (Matt. 16:14), wandering about like sheep without a shepherd. It's in direct response to this that Jesus says he's going to establish his Church upon Peter. Today, we see a Protestantism in which some say the rock is Christ himself, some say Peter as a representative of the Twelve, and some say Peter's confession of faith, and the existence of this theological chaos and biblical confusion points to the continued need for Peter and his successors. With that said, here are a few of the particular doctrinal points in dispute.

Is the "Rock" Jesus?

As I noted at the start of the chapter, A.T. Robinson says Jesus "could mean himself (Christ) by 'this rock,' *if he pointed to himself*."[238] Likewise, if we imagine that Jesus was holding construction plans, pointing to where he was going to build a chapel, we could interpret "this rock" as referring to a particular physical location. But neither interpretation is any good. Why? Because any biblical interpretation that turns on the existence of some never-mentioned detail (like Jesus holding construction plans, or pointing to himself) is bad exegesis. Furthermore, this interpretation butchers the metaphor, as the Presbyterian minister Marvin Richardson Vincent explains:

> The reference of [*petra*] to Christ is forced and unnatural. The obvious reference of the word is to Peter. The emphatic *this* naturally refers to the nearest antecedent; and besides, the foundation is thus weakened, since Christ appears here, not as the *foundation*, but as the *architect*: "on this rock *will I build*."[239]

Nothing *within* the text itself supports interpreting it as saying "Christ will build the Church upon Christ." Instead, the major reason for viewing the "rock" as Jesus is that *other* parts of Scripture use "rock" language to refer to God (and sometimes specifically to Jesus). For example, a few chapters later in Matthew's Gospel, Jesus will apply to himself Psalm 118:22, "the very stone which the builders rejected has become the head of the corner," thereby describing himself as the cornerstone.

This has led some Protestants to make sweeping, false statements, like that "God himself is clearly described as the unfailing 'rock' of our salvation throughout the entire Old

Testament. . . . In fact, the Bible declares that God is the *only* rock" or that "any first-century Orthodox Jew familiar with the Tenach (what Jews call the Old Testament scriptures), like Peter or Paul, knew that the God of Israel identified himself as the 'rock' of salvation in Israel's divine history, and would never have taken it to mean anything else."[240] These claims are simply untrue. Although the Old Testament typically applies the "rock" imagery to God, Isaiah 51:1–2 applies it to Abraham:

> Hearken to me, you who pursue deliverance, you who seek the Lord; look to the rock from which you were hewn, and to the quarry from which you were digged. Look to Abraham your father and to Sarah who bore you; for when he was but one I called him, and I blessed him and made him many.

Joseph Benson, one of the early Methodist ministers, explains that in this Isaiah passage, God "compares the bodies of Abraham and Sarah unto a rock, or pit, or quarry, out of which stones are hewn or dug; thereby implying, that God, in some sort, actually did that which John the Baptist said he was able to do, (Matthew 3:9,) 'even of stones to raise up children unto Abraham.'"[241] In other words, when John the Baptist warns the Pharisees and Sadducees, "Do not presume to say to yourselves, 'We have Abraham as our father'; for I tell you, God is able from these stones to raise up children to Abraham" in Matthew 3:9, he seems to be building upon this image of Abraham as the rock. If it's okay to refer to Abraham as the "rock" in the Old Covenant, there's no good reason to pretend it's blasphemous to call Peter the "rock" in the New Covenant, particularly given the parallels in the covenantal language used for the two men.

One obvious problem with these objections is that they rely on overextending metaphorical language. There's no reason why a metaphor must always mean the same thing each time it's used or must always be applied to the same person or referent.[242] For instance, Jesus is described both as a shepherd (John 10:11) and as a lamb (1:29), and he sends out his followers "as lambs in the midst of wolves" (Luke 10:3) and calls upon Peter to "feed my lambs" (John 21:15). In Matthew 16, Christ is the builder, building upon "the rock." But in 1 Corinthians 3:10, St. Paul refers to *himself* as "a skilled master builder" who "laid a foundation" among the Corinthians; this time, Jesus is the foundation, not the builder.

John MacArthur says the Catholic interpretation of Matthew 16 is "presumptuous and unbiblical, because the rest of the New Testament makes abundantly clear that Christ alone is the foundation and only head of his Church."[243] Here, again, we have a false argument premised upon overextending metaphorical language. It's true that Paul says that "no other foundation can any one lay than that which is laid, which is Jesus Christ" (1 Cor. 3:11), but taking this overly literally misses the point...and contradicts the rest of Scripture.

Revelation 22:14 says that "the wall of the city had *twelve foundations*, and on them the twelve names of the twelve apostles of the Lamb." Paul refers to the Christians at Ephesus as "fellow citizens with the saints and members of the household of God, built upon the foundation of the apostles and prophets, Christ Jesus himself being the cornerstone" (Eph. 2:19–20). This time around, Christ is the cornerstone, the apostles are the foundation, and the rest of us make up the house built upon this apostolic and Christological foundation. MacArthur knows this, acknowledging that this passage "equates the apostles with the church's foundation" and that this is how the earliest Christians understood the Church's foundation:

> Ignatius (c. A.D. 35–115) in his *Epistle to the Magnesians*, spoke in the past tense of the foundation-laying work of Peter and Paul. Referring to the book of Acts, Ignatius wrote, "This was first fulfilled in Syria; for 'the disciples were called Christians at Antioch,' *when Paul and Peter were laying the foundations of the Church.*" Irenaeus (c. 130–202) referred to the twelve apostles as "the twelve-pillared foundation of the church." Tertullian (c. 155–230) similarly explained that "*after* the time of the apostles" the only doctrine that true Christians accepted was that which was "proclaimed in the churches of *apostolic foundation.*" Lactantius (c. 240–320) in his *Divine Institutes* likewise referred to the past time in which the apostolic foundations of the church were laid.[244]

In short, arguments based on the idea that all metaphors involving a "rock" or a "foundation" must refer to God alone are bad arguments that both misunderstand the nature of metaphors and are contradicted by Scripture itself. Since this is the primary argument behind the theory that the "rock" of Matthew 16 is Christ, that interpretation should be judged weak.

Is the "Rock" Peter's Confession of Faith?

A stronger case can be made for the idea that the "rock" of Matthew 16 is Peter's confession of faith. After all, Jesus' words to Peter are certainly in direct response to Peter's confession of faith. And so there is a limited sense in which it's right to connect the "rock" with Peter's confession as the rock. In the aftermath of Barack Obama's re-election, a tech article explained that "it wasn't the super-expensive ads on the national networks that won the election, but the very careful micro-targeting of messages tailored to each reader."[245] You could say, without contradiction, that either "Barack Obama won the election" or "good messaging won the election." One of those tells you *who*, and the other tells you *how* or *why*. The way to express both ideas is to say Obama won re-election because of his strategy of targeted messaging. Likewise, the Southern Baptist Theological Seminary's Gregg Allison is right that we can say that "the rock is Peter by virtue of his confession."[246] If people connecting the "rock" with Peter's confession mean only this, they are right.

The trouble, as Allison realizes, is that oftentimes Peter's confession "is then shorn of any connection with the person of Peter: it is the confession itself, not Peter as confessor, that is emphasized as the foundation of Messiah's church."[247] It becomes just another Protestant interpretation of this personalized blessing that removes Peter from the moment in which he is given a new name. Such a view drives "a wedge between the person of Peter and his divinely revealed confession," and *Peter's* confession of faith quickly becomes simply *any* confession of faith. This is also the case for those who say the rock is about Peter, but as "representative of the Twelve."[248] In one sense that's perfectly true: Peter is speaking and acting on behalf of all of the apostles, and even all of the Church, just as the pope speaks and acts for the episcopacy and the Church today. No gifts are given for our private benefit, but are given "for the work of ministry, for building up the body of Christ" (Eph. 4:11–13). But often, those who argue for "Peter as a representative" really mean that Peter isn't particularly important and that Jesus meant these words for all of us.

This tendency to strip Peter of his blessing is explicit in the first Protestant Reformers. Martin Luther interprets Jesus' "upon this rock" as meaning "upon thy confession of faith, which makes thee a rock and upon this doctrine I will build my church."[249] But Peter is quickly sidelined, as Luther concludes that "Christ permitted Peter to fall, that we should not regard him as *the* rock, nor build upon him," and that "we also should all be called Peters (rocks)."[250] John Calvin's reading goes farther, suggesting that even the words "you are Peter" extend "no doubt, to all believers, each of whom is a temple of God," and that "the name *Peter* comes to be applied both to Simon individually, and to other believers."[251] At this point, nothing is personal to Peter, not even his name. Every Christian is Peter.

By this reasoning, we should expect to see a whole lot of Christians in the New Testament getting their names changed to Peter. But we see only one: Simon Peter. At the very least, if Luther and Calvin were correct, we should see Jesus changing the name of the first person to correctly confess him as the Christ. But we see nothing of the sort. This is most apparent if we look at the first chapter of John's Gospel. There, John the Baptist proclaims, "Behold, the Lamb of God, who takes away the sin of the world!" (John 1:29). Recognizing that "this is he of whom I said, 'After me comes a man who ranks before me, for he was before me,'" John concludes that "this is the Son of God" (John 1:30,34). One of John's disciples, Andrew, leaves John the Baptist to follow Christ. He brings with him his brother, Simon, to whom he says, "We have found the Messiah," a title that the Evangelist reminds us means "Christ" (1:41). Another disciple, Philip, tells Nathaniel that "we have found him of whom Moses in the law and also the prophets wrote, Jesus of Nazareth, the son of Joseph" (1:45). After encountering

Jesus, Nathaniel is then led to confess, "Rabbi, you are the Son of God! You are the King of Israel!" (1:49).

If Luther's or Calvin's argument is correct, we should see Jesus changing the names of John the Baptist, Andrew, Philip, and Nathaniel to Peter. Nathaniel's confession of faith in particular is remarkably similar to what Simon Peter will confess much later, in Matthew 16. But Jesus doesn't do that. In the span of these twenty-one verses, there's only one person named who *isn't* depicted as confessing Christ, and that's Simon. Although he's mentioned by name in the passage, John doesn't describe him saying anything remarkable. And yet right in the midst of this passage, Jesus says to Simon, and not to any of these others, "So you are Simon the son of John? You shall be called Cephas," a name that John helpfully translates for us as "Peter" (John 1:42). If the "rock" were simply "confession of faith," everyone *other than* Peter would be the rock in John 1. But Jesus clearly sees things differently.

Do *Petros* and *Petra* Mean Different Things?

Underlying nearly every Protestant rejection of Peter as the "rock" of Matthew 16 is the supposed difference between the Greek *Petros* and *petra*. After all, if *Petros* and *petra* mean the same thing, it seems quite clear that Jesus intends each to refer to Simon Peter: "You are Rock, and upon this rock I will build my church," with the only difference being that in the first case, "rock" is being used as a proper name or a title.[252]

And so we regularly find Protestants claiming that *Petros* means a small rock, even a pebble, whereas *petra* means a boulder or an immovable rock.[253] William Cathcart (the nineteenth-century president of the American Baptist Historical Society) writes that "*Petros* is a stone, a movable stone;

petra is a rock, a mass of rocks, a cliff. The one, such a stone as a maid-servant in the hall of judgment might upset; the other was the Rock of Ages—the confession that Peter made that Christ was the Son of the living God." According to Cathcart, the fact that Matthew used both *Petros* and *petra* meant that *Petra* "MUST refer to something different from Peter."[254]

In 1980, John MacArthur reworded Jesus' declaration to Peter this way: "You are *petros*—'you are a pebble Peter, you are a boulder'—but upon this *petra*—'rock bed foundation'—I will build my church." And what was that "rock bed foundation"? Peter's "confession of faith."[255] Notice that MacArthur's interpretation has Jesus saying, "You are Peter *but* upon this rock I will build my church," whereas Jesus actually says, "You are Peter *and* upon this rock I will build my church." This understanding of the passage requires introducing an opposition between *petros* and *petra* not actually found in the text, and so, eight years later, we find him arguing against his old interpretation, saying that "it seems more likely that, in light of other New Testament passages, that was not Jesus' point."[256]

At this point, he decides that "Jesus addressed Peter as representative of the Twelve," even though the Twelve are there present, and that "the use of the two different forms of the Greek for rock would be explained by the masculine *petros* being used of Peter as an individual man and *petra* being used of him as the representative of the larger group."[257] He continues to hold to the position that "it was not on the apostles themselves, much less on Peter as an individual, that Christ built his Church."[258] Anything but that.

The problem with this line of argumentation can be seen in an old, probably apocryphal account of the building of St. Paul's Cathedral in London. As the story goes, Sir Christopher Wren's design was chosen because it was "the most awful and artificial." Later versions of the story have it that the design was chosen because it was "amusing, awful, and artificial."[259] The punchline is that back in 1675, *amusing, awful,* and *artificial* were all words a church architect would love to hear, meaning "amazing," "awe-inspiring," and "artistic," respectively, but these words had come to mean something quite different by the twentieth century. I bring this up simply to point out the obvious: the meaning of words can shift, often dramatically, over the course of centuries. This is no less true of Greek than of English, which is why it's problematic that Protestants arguing for a sharp distinction in meaning between *petros* and *petra* are basing their arguments on poetry from centuries earlier.

Protestant exegetes who examine the matter closely tend to admit that there was actually no clear difference between *petros* and *petra* at the time of Christ, and so I will confine myself to only Protestant scholarship for the remainder of this section. The Lutheran theologian Oscar Cullman admits that "the difference in meaning between the two Greek words is not fixed."[260] Furthermore:

> The idea of the Reformers that he is referring to the faith of Peter is quite inconceivable. . . . For there is no reference here to the faith of Peter. Rather, the parallelism of "thou art Rock" and "on this rock I will build" shows that the second rock can only be the same as the first. It is thus evident that Jesus is referring to Peter, to whom he has given the name Rock. He appoints Peter, the impulsive, enthusiastic, but not persevering man in the circle, to be the foundation of his *ecclesia.*[261]

D.A. Carson[262] goes farther, arguing that "if it were not for Protestant reactions against extremes of Roman

Catholic interpretation, it is doubtful whether many would have taken 'rock' to be anything or anyone other than Peter."[263] One of the reasons Carson holds this is that "although it is true that *petros* and *petra* can mean stone and rock respectively in earlier Greek, the distinction is largely confined to poetry."[264]

At this point, you may well be frustrated. With scholars saying opposite things about first-century Greek, how can a reader who doesn't know ancient Greek possibly know which side to believe in this debate? Fortunately, the evidence is quite clear by looking to other ancient Greek writings. For example, Apollonius of Rhodes, a Greek poet from the third century B.C., wrote the *Argonautica*, the now famous epic of Jason and the Argonauts and their quest for the Golden Fleece. At one point, he describes how Jason "seized from the plain a huge round boulder, a terrible quoit of Ares Enyalius; four stalwart youths could not have raised it from the ground even a little."[265] The word he chose for this "huge round boulder," so large that four men couldn't budge it? *Petros.*[266] Does that sound like a "pebble" to you? And so we see that *petra* and *petros* had already come to mean the same thing even hundreds of years before Christ.

Caragounis finds some equivalency in meaning between *petros* and *petra* in ancient Greek texts, adding that "in later literature this interchangeability becomes more frequent, until finally [*petros*] falls into disuse" and "[*petra*] comes to signify 'stone.'"[267] Once *petros* and *petra* come to mean the same thing, Greek speakers stop using the now-redundant *petros*. At this point, they use *lithos* or stones, which can be anything from a pebble to a boulder. It's *lithos* that St. Matthew uses for everything from the stone you wouldn't hand to your child (Matt. 7:9) to the "great stone" over the Tomb of Christ (27:60). Neither he nor any other New Testament author ever uses *petros* in the way Protestant exegetes claim they should. Instead, the only time *petros* is used is to refer to Peter.

One final point to consider is that Jesus refers to himself as "the very stone which the builders rejected," which becomes the cornerstone (Matt. 21:42). If Jesus was trying to make a subtle theological argument based on the alleged difference in meaning between "small rock" and "big rock," he certainly seems to undercut it when he refers to himself as a "stone," using the word *lithos*. The obvious conclusion is that he was never making such a distinction, but instead meant exactly what a first-century speaker would understand him to mean: "You are Rock, and upon this rock I will build my church."

Did Jesus Say These Words in Greek?

The whole argument about what Jesus meant in saying *Petros* and then *petra* presupposes that Jesus said these words to Peter in Greek. But we know that this isn't true. Although the New Testament was written in Greek, it records and translates conversations that would have been primarily in Aramaic. But how can we know for certain that Matthew 16 was in Aramaic, rather than Hebrew or Greek? There are three ways. First, because Jesus' "denoting of Peter's father by bar-Jona," which is a Semitic expression, not a Greek one.[268] Second, because St. Paul nearly exclusively refers to Peter as Cephas (pronounced like "Kephas," not like "Sephas"), which is a transliteration of the Aramaic *Kefa*.[269] Why would he translate a Greek name like *Petros* into Aramaic and then transliterate it back to Greek?

The third reason why we know that the new name was originally given in Aramaic is that St. John tells us so. "Jesus looked at him, and said, 'So you are Simon the son of John? You shall be called Cephas' (which means Peter)" (John 1:42). John's account here is important for harmonizing the New Testament, because he's letting us know that when Paul speaks of "Cephas," it's the same guy whom the Evangelists call "Petros," or Peter. And John is clear that Simon's name is originally Aramaic, and is translated into Greek as *Petros*.

Why does this matter? Because the original name Jesus gave Peter means "rock." D.A. Carson explains that "the Aramaic which underlies the Greek, means '(massive) rock.'"[270] So Jesus didn't actually say "*Petros . . . petra*," but seems to have said "*kepha . . . kepha*." Cullman notes that "the pun can be fully appreciated only in Aramaic, which has the same word *kepha* both times, not *petros* [and] *petra* as in Greek."[271] In other words, "You are Rock, and on this rock, I will build my church."

But if the Aramaic says *kepha* both times, why doesn't Matthew say *petra* both times? Because, unlike Aramaic or English, Greek words have genders. It's common to hear Catholics say Matthew chose to translate Peter's name as *Petros* because *petra* is feminine, and he didn't want to give him a girl's name. But that's not quite right. By the time Matthew wrote his Gospel, everyone knew Peter as *Petros*. When the angel appears to Cornelius, he tells him to "send men to Joppa, and bring one Simon who is called Peter [*Petros*]" (Acts 10:5). Paul refers to him either as *Cephas* (from the Aramaic) or as *Petros* (Gal. 2:7–8). Most importantly, *Petros* is how St. Peter introduces himself in 1 Peter 1:1 and 2 Peter 1:1. In that case, why not use *petros* both times? Because *petros* was no longer a regular part of ordinary Greek vocabulary.[272] As noted above, in the dozens of references to rocks and stones in the New Testament, we find *lithos* used 60 times, *petra* used 15 other times, and *petros* never used at all, except as a name for Peter. By the time

St. Matthew writes his Gospel, *Petros* is how Peter introduces himself, but *petros* isn't a commonly used word for rock anymore, so Matthew translates the Aramaic using the best options open to him: by using the commonly used Greek name for Peter and the commonly used Greek word for a large rock.

All of this is to say that the most accurate English translation of Matthew 16:18 would be, "And I tell you, you are Rock, and on this rock I will build my church, and the gates of Hades shall not prevail against it."[273] Rendered that way, it's transparent that the "rock" in both cases is Simon Peter, Jesus' addressee. It's understandable why this meaning wasn't as transparent to those, like St. Augustine, who spoke neither Greek nor Aramaic. But this is one area in which centuries of scholarship around the Greek and Aramaic, around the Jewish meaning to these phrases, and around the structure of the passage have actually proven helpful in moving scholars toward a consensus that yes, Peter is the rock upon which Jesus built the Church.

10

YOU ARE PETER

PERHAPS YOU'RE unconvinced by the prior chapter about the "rock" being St. Peter, or still uncertain. That's fine! There's a reason why scholars favor the reading I just described, and it's got a wealth of biblical and patristic support, but it's also true that great saints have interpreted the "rock" in a different way. Let's set that question aside now, because there's a lot more in this passage that often gets overlooked as everyone focuses on the meaning of "rock." Even if you elided over the "rock" section entirely, you would still have Jesus saying to Peter, "Blessed are you, Simon bar-Jona!" ascribing his confession of faith to divine revelation, and giving him the keys to the kingdom and the power to bind and loose sins. And these parts of the passage have the great advantage that they are unmistakably said to, and about, Simon Peter. So let's see what else this passage has to tell us.

The Four Models of Church Governance

In ascending order of polity, there are essentially only four models of Church governance: congregational, presbyterial, episcopal, and papal.[274] The lowest two of these polities are democratic, as "democratic ecclesiologies typically result in congregational or representative churches with no bishops (e.g., the Presbyterian)."[275] The first of these, congregational governance, is "direct government of the church by the people who make up the congregation," and it "comes close to being pure democracy in action."[276] Nearly all Baptist churches are congregational. Presbyterian congregations are "governed by a group of presbyters elected by the congregation and known as the session."[277] Without denying the legitimate authority of the laity, presbyterianism argues for a higher authority. If congregationalism is "pure democracy," presbyterianism is akin to republican democracy.

Above this is episcopal governance, "the form of church government that is carried out by means of bishops."[278] In American Episcopalianism, bishops are elected, but in England, they're "designated."[279] The importance here is not only that authority resides with a smaller group of leaders, but that this is top-down leadership. Continuing the political metaphor, this model is akin to something like an aristocracy, not in the pejorative sense of "snob," but in the original sense in which Aristotle used the term: as "rule of the few (but of more than one person)."[280]

The most hierarchical is the papal model found in the Catholic Church. Although there are various levels of authority, the buck stops with one man, the pope. This understanding of Church governance is expressly monarchical, and not simply in a metaphorical way. As one political science textbook describes it: "A truly global church with a hierarchical structure headquartered in its own sovereign nation (Vatican City), the Catholic Church is literally the oldest continuously functioning institution in the world."[281]

From an American perspective, this monarchical character of the Catholic Church has always been something of an embarrassment. Liberal Catholics like Paul Lakeland lament (and not without cause) that "it is ironic that a culture of participatory democracy like that of the United States should be served by a group of bishops who collectively seem to be allergic to the democratic process."[282] The advantages of a representative and democratic system are relatively clear to most of us in the West, and the pitfalls of clericalism, secrecy, cronyism, and a lack of accountability are painfully clear at present in the Catholic Church in America and around the world. What may be less clear are the advantages of a hierarchical system, or the disadvantages of a democratic church. Fortunately, Jesus seems to highlight them in his conversation at Caesarea Philippi.

Consider the discussion in light of the alternative models of church governance. Jesus' first question is, as it were, a democratic one: "Who do men say that the Son of man is?" (Matt. 16:13). Right away, the problem becomes clear, as the apostles respond, "Some say John the Baptist, others say Elijah, and others Jeremiah or one of the prophets" (14). Left to our own devices, we are prone to come to contradictory theological opinions. This is true not just of the crowds in general, but of Christians as well. These contradictory opinions are not from the people who believed Jesus was a charlatan or a false prophet. It was those who believed in him who still weren't sure just what they believed about him or who they thought he was.

Martin Luther taught that "nothing whatever is left obscure or ambiguous" in the Bible, but instead that "all things that are in Scripture, are by the Word brought forth into the clearest light, and proclaimed to the whole world."[283] The idea is simple—Scripture is so clear that we don't need the pope, or the Church, or Tradition, or anything else to interpret its meaning. But if this were true, we should find all serious Christians in a single denomination and in total agreement on doctrine. At the very least, we should expect, as time went on, to find fewer and fewer Protestant denominations. But we see the exact opposite: as the Bible becomes easier and easier to access, as theological resources become more abundant, as a library that would have stunned the scholars of old is available for free at the fingertips of anyone with a computer or a library card, we find that there is *more* disagreement and that the number of denominations is growing rather than shrinking. "Some say John the Baptist, others say Elijah" turns out to be a perennial and inescapable problem. You and I will simply not interpret the Bible the exact same way. Multiply that disagreement by the world's 2.18 billion Christians, and you can see the size and scope of the problem.

Denominationalism is the natural result of a democratic church. There is no religious authority that all parties trust other than Scripture, and it's on the interpretation of Scripture that they disagree. (Failure to grasp this basic distinction is how you end up with John MacArthur calling biblical interpretations he disagrees with "unbiblical.") Those who believe that Jesus is John the Baptist disagree with those who believe he's Elijah, or Jeremiah, etc., and eventually they'll part company. The scholars Craig Atwood and Roger Olson (a Moravian and a Baptist, respectively) have explained that "the old Reformation slogan of 'Scripture alone' produced a cornucopia of denominations in the United States as ordinary individuals took up the challenge of interpreting the Bible and judging religious authorities," leading to "a bewildering variety of Protestant groups" within America.[284]

But it's not just that the crowds come to contradictory conclusions. They're also all wrong. The crowds speculate that Jesus is John the Baptist, or Elijah, or Jeremiah, or "one of the prophets," but none of them ventures a guess that he might be "the Christ," or the Second Person of the Trinity. In eliciting the answer to his first question, Jesus shows the folly of the democratic slogan *vox populi, vox dei* (the voice of the people is the voice of God). Indeed, the first recorded instance of this phrase is actually from St. Alcuin of York (735–804) explaining to Charlemagne what a foolish idea it is:

> The people in accordance with divine law are to be led, not followed. And when witnesses are needed, men of position are to be preferred. Nor are those to be listened to who are accustomed to say, "The voice of the people is the voice of God." For the clamor of the crowd [*vulgi*] is very close to madness.[285]

What makes democracy work in the political realm is that there's no reason to believe that any voter, or any politician, or any party has really figured out the absolute truth in politics.[286] We're free to disagree because, to some extent, we know we're all guessing: guessing at how the politician will be if elected, or how well the policy will work if passed, etc. But Christianity is built on the idea that we aren't just left with our best guesses about God. Instead, God enters history and reveals himself to us. And so we need not, and should not, be left with just "some say John the Baptist, others say Elijah, and others Jeremiah or one of the prophets." It's possible to know the truth, but it won't be from the *populi*.

So much for the democratic idea of church governance. Christ's second question is to the Twelve about themselves. Recall again that aristocracy, in its original meaning, just meant "rule of the few (but of more than one person)."[287] That seems to be a good description of the Twelve, those to whom Christ said, "You are those who have continued with me in my trials; as my Father appointed a kingdom for me, so do I appoint for you that you may eat and drink at my table in my kingdom, and sit on thrones judging the twelve tribes of Israel" (Luke 22:28–30). Jesus asks these Christian "aristocrats" about their own views: "But who do *you* say that I am?" (Matt. 16:15). The question is addressed to all twelve of them, and that "you" is in the second-person plural. But whereas "they" were happy to answer the first question about the crowds (cf. Matt. 16:14), all but one suddenly fall silent when asked for their own views. Were it not for St. Peter speaking out, guided by divine inspiration, it's not clear that the question would have been answered by any of the others.

This apostolic silence is a feature of the Eastern Orthodox Church. As Bishop Ware explains, "there is in Orthodoxy no one with an equivalent position to the pope in the Roman Catholic Church."[288] The highest-ranking bishop, the Ecumenical Patriarch of Constantinople, has an office that better "resembles that of the Archbishop of Canterbury in the worldwide Anglican Communion." The result is a "decentralized system of independent local Church."[289] One consequence of this decentralized system is comparative silence on the theological and moral challenges buffeting the Church. After the eleventh-century schism between the Catholic Church and the Eastern Orthodox Church, there are no more councils within Orthodoxy that are recognized by all the Orthodox. Without Peter, the other apostles fall relatively silent. Earlier in the Gospel of Matthew, Jesus has compassion on the crowds because "they were harassed and helpless, like sheep without a shepherd" (Matt. 9:36). Without the leadership of a shepherd, we are not only prone to contentious disputations. We're also left unprepared, helpless to handle the challenges we face as a church.

Even today, the Eastern Orthodox Church still "has never defined its official position on the scriptural canon in any ecumenical or Pan-Orthodox council."[290] That is, there's still no official consensus within Orthodoxy as to which books belong in the Bible. Perhaps needless to say, there are also no clear Orthodox answers on more recent moral and bioethical questions. On its website, the Greek Orthodox Church in America's article on "The Stand of the Orthodox Church on Controversial Issues" explains that "very few claims to uncontroverted teaching can be made" on issues like "artificial insemination, artificial inovulation, in vitro fertilization, sterilization, genetic counseling and genetic screening as well as genetic engineering" and that the Orthodox are only in "the earliest stages in the process of dealing with controversial issues."[291]

If the answer to Jesus' first question showed the difficulties with a purely democratic system of Church governance, the general silence to his second question showed the difficulty with a purely-aristocratic polity. What is needed is one "aristocrat" capable of answering for the rest, one apostle able to speak on behalf of all of the apostles, even able to speak on behalf of the entire Church. And this is exactly what we find when Simon Peter answers on behalf of the rest, declaring, "You are the Christ, the Son of the living God" (Matt. 16:16). This is not simply Simon Peter's natural impetuousness. It is instead his openness to the promptings of providence. As Jesus says in reply, "Blessed are you, Simon bar-Jona! For flesh and blood has not revealed this to you, but my Father who is in heaven" (16:17).

This is not to say that Peter is all that the Church needs—only that his individual role is integral. Christ calls all twelve, but the Father gives the answer through one of them in particular. Long before the Great Schism between Catholicism and Orthodoxy, this was expressed in a beautiful way in the East. We see a strong affirmation of the papacy from St. John Chrysostom (349–407), who refers to Peter as "the chosen one of the apostles, the mouth of the disciples, the leader of the band," into whose hands Jesus places "the chief authority among the brethren." But the nuanced beauty of John's expression is lost in the translation from Greek. Behind the "leader of the band" language is the Greek word *coryphaeus*, which referred to the chorus leader in ancient Greek theater. The role was a complex one:

> The leader of the chorus, or *coryphaeus*, had several roles that required him to be a skilled dancer and musician. He assisted with rehearsals and arranged the chorus in formation. As the lead dancer, he cued the chorus to enter the stage and begin the dance. Onstage he tapped his feet to keep time. Sometimes he was given a short solo in the dithyramb.[292]

The task of the *coryphaeus* was a difficult one, and it required a certain humility. After all, a leader who treated the rest of the chorus as irrelevant (or a threat to his glory) would fail to lead effectively. And so, Peter is the leader, but one called to enable the rest of the "chorus" of apostles to rise to new heights of excellence. That's the Peter we see here in Matthew 16, answering on behalf of the Twelve, in such a way that they are all given a new insight into Christ's glory.

The Rock and the Stumbling Block

By the structure of Matthew 16, Jesus seems to be showing the necessity of the papal polity over the weaknesses of a silent aristocracy or a self-contradictory democracy. But he shows the problems with a papal system as well. Immediately after this, Jesus tells his disciples about how he must suffer, die, and rise from the dead, and Peter "took him and began to rebuke him, saying, 'God forbid, Lord! This shall never happen to you'" (Matt. 16:22). The pope's attempt to rebuke the living God does not go well. Jesus says to him, "Get behind me, Satan! You are a hindrance to me; for you are not on the side of God, but of men" (23). When Peter proclaims Jesus as the Christ, it's because Peter has been led into this by the Father; when he starts trying to tell Jesus how to conduct his ministry, it's because he is thinking as a man rather than being on the side of God.

This complexity in Peter's character is captured by clever wordplay.[293] Jesus has just called Peter the "rock." Now he calls him a *skandalon,* meaning a "hindrance," or better yet, a "stumbling stone." For "no sooner does Jesus make Peter the rock of his Church than Peter makes himself a stumbling stone to Jesus. The figurative sense of 'stone' in *skandalon* stands in direct contrast to Peter as 'rock' and foundation of the Church."[294] Peter is both the rock upon which Jesus will build the Church and (through the sinfulness of Peter and all of his successors) that rock on the path that scandalizes the faithful, causing them to stumble. Indeed, it's from this word *skandalon* that we get the English *scandal.* So Peter is at once both the rock and the stumbling stone.

In a 1969 essay, Fr. Joseph Ratzinger says we are too "accustomed to make a clear distinction between Peter the rock and Peter the denier of Christ," with Peter as denier of Christ being the pre-Easter Peter and Peter as the rock being the post-Pentecost Peter, "the Peter of whom we have constructed a singularly idealistic image."[295] For in reality,

Ratzinger says, "he was at times both of these." After all, it was the "pre-Easter" Peter who proclaimed the beautiful words, "Lord, to whom shall we go? You have the words of eternal life; and we have believed, and have come to know, that you are the Holy One of God" when other disciples were abandoning Christ (John 6:68–69). On the other hand, it was the "post-Easter" Peter whom St. Paul had to rebuke in Galatia for undermining his own teaching about the equality of the Gentile Christians (Gal. 2:11–14). The future pope concluded, "Has it not been thus throughout the history of the Church that the pope, the successor of Peter has been at once *Petra* and *Skandalon*—both the rock of God and a stumbling block?"[296]

Understanding this complex dimension of both Peter and his successors is critical to understanding the real (as opposed to exaggerated) case for the papacy. Consider John Calvin's arguments against a papal interpretation of Luke 22:

> The thing is too childish in itself to need an answer: for if they insist on applying everything that was said to Peter to the successors of Peter, it will follow, that they are all Satans, because our Lord once said to Peter, "Get thee behind me, Satan, thou art an offense unto me." It is as easy for us to retort the latter saying as for them to adduce the former.[297]

But this is exactly the point. Jesus doesn't promise that the popes (or even the apostles) will be holy or brilliant. But he picks them anyway. As I have written elsewhere:

> Several times in history, the papacy has endured seemingly despite the pope. We might want a papacy in which every pope is sinless, or at least a future saint. But the papacy was founded by Jesus, who once said of his handpicked

apostles, "Did I not choose you, the Twelve, and one of you is a devil?" (John 6:70).[298]

Too many Catholic arguments in favor of the papacy turn a blind eye to the real hindrances that popes (past and present) have proven to be in the promulgation of the gospel. Jesus suffers from no such blindness. God chooses to work through Peter, despite knowing full well that he's a hindrance as well as a rock. Winston Churchill popularized the quip that "democracy is the worst form of government except for all those other forms that have been tried."[299] We can likewise conclude from Matthew 16 that the papacy is the worst form of church governance . . . except for all those other forms that have been tried.

The Keys to the Kingdom

After Simon confesses Jesus as the Christ, Jesus responds by calling Simon "Peter" and declaring "on this rock I will build my church." But then he says, "I will give you the keys of the kingdom of heaven" (Matt. 16:19). Consider that St. Matthew earlier summarized Jesus' public ministry by saying he taught, "Repent, for the kingdom of heaven is at hand" (4:17). Now this same Jesus is giving the keys to that kingdom to one man, Simon Peter (and yes, the grammar is all in the singular here, lest there be any confusion). What could such a gift possibly mean?

According to Luther, and many Protestant exegetes after him, very little. In response to those who say the keys are given to Peter alone, Luther points out that the binding and loosing is given to the whole Church in Matthew 18. Assuming (without explanation) that the keys and the binding and loosing are the same gift, Luther concludes that, therefore, "nothing special was given to St. Peter for his own person." These days, the Evangelical scholar Robert Gundry argues that "the figure of keys represents Jesus' words just as the figure of bedrock does," and "to use the keys will be to teach these words to future disciples."[300] And "the Great Commission will expand the authority to use these keys to include the others along with Peter just as [Matt.] 18:18 will also expand the authority to bind and loosen to include all of them together."[301]

Christ warns against the elders "making void the word of God through your tradition which you hand on" (Mark 7:13). But what would nullify the word of God more effectively than to say Jesus means *nothing* by giving these gifts to Peter? This exegesis makes the rock, the keys, and the binding and loosing redundant, so that the three gifts are really just one (the ability to proclaim the gospel), and then views Jesus as giving gifts to the whole Church that render his gifts to Peter redundant. A helpful question: If this passage were removed from the Bible, what would be lost? If the exegesis of Luther, Gundry, and so many other Protestants is correct, seemingly nothing.

Far better is the exegesis of the early Methodist minister Joseph Benson, who saw in the keys

> a significant emblem of the power of opening and shutting, or binding and loosing, of letting inferiors into an office, or putting them out of it; whence the delivering of the keys of a house or city in a person's hands signifies the giving him the power and possession of it, or the confirming to him of such a grant.[302]

To better understand the meaning of the "keys," though we need to recover the Jewish backdrop to Jesus' words. For this, we should turn to the book of Isaiah, where God says to the self-serving Shebna:

> I will thrust you from your office, and you will be cast down from your station. In that day I will call my servant Eliakim the son of Hilkiah, and I will clothe him with your robe, and will bind your girdle on him, and will commit your authority to his hand; and he shall be a father to the inhabitants of Jerusalem and to the house of Judah. And I will place on his shoulder the key of the house of David; he shall open, and none shall shut; and he shall shut, and none shall open. And I will fasten him like a peg in a sure place, and he will become a throne of honor to his father's house.(Isa. 22:19–23).

If we want to understand what it means for Jesus to give the keys to Peter, it might help to understand what it means for God to give the key to "Eliakim the son of Hilkiah." We are assisted in understanding this by looking at the Targums, which are "the Aramaic translations of the Hebrew Bible done by Jews during the rabbinic period." To the Aramaic-speaking Jewish congregations, "the Targum *is* Scripture."[303] The Targum of Isaiah explains that this is "the key of the sanctuary house and the rule of the house of David."[304] In other words, what's promised in the bestowing of the key upon Eliakim is at once royal and priestly.

The first-century Jewish historian Josephus says Eliakim was "the high priest," for reasons we'll get to in a moment.[305] But it's clear that Eliakim is not only the high priest; he is also an important part of the royal government. In 2 Kings 18, the Assyrian king Sennacherib and his troops come up to Jerusalem, and "when they called for the king, there came out to them Eliakim the son of Hilkiah, who was over the household, and Shebnah the secretary, and Joah the son of Asaph, the recorder" (2 Kings 18:18). It's Eliakim who acts in the person of the king, with the now-demoted Shebnah and the recorder Joah (Asaph's son) alongside him.[306]

This understanding of Eliakim as a sort of priest-king is shocking, but as the University of Copenhagen's Frederik Poulsen notes, the portrait of Eliakim in Isaiah 22 is itself "astonishing," since "as has often been noticed, the royal and priestly imagery brings the character closer to a king or high priest than a steward."[307] Poulsen highlights six important details we might otherwise miss. First, God refers to Eliakim as "my servant," a term of honor usually reserved for the religious and political leaders of Israel. Second, there's the imagery of the "robe" and the "girdle," which were the priestly vestments (see Exod. 28:4–5,40; Lev. 8:7). Third, Eliakim is to be "a father to the inhabitants of Jerusalem and to the house of Judah" (Isa. 22:21). Fourth, "the key of the house of David" is to be placed "on his shoulder." Both the government upon the shoulders and the image of fatherhood are royal images, evoking the coming messianic king, promised earlier in the book with the words that "the government will be upon his shoulder, and his name will be called 'Wonderful Counselor, Mighty God, Everlasting Father, Prince of Peace'" (9:6).

God promises to fasten Eliakim "like a peg in a sure place" (Isa. 22:23), a symbol of security for the land and the people. The dependence of "the whole weight of his father's house, the offspring and issue" is compared to "every small vessel, from the cups to all the flagons" hanging from Eliakim the peg.[308] This again is priestly imagery; upon the table of the bread of presence in the temple were "the vessels of pure gold" and the "bowls and flagons with which to pour libations" (Exod. 37:16). Finally, in the most obviously royal language, he is described as "a throne of honor to his father's house" (Isa. 22:23).[309]

How do we make sense of this picture of Eliakim, given that we know he is *not* the king but follows orders from the true king, Hezekiah (2 Kings 18:36–37)? Here, we must dig deeper into the Old Testament. After Joseph interprets Pharaoh's dream, Pharaoh responds by declaring, "You shall be over my house, and all my people shall order themselves as you command; only as regards the throne will I be greater than you" (Gen. 41:40). Joseph is ritually enrobed and made second to Pharaoh, and he seems to be in charge of much of the actual day-to-day administration of the empire (cf. Gen. 41:42–43). So it is not an exaggeration to say Pharaoh "set him over all the land of Egypt" (Gen. 41:43), even though Pharaoh's throne remains greater. Likewise, when Jotham was co-regent alongside his father Azariah, before he became king, he too was described as ruling "over the household, governing the people of the land" (2 Kings 15:5). So it is with Eliakim: he is the one "who was over the household" of David, but he is such as a vicar of King Hezekiah.

And so it is with Peter, who is given the keys, not simply to the "household of David," but to the kingdom of heaven. Peter testifies that we "are a chosen race, a royal priesthood, a holy nation, God's own people" (1 Pet. 2:9). We all share, in some sense, in the royal and the priestly office of Christ. But if Peter is the new Eliakim, and the recipient of the keys, then Jesus is making him both the top priest in the Church and its top administrator, both offering sacrifice for the kingdom and governing its earthly affairs.[310]

To Bind and to Loose

What does it mean when Jesus gives Peter the ability to "bind on earth" and to "loose on earth" (Matt. 16:19)?

Mark Allan Powell, New Testament professor at Trinity Lutheran Seminary, points out that Martin Luther and others "thought the terms referred to the church's authority to forgive or retain sins." But as the *Jewish Encyclopedia* notes, Luther's interpretation was "quite different" from the "Judaic and ancient view."[311] It's true that Jesus also gives that authority to the Church (in the person of the Twelve) in John 20:22–23, when he breathes the Holy Spirit upon them after the resurrection. But that's not going on here. Instead, as Powell explains, "a majority of scholars now recognize that the terms 'to bind' and 'to loose' are best understood with reference to a practice of determining the application of scriptural commandments for contemporary situations."[312]

To see what "binding" and "loosing" meant in a first-century context, look at what the Jewish historian Flavius Josephus (A.D. 37–100) had to say about the Pharisees under Queen Alexandra. When the queen came to power around 76 B.C., Josephus tells us that a group of "Pharisees joined themselves to her, to assist her in the government." Little by little, they became "the real administrators of the public affairs: they banished and reduced whom they pleased, they bound and loosed [men] at their pleasure; and, to say it all at once, they had the enjoyment of the royal authority" to the extent that the queen "governed other people, and the Pharisees governed her."[313]

This authority of governance included with it the ability to determine what was or wasn't acceptable theologically, morally, and ceremonially. The Babylonian Talmud thus encourages readers to "procure for thyself an understanding heart to hear the words of those who declare unclean and the words of those who declare clean, the words of those who bind and the words of those who loose, the words of those who disqualify and the words of those who pronounce ceremonially pure."[314] It was an enormous authority over the moral lives of the people. And it seems clear from Matthew 23 that this is exactly what Jesus has in view, for he says (Matt. 23:2–4):

> The scribes and the Pharisees sit on Moses' seat; so practice and observe whatever they tell you, but not what they do; for they preach, but do not practice. They bind heavy burdens, hard to bear, and lay them on men's shoulders; but they themselves will not move them with their finger.

It's telling that the Pharisees bind but don't loose. They restrict, but they don't permit. But even as they abuse this authority, Jesus recognizes that they *have* the authority, because they "sit on Moses' seat." And it's striking that in the theological debates between the Pharisees and the Sadducees described in Acts 23:8, the Pharisees were right on all counts. This concept of the seat (*cathedra*, in Latin) is critical for understanding this grant of authority: it's not about personal holiness or orthodoxy, but about protecting the faith of the people from corruption.

There is some scholarly debate about whether the binding and loosing should be understood as giving Peter the authority to define doctrine or the authority to communicate and excommunicate, but there's no reason to oppose these two. Gundry explains that "in rabbinic literature, binding and loosing usually signify interpretative decisions of prohibition and permission; but they also signify condemnation and acquittal in disciplining members of the synagogue who disobey the interpretative decisions."[315] After all, the ability to define orthodoxy and the ability to police heresy go hand in hand.

How Might a Protestant Respond?

Yale's Richard H. Hiers sums things up neatly when he says Protestant commentators on Matthew 16 "tend to argue that the sayings either are inauthentic, since found only in Matthew, or else must surely mean something other than that Jesus bestowed sacerdotal authority on Peter or other apostles."[316] Hiers himself is no exception: he argues that "the terms 'binding' and 'loosing' refer to the binding of Satan or satanic beings (e.g., demons) and the loosing of such beings or their erstwhile victims."[317] Besides the fact that, even by Hiers's admission, neither Matthew 16 nor Matthew 18 has anything to do with demons or exorcisms, there's another glaring difficulty: why would anyone want to *loose* a demon? As Joel Marcus notes, Hiers has no good answer to this question: "At one point he asserts that the reference is not to the demon but to the human being who is loosed when the demon is bound, while at another point he interprets the loosing as referring to the demon, but as being totally hypothetical." [318]

A more plausible and popular theory is articulated by Malcolm Yarnell, who teaches systematic theology at Southwestern Baptist Theological Seminary. Yarnell cites Martin Luther as support for the idea that "although the preacher of the Word is instrumental and necessary, the work of binding and loosing is reserved for God."[319] You might notice that this is a strange conclusion to draw from the promise that "*whatever you bind on earth* shall be bound in heaven, and *whatever you loose on earth* shall be loosed in heaven." But that's because this exegesis isn't really starting with the biblical text. It's starting with a theological presupposition and forcing it onto the text, even where the text seems to say the exact opposite. The support Yarnell cites is Luther's 1545 screed *Against the Roman Papacy, an Institution of the Devil*, in which he says, "To retain or forgive sins is the work of the divine majesty alone."[320] (Contrast this with Jesus' words in John 20:22–23, "Receive the Holy Spirit. If you forgive the sins of any, they are forgiven; if you retain the sins of any, they are retained.")

So how can these exegetes come to conclusions so much at odds with what the text actually says? The first way is by reversing the meaning of the passage by changing the wording. Most Bibles, including Protestant translations like the KJV, NKJV, RSV, NRSV, ESV, NIV, and NLT, have the verbiage in the future tense: that whatever Peter binds on earth *will be* bound in heaven. But there are a handful of Protestant scholars who argue that this should actually read that whatever Peter binds on earth "shall *have been* bound" to ensure that "heaven's prior decision is later ratified by the church."[321] Jonathan Leeman explains that "both translations may be technically legitimate, but Protestants have feared that a simple future translation suggests that the church can confer salvation."[322] In other words, it's Protestant theology driving the translation of the Scripture.

For a while, the Protestant argument seemed like a strong one, grammatically, on the basis that the verbiage wasn't in the future tense ("I will do it"), but in the future perfect tense ("I will have done it"). But the future perfect *isn't actually what is being used here*. Indeed, the future perfect tense isn't actually used anywhere in the New Testament.[323] Instead, the verbiage here uses what's called the "periphrastic future perfect." Ernest DeWitt Burton, the Protestant biblical scholar who served as president of the University of Chicago, wrote an entire book on the "moods and tenses" of New Testament Greek and found only four instances of the "periphrastic future perfect" being used. In each case, the verb was simply "expressing a future state."[324] In other words, the traditional rendering "whatever you bind on earth will be bound in heaven" is the one most consistent with the language of the New Testament.

But even while admitting that the grammatical case was worse than was once thought, Protestant exegetes like Grant R. Osborne continue to cling to the "shall have been bound" translation for theological reasons:

> The more recent appraisal of the perfect tense shows that it often does not have past time sense but rather is stative in force, thus emphasizing the present and future aspect ("will be bound/loosed"). So some make God's decision subsequent, thus ratifying Peter's/the church's decision. Surely, this cannot be correct, as if God is bound to accept the church's decisions.[325]

Osborne is refreshingly clear. He holds to his position not because of what the Bible actually says. He holds to it because he refuses to accept even the possibility that Jesus might give such an audacious gift to Peter or the Church. Yarnell likewise makes his argument on purely theological, rather than grammatical or scriptural grounds:

> If a person is loosed from sin upon earth through faith in the proclamation of a Christian disciple, it is because God is applying his grace at a spiritual level. It is only the disorderly hubris like that of some medieval popes that would demand that a spiritual leader on earth automatically obligates divine application and human salvation.[326]

D.A. Carson favors a future perfect reading but admits that "scholars have at times tried to bleed a bit too much theology out of their grammatical conclusions."[327] The attempts to retranslate Matthew 16:19 and 18:18 are transparently motivated by a desire to preclude the papal reading. But Carson also recognizes that this motivated retranslating doesn't succeed:

> For instance, if the tense is translated as a future ("shall be bound"), the passage could be taken to justify some form of extreme sacerdotalism without unambiguous defense elsewhere in the NT. But if it is translated as a future perfect ("shall have been bound"), it could be taken to support the notion that the disciple must therefore enjoy infallible communication from God in every question of "binding and loosing," a communication that is the role of the so-called charismatic gifts.[328]

Carson is wrong to think infallibility involves some kind of special "communication from God," but he's right to point out that whether you say the pope will always agree with God or that God will always agree with the pope, you haven't really avoided a reading suggestive of infallibility. And it's possible that the whole chicken-egg debate is meaningless, as well, since it treats God as an act *inside* time, rather than acting from all eternity.[329]

Given everything Carson points out about the weakness of the Protestant arguments against the heavenly ratification of binding and loosing, how does he avoid the conclusion himself? Simple: by assuming that Jesus doesn't mean this literally. As he puts it, "to press the 'whatever' absolutely not only misunderstands the context but fails to reckon with Jesus' tendency to use absolutist language, even when he cannot possibly mean to be taken that way."[330] In other words, when Jesus says, "Whatever you bind on earth shall be bound in heaven," he doesn't *really* mean "whatever." R.J. Rushdoony argues that "it is the law of God, not the church which binds or looses men, and only as the church faithfully declares the law is there any true binding or loosing. Whenever the church attempts to bind or loose men's conscience and conduct apart from the law-word of God, it is itself bound, that is, it is itself under judgment."[331] Or as Benjamin Merkle says, "The church's binding and loosing is only authoritative when it corresponds with the divine will."[332]

In other words, the Church is right if it happens to agree with God. You'll notice that this is less of a promise and more a basic logical axiom. Suppose someone tells you, "You're going to watch two people perform. The one you rate highest shall be the winner." That's a pretty clear delegation of authority: you're being made the judge of some kind of competition. But let's say this someone comes back and says, "Oh, by that we mean, the one you rate highest will have *already* won, and that's why you'll have rated him the highest." At this point, you may conclude that your time is being wasted, but at least the person is praising you by assuming that you have the good taste to spot a winner from a loser, even if your vote doesn't actually turn out to count. But now let's say that this someone comes back and says, "Well, actually, your decision as to who wins and who loses is 'authoritative' only if it matches up with what the judges already decided." At this point, you would be right to ask, "What on earth did you mean when you said, 'The one you rate highest shall be the winner'?" Now not only are you not the judge, but you're not even a reliable observer. The original words to you have been stripped of any meaning.

So it is here. In a desire to avoid reading Jesus as giving Peter real, binding authority, these Protestant exegetes have redefined Christ's promise to him in Matthew 16:19 into meaninglessness. If all Jesus meant was that Peter's decisions are right when they correspond with the divine will, that's another way of saying Peter is right when he's right and wrong when he's wrong. If that was all Jesus meant to say, he could have saved his breath, and St. Matthew could have saved his ink.

Instead, the full weight of the grammar, the context of the passage being a blessing, and the meaning of these words from a Jewish framework all point to one thing: that Jesus gave to Peter the ability to define the boundaries of the Church, including both *who* is within the boundaries and *which beliefs* are within the boundaries. But these Protestant critics are right to recognize that this interpretation entails Jesus promising Peter infallibility. That's true, so we'll turn to that next.

11

WHATEVER YOU BIND ON EARTH

ONCE WE UNDERSTAND Jesus' words to Peter in the framework of their Jewish background, the meaning of the binding and loosing become clear. The Lutheran professor Tord Fornberg explains that "Peter stands out as a kind of Chief Rabbi, who binds and loosens, in the sense of declaring something to be forbidden or permitted."[333] In support of this interpretation is the promise Jesus gives with the authority. Not only is Peter given the ability to bind and loose, but "whatever you bind on earth shall be bound in heaven, and whatever you loose on earth shall be loosed in heaven" (Matt. 16:19).

This promise of heavenly ratification is extremely Jewish. Hans Bayer, a Presbyterian theologian, concedes that in rabbinic usage, "binding" and "loosening" signify that "various decisions especially of the Sanhedrin," primarily interpreting the law or including or excluding members from the community, were "viewed as subsequently sanctioned by God."[334] As Rabbi Kauffman Kohler explains:

The various [rabbinical] schools had the power "to bind and to loose"; that is, to forbid and to permit; and they could bind any day by declaring it a fast-day. This power and authority, vested in the rabbinical body of each age or in the Sanhedrin . . . received its ratification and final sanction from the celestial court of justice.[335]

For instance, the rabbis taught that the liturgical year was set by the earthly authorities and that this calendar was then ratified in heaven.[336] It's within this context that we can understand the prophet Joel's admonition to the priests to "sanctify a fast" and "call a solemn assembly" (Joel 1:13–14). Such an authority might sound trivial today, but the Jewish people centered their lives on the liturgical calendar. We get hints of this in the New Testament. When Jesus returned to Galilee, "the Galileans welcomed him, having seen all that he had done in Jerusalem at the feast, for they too had gone to the feast" (John 4:45). A few verses later, Jesus returns to Jerusalem, because "there was a feast of the Jews" (5:1). The religious leaders capable of setting these feasts thus wielded a tremendous amount of authority over the daily lives of the people.

This authority wasn't limited to liturgical determinations. It also included the ability to settle disputes about the interpretation of Scripture. The Levitical priests were traditionally the authoritative interpreters of the Torah, which is why God laments that for "a long time Israel was without the true God, and without a teaching priest, and without law" (2 Chron. 15:3).[337] If there were questions about "one kind of legal right and another," if a case became "too difficult for you," then you could bring it to the priests, whereby "you shall consult them, and they shall declare to you the decision," and whatever "the decision which they pronounce to you, you shall do; you shall not turn aside from the verdict which they declare to you, either to the right hand or to the left" (Deut. 17:8–13; cf. 2 Chron. 19:8–11). This commandment is shocking, since the language mirrors the fidelity we owe to God's own commands: "You shall be careful to do therefore as the Lord your God has commanded you; you shall not turn aside to the right hand or to the left" (Deut. 5:32).

The priest, and particularly the high priest, was viewed as being divinely protected with a sort of infallibility, in the particular context of binding and loosing. It's for this reason that, when Jesus and the apostles are arrested, they are brought before the high priest and the Sanhedrin (John 18:19–40; Acts 5:17–52).[338] At first blush, this seems to be the most obvious counter-example to the idea of any sort of high priestly infallibility: how could the high priest Caiaphas have been infallible in any context, given how he treated Jesus? But that's not how the Evangelists saw it. A few chapters earlier, when the Sanhedrin were debating whether or not to arrest Jesus in the first place, St. John presents the pivotal moment in this way:

> One of them, Caiaphas, who was high priest that year, said to them, "You know nothing at all; you do not understand that it is expedient for you that one man should die for the people, and that the whole nation should not perish." He did not say this of his own accord, but being high priest that year he prophesied that Jesus should die for the nation, and not for the nation only, but to gather into one the children of God who are scattered abroad (John 11:49–52).

The Holy Spirit was working through the high priest, enabling him to speak prophetically, perhaps even in spite of himself, *because* he was "high priest that year." What's fascinating is that at one and the same moment, you see the evil of the man and the orthodoxy of what he's teaching. It was evil of Caiaphas to want Jesus dead. But it was true (and, John tells us, prophetic!) for him to say Jesus should die for Israel and the whole people of God.

If Jesus means his words to Peter in the way a Jewish listener would understand them, then he seems to be giving him something like infallibility, by promising that the Holy Spirit will work through Peter to ensure that he doesn't teach anything contrary to divine law and that his earthly decisions will be ratified in heaven. To readers who are approaching this from a Protestant background, this might all seem shocking. Keith Mathison speaks for many a Protestant when he warns that "if the church is infallible, appeals to history, tradition, and Scripture are superfluous."[339] After all, didn't the Jewish leaders nullify the word of God by imposing their manmade tradition (Mark 7:13)?

It's a reasonable objection, but it begs the question. The whole point of infallibility is that the pope won't (and can't!) contradict God, so a question that begins by asking what happens when he does is a bit like "disproving" the inerrancy of Scripture by asking, "But what do you do when Scripture *is* wrong?" In fact, far from rendering Scripture superfluous, infallibility is the *only* way of living out full obedience to what Christ commands in Scripture. That's a big claim, but I think that it can be proven through four relatively uncontroversial points.

Point #1: Christ Demands Church Unity

St. Paul tells the Philippians to "stand firm in one spirit, with one mind striving side by side for the faith of the gospel," and to have "the same love, being in full accord and of one mind" (Phil. 1:27, 2:2). He's clearly calling them to a unity that is both exterior and interior. And that's Jesus' prayer for all of us, as we see from John 17:20–23:

> I do not pray for these only, but also for those who believe in me through their word, that they may all be one; even as thou, Father, art in me, and I in thee, that they also may be in us, so that the world may believe that thou hast sent me. The glory which thou hast given me I have given to them, that they may be one even as we are one, I in them and thou in me, that they may become perfectly one, so that the world may know that thou hast sent me and hast loved them even as thou hast loved me.

There are a few things worth noting here. First, this is one of Jesus' final prayers before his passion—that's how important it is. Second, as far as I can tell, it's the only time he explicitly prays for us, the future generations who come to believe through the testimony of the apostles. Third, the *only* thing he prays for is that we'll be united. Fourth, he describes this unity as crucial to the success of the gospel. We need to be one, not just because it feels good to be united, but "so that the world may know that thou hast sent me and hast loved them even as thou hast loved me." Conversely, then, when we Christians are at each other's throats, we make nonbelievers skeptical of Jesus' claims, and we even make them doubt God's love for his people. Christian unity, in other words, is not some optional bonus, or a goal to be achieved once we're done with bringing everyone to Christ. It's a necessary condition for the success of the Great Commission.

And to be sure, Christian unity is broader than the healing of the scandal of denominationalism: two Catholics who hate each other are acting contrary to the gospel as well. But certainly we can say that, at a minimum, having multiple denominations teaching contrary doctrines is a failure to live out what Christ desires for his Church. The Methodist scholar Ben Witherington is right to say that Jesus' words here "raise disturbing questions of whether the theology of denominationalism, which, after all, is a late invention caused originally by the Protestant Reformation, is biblically valid and whether the modern ecumenical movement is the way to bring about church unity."[340]

Factionalism is destructive, both personally and collectively. On a personal level, Paul warns that enmity, strife, dissension, and "party spirit" are "works of the flesh," and that "those who do such things shall not inherit the kingdom of God" (Gal. 5:19–21). But it's not just ourselves whom we're destroying, or our evangelical mission. A church that tears itself apart has little to offer the world and ultimately cannot endure. In Greek mythology, Erysichthon dies after being cursed with an insatiable hunger that causes him to devour everything around him, until eventually the "wretch consumed his body / feeding upon a shrinking self."[341] To take a more Christian image, the Church is "the household of God" (1 Tim. 3:15), but "if a kingdom is divided against itself, that kingdom cannot stand. And if a house is divided against itself, that house will not be able to stand" (Mark 3:24–25).

Point #2: Christ Demands Orthodoxy

Jesus' message is bracingly clear: "I am the way, and the truth, and the life; no one comes to the Father, but by me" (John 14:6). So an ecumenism that obscures or minimizes the truth obscures Christ and makes the way to the Father harder for searchers to find. The consequences are fatal. St. Peter warns that "there will be false teachers among you, who will secretly bring in destructive heresies, even denying the master who bought them, bringing upon themselves swift destruction," and that "because of them the way of truth will be reviled" (2 Pet. 2:1–2). Peter describes the ones creating heresy and division as "bold and willful," saying they "despise authority" (10).

St. Paul likewise tells Titus that a bishop "must hold firm to the sure word as taught, so that he may be able to give instruction in sound doctrine and also to confute those who contradict it," and that Titus himself must "teach what befits sound doctrine" (Titus 1:9, 2:1). Paul warns him that "there are many insubordinate men, empty talkers and deceivers, especially the circumcision party," who "must be silenced, since they are upsetting whole families by teaching for base gain what they have no right to teach." He instructs Titus to "rebuke them sharply, that they may be sound in the faith" (1:10–13).

Point #3: This Creates a Catch-22 for Protestantism

Given that, as we've just seen, Christ calls his people to *both* unity and truth, is it possible for Protestantism to answer this call? A 2017 article in the *Atlantic* asks, "Why can't Christians get along, 500 years after the Reformation?" and answers that "while relations among Christians are far more peaceful today than they were 500 years ago, the tension between theological particularity and yearning for universal fellowship is still just as complicated."[342] In other words, the last 500 years have shown the inherent pitfall of denominationalism: constantly pitting truth and unity against one another. Ben Witherington, the Methodist theologian I quoted earlier, does a good job of showing that Protestantism must inevitably choose to disobey Christ in one or the other of these commandments:

There is always a tension in the Church between unity among believers and truth as it is understood and held by believers. Protestantism has tended to uphold Truth, with a capital T, while intoning unity with a lowercase u, with the end result that Protestant churches and denominations have proved endlessly divisive and factious. On the other hand, Catholicism and Orthodoxy have held up Unity with a capital U, and at least from a Protestant viewpoint this has been at the expense of truth. In other words, no part of the church has adequately gotten the balance between truth and unity right, it would seem.[343]

If there's no such thing as an infallible authority to interpret the Bible, then we're all left to interpret it to the best of our own abilities. And no two Christian denominations (indeed, perhaps no two Christians), left to their own devices, interpret the Bible the exact same way. If they did, there probably wouldn't be distinct denominations.

In the early days of the Reformation, there were Reformers who were convinced that if everyone just read the Bible, unshackled by the authority of the Catholic Church, the plain truths of Christianity would be transparent for all to see. Martin Luther declares to Erasmus that "if you speak of the external clearness [of Scripture], nothing whatever is left obscure or ambiguous; but all things that are in the scriptures, are by the Word brought forth into the clearest light, and proclaimed to the whole world."[344] Coupled with this external clarity, Luther argues, is an internal clarity, brought about by the Holy Spirit, since "the Spirit is required to understand the whole of the Scripture and every part of it."[345] In other words, instead of the Holy Spirit leading the Church corporate, or the leadership of the Church, into the fullness of truth, Luther's view is that the Holy Spirit leads each individual believer to understand every part of Scripture. In place of papal infallibility, Luther has declared himself (and all Spirit-led believers) infallible.

If Luther is correct, we should find exactly one Protestant denomination, since all of the Spirit-led believers will naturally agree on everything. But of course, we find the exact opposite. The Evangelical group Focus on the Family explains on its website that the result of the Protestant Reformation "was a veritable explosion of new ideas and conflicting opinions about the interpretation of various biblical passages."[346] Most of these Protestants agree that we should believe what's taught within the Bible alone and even agree with each other that there are only sixty-six books that make up this Bible. But they can't agree on the *meaning* of these texts. Five hundred years after the fact, Protestants sometimes imagine that the controversy at the heart of the Reformation was over whether or not to follow the Bible. It wasn't. It was about how to interpret the Bible. Martin Luther himself acknowledged that "both we and our opponents, the pope and the other sects, are appealing to the same Scripture and laying claim to one gospel and word of God."[347]

Centuries earlier, St. Jerome warned the heretics of his day not to "flatter themselves if they think they have Scripture authority for their assertions, since the devil himself quoted Scripture, and the essence of the scriptures is not the letter, but the meaning."[348] You can twist Scripture to support almost any position, and even readers trying their best to understand the meaning won't always do so accurately unassisted. Scripture itself bears witness to this fact. St. Peter warns that St. Paul's writings have "some things in them hard to understand" (2 Pet. 3:16). When St. Philip approaches the Ethiopian eunuch reading the book of Isaiah, he asks him, "Do you understand what you are reading?"

to which the man humbly replies, "How can I, unless some one guides me?" (Acts 8:30–31). The eunuch was not arrogant enough to assume that the Holy Spirit was going to internally guide him personally into all truth. He needed the guidance of the visible Church.

Left without the guidance of the Church, these conflicting Protestant sects eventually hardened into the denominational families we know today. Catholics often misunderstand Protestants by assuming they believe everything their respective denominations teach. But the truth is much stranger than that. Baptists don't go around preaching, for instance, that their particular church has everything right. Even moderately self-aware Protestants will admit that their denominations may well be wrong on a wide swath of issues. As Focus on the Family notes, the denominations we know today emerged simply as "a collection of people who more or less agreed on what they considered the major points of the faith."[349] Even the question of which are the "major points of the faith" has proven endlessly divisive. Is it important to believe in (or reject) infant baptism? Young-earth Creationism? Saturday (or Sunday) worship? The dual natures of Christ? Pacifism? Dispensationalism? Trinitarian theology? Male-only ordination? *Sola fide*? A particular eucharistic theology? And most importantly, *who gets to decide*?[350] In practice, it's up to each individual believer, even within his own denomination, to decide how much truth to sacrifice for unity or how much unity to sacrifice for truth.

The point here isn't merely historical. Suppose that a Baptist, after carefully studying Scripture, concludes that his own denomination is wrong to reject infant baptism. And suppose that, at the same time, his Presbyterian neighbor has arrived at the opposite conclusion. What are they to do? Should they stay in their original denominations out of respect for Christian unity? Should they switch to one another's denominations in pursuit of the truth? Should each of them create his own denomination, to avoid having to compromise on the truth at all? This leads to a catch-22. The internal logic of Protestantism is forcing each of these men to choose either heresy (submitting to teachings that he knows or believes is false) or schism. Whichever he chooses, he's disobeying some part of Christ's call to unity in the truth.

Nor is this merely a matter of disobedience. It's also a matter of disbelief. Christ prays that his followers "may become perfectly one, so that the world may know that thou hast sent me and hast loved them even as thou hast loved me" (John 17:23). In other words, Christ's teaching is that the oneness of the Church is an essential part of the proclamation of the gospel, and "capital U" unity is necessary for the conversion of the world to "capital T" truth. We cannot believe Christ on this point and still insist that there is "always a tension" between truth and unity.

Point #4: Infallibility Offers the Only Way Out of This Catch-22

Whether or not you believe that the Church or the pope is infallible, hopefully you can at least see that *if* infallibility is true, it solves this apparent contradiction. Witherington even implicitly concedes this when he describes the tension between truth and unity as existing within "a Protestant perspective." If infallibility is true, then it's possible to "obey your leaders and submit to them; for they are keeping watch over your souls, as men who will have to give account" (Heb. 13:17). If we can know that the official teaching of the Church is true, then the closer we draw to that teaching, the closer we'll draw both to the truth and to one another. If the

Protestant view that Witherington describes so well is unity *against* truth, the Catholic view is unity *in* truth.

It's worth noting that the New Testament clearly pre-supposes unity in truth. When Paul writes to the Philippians, he hopes they will "stand firm in one spirit, with one mind striving side by side for the faith of the gospel," and "complete my joy by being of the same mind, having the same love, being in full accord and of one mind" (Phil. 1:27, 2:2). They aren't forced to choose between "the faith of the gospel" and being "of one mind." The two go hand in hand. But without infallibility, this kind of unity in truth is impossible, since you cannot place that kind of trust in any merely human leadership. That's the heart of C.S. Lewis's objection to Catholicism, after all, as we saw back in the first chapter:

> The real reason I cannot be in communion with you is not my disagreement with this or that Roman doctrine, but to accept your Church means, not to accept a given body of doctrine, but to accept in advance any doctrine your Church hereafter produces. It is like being asked to agree not only to what a man has said, but what he's going to say.[351]

If you can't trust that the Church will continue to teach the truth tomorrow, then you're unable to enter fully into communion with it, even if you don't yet have a theological objection. Lewis's witness demonstrates this reality. Without infallibility, we can therefore never have a lasting unity in truth. Yet that's precisely what Christ calls us to, and what the New Testament presupposes. So infallibility doesn't render the New Testament *superfluous*. It makes the New Testament model of truth in unity *workable*.

The Spirit of Truth

I mention these last four points about unity in truth versus unity against truth to explain what I understand to be the *why* behind Jesus' promise of infallibility. But it's worth hearing his promises from his own lips. Unlike the keys, which are given only to Peter, Jesus gives the infallible "binding and loosing" both to Peter specifically and to the Church collectively. In addressing controversies among believers, the highest court of appeal is the Church, and if a sinning brother "refuses to listen even to the Church, let him be to you as a Gentile and a tax collector. Truly, I say to you, whatever you bind on earth shall be bound in heaven, and whatever you loose on earth shall be loosed in heaven" (Matt. 18:17–18).

Couple this with Jesus' words to the seventy, that "he who hears you hears me, and he who rejects you rejects me, and he who rejects me rejects him who sent me." To the Twelve, he goes farther, promising that "when the Spirit of truth comes, he will guide you into all the truth; for he will not speak on his own authority, but whatever he hears he will speak, and he will declare to you the things that are to come" (John 16:13). This Holy Spirit "will teach you all things, and bring to your remembrance all that I have said to you" (14:26).

And so when the Church acts in the New Testament, it does so with the full assurance of being guided by the Holy Spirit. This is most clearly seen in Acts, in the discussion of the so-called "Judaizer controversy" and the subsequent Council of Jerusalem. In Acts 10, Peter is led by God to dine with a Gentile named Cornelius. Cornelius and those with him hear the gospel and are converted. Peter then commands that these Gentiles be baptized, creating the first non-Jewish Christians in history (Acts 10:47–48).

This is immediately controversial, with Jewish Christians complaining, "Why did you go to uncircumcised men and eat with them?" (11:3). Peter recounts what happens, and even the objectors rejoice, saying, "Then to the Gentiles also God has granted repentance unto life" (18). But an important question is left unanswered. Given that Gentiles can be saved, do they have to follow the Jewish law to do so? And so Acts 15 opens on a group of preachers teaching that "unless you are circumcised according to the custom of Moses, you cannot be saved" (15:1).

As you might expect, this leads to a huge theological spat, and Paul and Barnabas (who had "no small dissension and debate" with these preachers) quickly send the problem to Jerusalem. The problem is big for two reasons. One, from an evangelical standpoint, the spread of Christianity is going to be stunted if grown men are required to be circumcised in order to be saved. But two, these preachers have what appears to be a scriptural case. When God speaks to Abraham, he says, "This is my covenant, which you shall keep, between me and you and your descendants after you: Every male among you shall be circumcised" (Gen. 17:10). Twice, he describes this to Abraham as an "everlasting covenant" (7,13–14). The New Testament hasn't been written. If the early Christians had believed in *sola scriptura*, it's likely that the Judaizers would have won, or at least that the two groups would never have come to any sort of agreement and eventually formed separate denominations.

Thankfully, none of that happens. Instead, "the apostles and the elders were gathered together to consider this matter" at what we now call the Council of Jerusalem (Acts 15:6). Exercising its binding and loosing authority, the assembled Church declared that "it has seemed good to the Holy Spirit and to us to lay upon you no greater burden than these necessary things" (28). Unlike the Pharisees, who used their binding and loosing authority to "bind heavy burdens, hard to bear" (Matt. 23:4), the Church was conscious not to lay too heavy a burden. Simultaneously, it clarified the theological controversy at hand, rebuking those who were teaching "although we gave them no instructions" (Acts 15:24) and spelling out the proper doctrine. This is what it looks like to act in an infallible way, to bind and to loose. And Christ gives this to Peter specifically, as well as to the Church generally.

What Infallibility Is and Isn't

The logical case for infallibility, laid out above, is also important in dispelling many of the common misconceptions about just what it means to say Peter (or the Church, or subsequent popes) is infallible. It's probably not an exaggeration to say the biggest objection to infallibility is simply not understanding what's meant by the term. We also saw in the prior chapter D.A. Carson's description of it as a sort of hotline from God, in which God tells the pope the right answers. Mathison makes a helpful threefold distinction: "whereas God himself is the author of an inspired utterance, an infallible word remains the word of man although it is preserved from the possibility of error. In addition, infallibility does not mean impeccability. God may give the gift of infallibility to wicked men."[352] So infallibility *isn't* saying the pope is divinely inspired or that the pope is holy. Indeed, infallibility isn't even for the pope's own benefit. St. Paul tells us all of the gifts of God are

for the equipment of the saints, for the work of ministry, for building up the body of Christ, until we all attain to the unity of the faith and of the knowledge of the Son of God, to mature manhood, to the measure of the stature of the fullness of Christ; so that we may no longer be children, tossed to and fro and carried about with every wind of doctrine, by the cunning of men, by their craftiness in deceitful wiles (Eph. 4:12–14).

Infallibility is not at all different. The gift isn't a special hotline to God or a promise of the pope's salvation. It's a protection of the "unity of the faith" from the false doctrine and deceitful wiles of cunning men. The best way to understand infallibility is simply this: believers will never have to choose between membership in the visible Catholic Church and fidelity to the gospel. We'll never have to choose schism or heresy.

This also reveals the "boundaries" of infallibility. If you're wondering if a particular statement is protected from error, ask this: *am I required to believe this to be a faithful Catholic?* If so, then you can be assured that the statement is infallible, for the simple reason outlined above: if the statement is heretical and you're required to believe it, then you're put in an impossible position, and God never commands the impossible.

Catholics are guilty of often overstating papal infallibility, as if every word that comes from the mouth of the pope is without error. The result is needless vexation and spiritual gymnastics. It's not just Pope Francis; there are countless examples of popes thinking and saying silly and even sinful things, and Protestants are right to be skeptical of any kind of whitewashed or triumphalist Church history.

Far better is the witness of the nameless Catholic cardinal who is alleged to have responded to Napoleon's threat to destroy the Church by saying, "Your majesty, we, the Catholic clergy, have done our best to destroy the Church for the last 1,800 years. We have not succeeded, and neither will you."[353] Or if you prefer, there is Hilaire Belloc's famous line: "The Catholic Church is an institution I am bound to hold divine—but for unbelievers a proof of its divinity might be found in the fact that no merely human institution conducted with such knavish imbecility would have lasted a fortnight."[354] These statements are not glib; they're expressing the profound truth that papal infallibility is an expression not of the greatness of the Church's shepherds, but of the need to protect us from the worst of their sinfulness and brokenness.

At the outset of the book, I presented the question that had vexed me: what do we do with Pope Francis's comments about the Zika virus, in which he seemed to suggest both that contraception might be okay and that the Ten Commandments might contradict each other? And what does it mean for papal infallibility? We've now come to a point where we can answer both of those questions in the same way: *very little.*

Pope Francis neither changed Church teaching nor stated it accurately. If you want to know what the Church teaches, that's not something determined by offhand comments in airplane interviews. That contraception is contrary to natural law is something the Church teaches authoritatively,[355] and even the popes who have spoken on it in an authoritative way do so by stressing it as something *already known.* In describing marital contraception as intrinsically evil, Pope Pius XI stresses that he is merely reaffirming "the uninterrupted Christian tradition" and points to support from both Scripture and St. Augustine (*Casti Connubii* 55–56). And as for the idea that some extreme circumstance, like Zika, might justify it, Pius explains that "no difficulty can arise that justifies the putting aside of the law of God which forbids all acts intrinsically evil," but this too comes from the explicit teaching of the Council of Trent, which condemns the opinion that "there are precepts of God impossible for the just to observe."[356] The Church's teaching on this matter is well known, and those who depart from it dissent from the fullness of the faith to which they've been called.

Time and time again, the pope or Church councils have taken up the moral questions related to the nature of marriage, the difficulty of living out the commandments of God, and the impermissibility of contraception. These teachings, given authoritatively, all point in one direction. Pope Francis's comments point, or at least seem to point, in the opposite direction, but he's not even pretending he's defining some doctrine as pope. A Catholic can (and in this case should) respectfully disregard his comments without dissenting from the Faith. In saying this, I'm not downplaying the scandal of a pope who seems to contradict Catholic teaching or who presents Church teaching so vaguely that it becomes a full-time job trying to make sense of what's even being said. But I'm also trying to ensure that we don't exaggerate the severity of it.

After all, by no means did this problem begin with Pope Francis. It goes directly back to the first pope, St. Peter. We've already seen that it was through Peter that God opened the doors of the Church to the Gentiles in a definitive way (Acts 10), and Peter was the first to preach that the Gentiles could be saved (Acts 11). But he didn't always practice what he preached. Paul recounts his famous confrontation with Peter at Antioch (Gal. 2:11–14):

> But when Cephas came to Antioch I opposed him to his face, because he stood condemned. For before certain men came from James, he ate with the Gentiles; but when

they came he drew back and separated himself, fearing the circumcision party. And with him the rest of the Jews acted insincerely, so that even Barnabas was carried away by their insincerity. But when I saw that they were not straightforward about the truth of the gospel, I said to Cephas before them all, "If you, though a Jew, live like a Gentile and not like a Jew, how can you compel the Gentiles to live like Jews?"

The same Bible that says Peter was in the wrong at Antioch also contains two inspired epistles from him, 1 and 2 Peter. Both Catholics and Protestants have to come to grips with the fact that Peter's teaching is infallible (and more than that, divinely inspired), but his personal witness and pastoral leadership weren't. And it's not just that Peter sinned, but that he was leading the other Jewish Christians badly here. Nothing in our understanding of either papal infallibility or divine inspiration prevents that from happening. If we can harmonize that for Peter, then it's easy to understand how we can respect Peter as pope without blindly following every word that comes forth from his mouth.

How Might a Protestant Respond?

One way that Protestants might respond is to find a different reason to accept 1 and 2 Peter while rejecting St. Peter's conduct at Antioch. Got Questions, a popular Protestant website that serves as a kind of theological FAQ, claims that "the Bible does not teach that the apostles were infallible, apart from what was written by them and incorporated into Scripture."[357] Nothing in Scripture supports this idea. In fact, St. Paul says the opposite: "So then, brethren, stand firm and hold to the traditions which you were taught by us, either by word of mouth or by letter" (2 Thess. 2:15). Paul is clear about the binding nature of the traditions he passed along both orally and in writing, and there's no way to faithfully interpret this as saying that it's only "what was written" that was considered to have this authority. Beyond this, much of the book of Acts is St. Luke writing down what the apostles *said*. For instance, when the apostles are before the Sanhedrin, Luke tells us what "Peter, filled with the Holy Spirit, said to them" (Acts 4:8). And so the attempt of Got Questions to get around the problem of Peter doesn't pass muster.

The broader Protestant objection is that we don't need infallibility since we have inspired Scripture. Some variation of this position goes back to Martin Luther's defense at the Diet of Worms in 1521: "Unless I am convinced by Scripture and plain reason—I do not accept the authority of the popes and councils, for they have contradicted each other—my conscience is captive to the word of God."[358]

Keith Mathison puts the argument this way: "Unlike Scripture, no one claims that everything found in tradition is inspired, or that every writing of every Church Father is inspired or that every official utterance of the Church is inspired. . . . Even if there were inspired traditions, all would have to admit that these inspired revelations are mixed with fallible uninspired human dross."[359] In other words, even granting that there are capital-T Traditions out there, how can we distinguish them from manmade, lowercase-t traditions? If we can't, Mathison concludes, then "the traditions, the Fathers, and the Church are all inherently fallible standards," whereas Scripture alone can claim "verbal and plenary inspiration."[360] That argument makes sense: if there really were no way of distinguishing fallible from infallible tradition, or fallible from infallible Church teachings, that would render infallibility meaningless.

But let's take the argument one step forward. "Scripture" just means "writing," and just as not every tradition is a capital-T Tradition, so not all scripture is capital-S Scripture. To be able to believe that the inspiration of Scripture is "plenary" (that is, unqualified and absolute), Mathison has to believe that there's some way that we can know exactly which books are which. But nowhere in Scripture are we given a divinely inspired table of contents. Historically speaking, the Bible was assembled by the Catholic Church, and Christians could know that the Bible was trustworthy because of the Holy Spirit's ongoing protection of the Church.

But that explanation doesn't work for Protestants. If you can trust that the Holy Spirit is guiding the visible Church, then there's no reason to split off and form a separate body. But if you *can't* trust that the Holy Spirit is guiding the visible Church, and if you believe that the Church has actually erred on important questions regarding the faith, then how can you trust that the Church got the Bible right? Short answer: you can't, which is why R.C. Sproul says that "the historic Protestant position shared by Lutherans, Methodists, Episcopalians, Presbyterians, and so on, has been that the canon of Scripture is a fallible collection of infallible books."[361]

What's more, it's a fallible collection that the Reformers think the Church got wrong. Most Protestant Bibles today are seven books shorter than the earliest Bibles, since the Reformers called into question the canonicity and inspiration of seven of the Old Testament books (known as the Deuterocanon or "Apocrypha"). But that was just the tip of the iceberg. In his German translation of the Bible, Martin Luther doesn't number Hebrews, James, Jude, or Revelation among the New Testament books, owing to his doubts about their inspiration or canonicity.[362] His contemporary

Andreas Karlstadt goes farther, questioning whether 2 Peter, 2 John, and 3 John belonged.[363] What does it mean to say you believe in "Scripture alone" if no one knows which books are and aren't Scripture?

And so the standard Protestant position is that the Church got the canon of Scripture wrong, that the Holy Spirit isn't guiding the process, and that we can't know for sure which books do and don't belong in the Bible. There's no reliable way to tell which books are divinely inspired Scripture and which ones are "fallible uninspired human dross," and the consensus of the early Christians can't be trusted. By Mathison's own reasoning, this reduces Scripture to the level of a fallible authority, since there's no good way to know whether a particular Bible verse is from an inspired book or not.

Put more positively, you can have infallible Scripture only if you have some way of knowing which books of Scripture are infallible, which requires an infallible Church. Mathison tries to counter this point by saying that "despite the fallibility of the Old Testament Jews, they managed to preserve the canon of Old Testament Scripture."[364] But anyone informed on the history of the Jewish canon knows that this isn't true. At the time of Christ, there was a shorter "Hebrew or Palestinian canon," corresponding to the Protestant Old Testament, but there was also a longer "Alexandrian or Septuagint canon" used by Greek-speaking Jews, corresponding to the longer Catholic Old Testament.[365] The New Testament mostly cites to the Septuagint version, and most early Christians use this as the basis for the Old Testament. But in addition to these two canons, there were too many variations to list.

For instance, the Sadducees accepted only the Torah, the first five books of the Bible, as inspired, and so all of Jesus' scriptural citations to them come exclusively from the

Torah.[366] This is particularly obvious in their debate with Jesus over the bodily resurrection, in which Jesus proves the resurrection by pointing to Exodus 3:6 (in which God calls himself "the God of Abraham, the God of Isaac, and the God of Jacob") rather than more explicit, but un-recognized, texts like Daniel 12:2 ("many of those who sleep in the dust of the earth shall awake, some to everlasting life, and some to shame and everlasting contempt") or 2 Maccabees 12:43 ("in doing this he acted very well and honorably, taking account of the resurrection").

As for the Samaritans, they also accepted only the Torah, but it was their version of the Torah, with a significantly different text and even a different set of Ten Commandments.[367] The biblical canon used by the Qumran community (who may have been Essenes) is downright mystifying: Rice University's Matthias Henze says that "of the close to 900 Dead Sea Scrolls discovered in eleven caves between 1947 and 1956, about a quarter, or 222, are biblical scrolls, whereas approximately 670 are nonbiblical."[368] But he quickly notes that even this terminology is anachronistic, since there didn't seem to be any sort of closed biblical canon at the time, making it impossible to know which of the books were and weren't treated as inspired. As the University of Edinburgh's Timothy Lim explains, "The closing of the Jewish canon may be seen as part of the Jewish reaction to knowledge of books of the New Testament and the increasing influence of Christianity."[369] In other words, the Jewish canon isn't solidified until *after* the time of Christ, and largely *in opposition to* Christians, so it's bizarre that so many modern Protestants think this is a good foundation for the Christian Old Testament.[370]

Only someone oblivious to the serious canon problems facing first-century Judaism could posit that they got along just fine knowing the contours of the biblical canon without an infallible authority. And so we're back where we started: if we want the infallibility of the Bible, we need the infallibility of the Church.

How Might an Eastern Orthodox Respond?

The bulk of this book is aimed at objections coming from within Protestantism—mostly (but not entirely) mainstream, conservative Protestantism. But it's worth addressing one of the major Eastern Orthodox arguments against papal infallibility because of how closely it mirrors the Protestant argument we just saw. Archpriest Victor Potapov, rector of the Russian Orthodox Cathedral of St. John the Baptist, argues *for* in the infallibility of ecumenical Church councils, since "for the whole Church to err would be tantamount to her spiritual death, but, by virtue of the Savior's promise, she cannot die."[371] But he argues against the infallibility of the pope, claiming that "the pope of Rome began to attribute the privilege of ecclesiastical infallibility to himself alone and, after long efforts, finally secured the recognition of his absurd pretension at the Vatican Council of 1870."[372]

Potapov's argument looks sound on its face, but it raises several problems. First, what role do ecumenical councils play? David Bentley Hart, perhaps the most famous living Orthodox theologian, argues that "Orthodoxy's entire dogmatic deposit resides in the canons of the seven ecumenical councils" but feels comfortable disregarding the authority of the Fifth Ecumenical Council on the question of Origenism and universal salvation.[373] Second, what makes a council an infallible ecumenical council? As Bishop Kallistos of Diokleia, Timothy Ware, explains:

This is a more difficult question to answer than might at first appear, and though it has been much discussed by Orthodox during the past hundred years, it cannot be said that the solutions suggested are entirely satisfactory. All Orthodox know which are the seven councils that their Church accepts as ecumenical, but precisely what it is that makes a council ecumenical is not so clear.[374]

There are plenty of Orthodox theologians (and armchair theologians) who have theories about how to know which are and aren't the true councils, but the truth is, the Orthodox Church itself doesn't know. The third problem is even more fundamental: how many ecumenical councils are there? It turns out that even the idea that there are only seven councils isn't something that "all Orthodox know." In 1848, the Orthodox patriarchs of Constantinople, Alexandria, Antioch, and Jerusalem wrote a scathing denunciation of Pope Pius IX, in which they referred to the so-called "Fourth Council of Constantinople" of 869–870 as the "eighth ecumenical council."[375] Other influential theologians, including Fr. John S. Romanides, speak even of a *ninth* ecumenical council from sometime in the fourteenth century.[376]

But even if we assume that there are only seven, we're left with a difficulty. In 449, in between the universally accepted Third Ecumenical Council (Ephesus, 431) and Fourth Ecumenical Council (Council of Chalcedon, 451), the Roman emperor Theodosius II convened a council, to be called "Second Ephesus." The would-be council was presided over by the Patriarch Dioscorus of Alexandria and attended by approximately 150 voting members.[377] From an exterior perspective, it seems to be an ecumenical council. But there's a huge problem: its declarations were heretical. It was advancing a Christology that muddled Christ's humanity and divinity.

In the providence of God, one word changed the course of this would-be council. As everything was drawing to a close, "while the orthodox bishops stood by trembling and silent, Hilary, the deacon of the Roman Church cried, '*contradicitur*,'" meaning simply "I object."[378] That was all he said, and all he needed to say. As Cara Berkeley describes it, "Hilary pronounced the one word '*Contradicitur*' and in the confusion escaped from Ephesus."[379] "Escaped" is probably not an exaggeration, as the "council" is remembered for its "tyranny and violence."[380] The French historian Alain Besançon paints the picture beautifully: "At that moment it was certainly not the cowering silent crowd of Orthodox Easterns which represented the Church of God. All the immortal power of the Church was concentrated in that simple, legal word spoken by the Roman deacon: *contradicitur*."[381]

All of the imperial pomp that the Byzantine Empire had to offer, the whole assembly of scores of patriarchs, metropolitans, and bishops, and all of the external trappings of an ecumenical council were no match for a single word from the deacon Hilary. Why? Because Hilary was the pope's legate, one of his only representatives at the council, and he was invoking the pope's own authority to object to the unsavory proceedings. Amazingly, neither Catholics nor Orthodox consider "Second Ephesus" to be a true ecumenical council, and it is mostly remembered today (if at all) by the scathing nickname Pope Leo the Great gave it: the "Robber Council."[382]

The clear lesson seems to be that the consent of the pope is required for an ecumenical council to be an ecumenical council, in a way that no other bishop's consent is. For instance, after hearing news of the Robber Council, Leo the Great immediately demanded that a true council be called to set things right. The emperor refused but then died abruptly in a riding accident.[383] The new emperor, Marcian, quickly called the Council of Chalcedon, with the result that many of the same bishops who had signed on to a Christological heresy two years earlier now publicly repented and declared the orthodox faith. Pope Leo sent along a letter accurately declaring orthodox Christology, called the "Tome" of Leo, and the council received it by declaring, "Peter has spoken through the mouth of Leo."[384]

But something else happened at Chalcedon: Dioscorus, the patriarch of Alexandria who had presided at the Robber Council, was deposed and exiled. And apparently, *he* couldn't just say *"contradicitur"* and nullify the proceedings, suggesting that the Orthodox understanding of ecumenical councils only makes sense if the pope, and the pope alone, can approve or veto their proceedings. This papal authority doesn't replace conciliar authority, just as the authority of the Church doesn't replace the authority of the Bible. Rather, the two work hand in glove. Without the pope, there's no good explanation of how many ecumenical councils there are, or why "Second Ephesus" is a false council, and Chalcedon is a true one, just as without infallibility, you cannot reliably say which books belong in the Bible.

12

THE POST-PETRINE PAPACY

THE SCOPE OF this book has been intentionally narrow. Rather than answering every possible objection against Catholicism, or even every question about the papacy, I've tried to answer only one: whether or not Jesus established the papacy with St. Peter. The three major questions left to be answered are these: did the Church that Christ founded fall into apostasy? If not, why doesn't the Church today look like the Church back then? And finally, how do we know that the papacy was ever intended to last beyond Peter? Let's consider each of those.

By way of an overview, it is worth considering that there are ultimately only three possibilities. The first is that the Catholic Church *isn't* the Church that Christ founded, but a later imposter. If that's the case, we should be able to trace the Church to its origins. If not Peter, then who was the first pope? The second is that the Catholic Church *is* the Church that Christ founded but fell into apostasy. Christ's promises seem to preclude this option. The third is that the Catholic Church is the Church that Christ founded and remained faithful. If this is true, then we should all be part of the Church.

The Gates of Hell Will Not Prevail

Nobody before the Protestant Reformation was a Protestant. That seems like a simple enough proposition, but it creates an "apostasy" problem for Protestants. Should the pre-Reformation Church, and all of the Christians before 1500, be treated as apostates? After all, the seventeenth-century Puritan John Owens described the Catholic Church as "a Church under a degenerating apostasy."[385] Such an attitude goes back to the start of the Reformation. In the *Treatise on the Power and Primacy of the Pope*, part of the Lutheran *Book of Concord*, we hear that "it is manifest that the Roman pontiffs and their adherents defend godless doctrines and godless forms of worship, and it is plain that the marks of the Antichrist coincide with those of the pope's kingdom and his followers"[386] and that "it is necessary to resist him as Antichrist."[387] This is an attack on not just the pope, but all of those centuries of Christians who accepted Church teaching, or even just didn't resist the pope.

The trouble is, if you take this view, it doesn't leave you much in the way of Christian history. John Milton, best known for his *Paradise Lost*, argues that the Church can be found in its purity only in "the most virgin times between Christ and Constantine."[388] But it turns out that even the Christians before Constantine are Catholic, and Milton is left lamenting "the foul errors, the ridiculous wresting of Scripture, the Heresies" that he perceives in "the volumes of Justin Martyr, Clement, Origen, Tertullian, and others of eldest time."[389] We really are dealing with the "eldest time" here: Justin Martyr lived from A.D. 100 to 165 and died for the Faith. If even he can't be trusted not to be a heretic, where can Protestants find what they would accept as orthodox Christianity in the 1,500 years between the apostles and Martin Luther?

On the other hand, if the pope *isn't* the Antichrist, and Catholicism *isn't* an apostate counterfeit Christianity, why in the world does Protestantism exist? The Protestant theologian Stanley Hauerwas points out that the Catholic Church has actually made most of the reforms that the Reformers hoped for, which should logically end the Reformation. Instead of returning to the Church, Hauerwas laments:

> Protestantism has become an end in itself, even though it's hard to explain from a Protestant point of view why it should exist. The result is denominationalism in which each Protestant church tries to be just different enough from other Protestant churches to attract an increasingly diminishing market share. It's a dismaying circumstance.[390]

Besides admitting or denying it, there's a third way of responding to the "apostasy" problem: simply ignoring it. Gavin Ortlund, a Baptist pastor, admits that "we contemporary evangelicals have a tendency to neglect" Church history before the Reformation, "acting as if the important stuff basically skipped from the first to the sixteenth century." He asks rhetorically, "How many Christians between the apostle John and Martin Luther do you think today's average American evangelical can name?"[391] Nor is this a problem for only the laity: Gregory Jackson tells the story of a Baptist seminary whose course on Church history skipped "from the apostolic era to the Reformation, as if nothing worthwhile had happened in the fourteen centuries between."[392] This is nothing new. One hundred seventy-five years ago,

St. John Henry Newman suggested that this "long neglect of ecclesiastical history" was at least somewhat intentional.[393] The habit "of dispensing with historical Christianity altogether, and of forming a Christianity from the Bible alone" was an implicit admission that "to be deep in history is to cease to be a Protestant" since "men never would have put it aside, unless they had despaired of it."[394]

But what does the Bible have to say about the idea of an apostasy? We've looked a lot at Jesus' promises to Peter in Matthew 16 in this book, but there's one part we haven't really examined. After Jesus says, "You are Peter, and on this rock I will build my church," he then says something that the RSV:CE translates as "and the powers of death shall not prevail against it" (Matt. 16:18). What he actually says is that the "gates of Hades" will not prevail against it. Once again, Jesus' promise to Peter uses language that is evocative of God's covenants with Abraham, this time to his promise that "your descendants shall possess the gate of their enemies" (Gen. 22:17). Christ fulfills this but directs us toward the real enemy: not the Canaanites, but Hades itself. The imagery of the "gates of Hades" recalls man's three enemies: sin, death, and Satan. Milton, despite his views on the Church, recognizes this; in *Paradise Lost*, he says that "within the gates of Hell sit Sin and Death," while their "great author," Satan, seeks the downfall of man.[395] It's these three enemies that Jesus promises won't overcome his Church.

Although the early Christians are "far more concerned about the hermeneutical possibilities in the concept of the Church's being built on the rock (Peter) than on implications of the gates of Hades not prevailing against it," they "are agreed that the ongoing permanency of the Church is promised."[396] And so it is: if the Church falls into apostasy, then sin prevails over the Church. If it simply fades away through lack of conversion, then death prevails. In either case, Satan and the gates of Hades triumph. And this is the case even if the Church is eventually restored. Judges 6:2 says that "the hand of Midian prevailed over Israel," and it didn't matter that Israel was later rescued. Christ's promise is that the gates of Hades *will not prevail*, not that they will prevail for only 1,500 years.

To be protected from Satan, sin, and death prevailing is the natural result of the Christian vision of the Church. St. Paul describes the Church as Jesus' "body, the fullness of him who fills all in all" (Eph. 1:23), and describes the "great mystery" of Christ and the Church by connecting it to God's promise in Genesis that "a man shall leave his father and mother and be joined to his wife, and the two shall become one flesh" (5:31–32). Christ has won the victory, and the apostasy of the Church would strip that victory from him.

Nebuchadnezzar's Messianic Dream

Another reason we can safely reject any theory of apostasy is that the messianic promises including the promise of a kingdom of God on earth that will have no end. The clearest example of this is from the prophet Daniel's interpretation of King Nebuchadnezzar's dream. The dream was of a giant image, in which "the head of this image was of fine gold, its breast and arms of silver, its belly and thighs of bronze, its legs of iron, its feet partly of iron and partly of clay" (Dan. 2:32–33). Each part of the statue represents a different kingdom, starting with Nebuchadnezzar himself (36–43).

Numbering and naming these four kingdoms is where things get complicated, but there are generally two views: a "Greek" view and a "Roman" view. The Greek view numbers the four kingdoms as Babylon, Media, Persia, and Greece. Daniel speaks of the fourth kingdom as "a divided kingdom," and this reading takes that to be a reference to the partition of the Greek Empire after Alexander's death. It was Antiochus IV Epiphanes (whose title means "God Manifest") who inherited part of Alexander's empire and who cruelly persecuted the Jews, setting up "a desolating sacrilege upon the altar of burnt offering" (1 Macc. 1:54).[397]

But there are some real problems with the Greek view. The first is that many of its adherents hold to it because they suppose (contrary to Matt. 24:15) that Daniel is writing history or current events, not really prophecy. As one scholar puts it, "It is clear from the abundant historical allusions that the book of Daniel was written in response to the crisis at the time of Antiochus IV."[398] According to proponents of this view, the alleged interactions between Daniel and Nebuchadnezzar in the sixth century B.C. are really a narrative device used to talk discreetly about the horrors of Antiochus in the second century B.C. But the second problem is internal to the text. The Median-Persian Empire has often been treated as one empire, rather than two (just as the Seleucid Empire of Antiochus IV is often treated as part of the Greek Empire). In a later prophecy, Daniel sees a ram with two horns fighting a he-goat (Dan. 8:1–8). The angel Gabriel explains the vision by saying, "As for the ram which you saw with the two horns, these are the kings of Media and Persia. And the he-goat is the king of Greece" (20–21). In other words, the numbering of the Greek view is wrong: Media and Persia are treated as one kingdom within the book of Daniel.

That points to the other major view, the "Roman" view. St. Jerome identified the four kingdoms as Babylon under Nebuchadnezzar, the Persian-Mede Empire, the Greek Empire under Alexander, and the Roman Empire.[399] Jerome was hardly alone in this. This is also the view taken by non-canonical Jewish sources like "4 Ezra" and "2 Baruch." As John Bergsma and Brant Pitre explain, this is one of the reasons that "there was great eschatological expectation among Jews during Jesus' earthly ministry": they knew they were living in the fourth kingdom that Daniel prophesied about.[400]

Jesus, his disciples, and the crowds are living in the fourth kingdom. And what happens then? In King Nebuchadnezzar's vision, "a stone was cut out by no human hand," and it struck the statue, destroying it, and "the stone that struck the image became a great mountain and filled the whole earth" (Dan. 2:34–35). Daniel explains to the king that this means that "in the days of those kings the God of heaven will set up a kingdom which shall never be destroyed, nor shall its sovereignty be left to another people. It shall break in pieces all these kingdoms and bring them to an end, and it shall stand for ever" (44).

This is the promise Jesus fulfills in building his Church: the creation of the kingdom of God on earth, a kingdom that "shall stand for ever," outlasting the Roman Empire and all successive empires. It's a guarantee that even though we may fall away from the Church, the Church will never fall away. And whether you love or hate the Catholic Church, it's hard to deny that this prophecy has been fulfilled in the Church. As a sheer historical fact, "the papacy is the world's oldest continuously functioning institution."[401]

The Apostasy Free-for-All

If the entire Church founded by Jesus Christ could go wrong for several centuries, until a German monk like Luther or a French lawyer like Calvin restored orthodoxy, is there any particular reason to believe that orthodoxy even *exists*

today? Norman Fox, a nineteenth-century Baptist professor, became convinced that everybody was wrong about
the meaning of the Lord's Supper other than himself. In his
book on the subject, he anticipates the obvious response:
"Do you really mean to say that the whole church has been
in error for so many centuries?"[402] But Fox is sly. He sees
that there is no way a Protestant could seriously object to
this. After all:

> The Baptists do not hesitate to declare that nearly the
> whole church fell into error regarding the subjects of
> baptism; the Presbyterians affirm the same regarding or-
> ders in the ministry, and the Congregationalists make the
> same assertion concerning church government.[403]

If it's believable that Christ let his entire Church fall into
error for 1,500 years, why not 2,000? Or, for that matter, why
not 30,000? And if it's believable that the whole Church could
err on the structure of the Church, why couldn't the whole
Church be wrong about the Trinity or any other doctrine?

Indeed, believing that we're still in a state of apostasy
would be more coherent than believing the standard Protestant views offered. As implausible as it is that Jesus allowed his
Church to almost immediately fail, it's a great deal *less* plausible that he then allowed it to be restored by a German monk
(Luther), a French lawyer (Calvin), etc. Mormon apologists
have been quick to point this out. Since Jesus himself founded
the early Church, they reason that the founder of the restored
Church must at least be a prophet, so it makes more sense to
follow Joseph Smith than Martin Luther.

James E. Talmage, regarded as an "apostle" within
Mormonism, points out that "the weakness of the Protestant
sects as to any claim to divine appointment and authority

is recognized by those churches themselves."[404] In other words, Protestant denominations don't even pretend to be the Church of Jesus Christ. Whereas "the Roman Catholic Church is at least consistent in its claim that a line of succession in the priesthood has been maintained from the apostolic age to the present," the Protestant denominations "are by their own admission and by the circumstances of their origin, manmade institutions, without a semblance of the claim to the powers and authority of the holy priesthood."[405] The point here isn't that Mormonism is right—it isn't. But Talmage is right about this much: the idea that the whole visible Church fell into apostasy makes more sense if you're arguing for Mormonism than if you're arguing for Protestantism.

Remnant Theories

Since apostasy theories are theologically untenable, some Protestants instead opt for "remnant" theories. The idea here is that the Church *did* survive, but not as the Catholic Church. In short, these tend to be different ways of denying the fact that nobody before the Protestant Reformation was Protestant. The first and strongest is the theory that Protestantism has "forerunners," pre-Reformation Catholics who said and taught many of the same things the Protestant Reformers and their followers would later say and teach. The validity of this argument depends on the topic: not *everything* that Protestantism taught was brand new. But much of it was, and the supposed "forerunners" tend to be (upon actually reading more than cherry-picked quotations) at radical odds with the Reformers. For instance, the Evangelical Anglican theologian Alister McGrath points out that "the theological question about which the Reformation turned is that of justification." But he concedes that the Protestant Reformers executed a "complete reversal of the accepted teaching on the nature of justification," and there "are no Forerunners of their doctrines of justification."[406]

The second is the claim by certain Baptists that there is an "unbroken line of faithful Christians" that can be traced from the time of the apostles to modern Baptists, consisting of "Montanists, Donatists, Cathars, Waldensians, and Anabaptists."[407] This theory was popularized by J.M. Carroll's *The Trail of Blood*, in which he claims that during the "Dark Ages," 50 million Anabaptists were martyred, but "great numbers" of them "still existed" by 1500.[408] (For the record, "by 700 or so, neither Rome nor Paris nor any other population center in Western Europe had more than 20,000 people in it, and those numbers were rare,"[409] and even by 1500, the total population of all of Europe stood at only around 60.9 million.[410]) As for those alleged pre-Reformation "Baptists," it might help to read their actual writings. For instance, the Cathars taught that "sex is bad, marriage worse, and reproductive sex the worst of all," based on their belief in a "dualist view of the material world as created by the devil."[411] Even the Baptist historian Albert Henry Newman "could find no common ground between modern Baptists and such early movements as Montanism, Novatianism, and Donatism or such later movements as the Paulicians and the Cathari."[412]

The third is that there's always been an invisible remnant out there, and we just don't know who or where. This is Luther's own position. He challenges Erasmus to "show me a single bishop discharging his office under the kingdom of the pope" or "a single council at which they dealt with matter of religion." Nevertheless, "Christ has preserved his Church, though not so as to be called the Church. How many saints do you think the Inquisitors alone have in time past burned and killed for heretical perversions, such as John Hus and those like him?"[413] Luther's position is like that of the Baptists above, but with even fewer details. The Baptists point to the heretics that they think are Baptists, and historians quickly dispel the identification. Luther points to no one, save Jan Hus, and just supposes that maybe these people existed.

What all these remnant theories have in common is that the more detailed they try to get, the more quickly actual historians disprove them. Besides being historically false, they're also theologically unsound. As we saw in chapter 3, Christ founds the Church to be a city on a hill and a light to the nations. If the Church's own members can't find it anywhere in history, that's a good sign that this isn't the Church Christ promised. Instead, we should be looking for a much larger church.

The Mustard Seed and the Missing Child

One of the most famous converts on the abortion issue is Bernard Nathanson, who was the co-founder of NARAL (the National Association for the Repeal of Abortion Laws) in 1969 and was once the director of the nation's largest freestanding abortion clinic. As he would later recount, his conversion on the issue only occurred after ultrasound technology "for the first time threw open a window into the womb."[414]

It's not that the science was unclear before that point. As neuroscientist Michael Gazzaniga concedes, scientifically speaking "a specific human life begins at conception."[415] We've known this for a long time. But a one-day-old embryo looks very little like a newborn, so it can still be hard to believe that they're the same species. Of course, the same can be said for comparing newborns to adults—so what's different? With newborns, you can watch them develop, day-by-day, into adults, and you can see that it's the same human being throughout. The ultrasound, as a "window into the womb," changed the debate about abortion by finally letting us do this for the development of the embryo into a newborn. In Nathanson's own words:

> Although we had a mound (literally) of empirical data attesting to the fact that a living human being had been destroyed in the act of abortion, it was not until after the advent of ultrasound technology that a true paradigm change took place. With ultrasound technology, we could not only know that the fetus was a functioning organism, but we could also estimate its age, watch it swallow and urinate, view it in its sleeping and waking states, and watch it move itself as purposefully as a newborn.[416]

Something similar is true with the Church. If all you know is the Church described in the book of Acts and the Catholic Church of today, perhaps it's hard to imagine that it's the same church. They look different, which is exactly what we should expect from Jesus' own words:

> The kingdom of heaven is like a grain of mustard seed which a man took and sowed in his field; it is the smallest of all seeds, but when it has grown it is the greatest of shrubs and becomes a tree, so that the birds of the air come and make nests in its branches (Matt. 13:31-32).

Seeing just the mustard seed, you wouldn't recognize the mustard tree. Many of the things that the Catholic Church is criticized for, including its wealth, its often-incompetent

bureaucracy, and the like, are unavoidable (or at least difficult to avoid) side effects of the growth Christ promises. Take
a corporate example. According to Steve Jobs's biographer,
Apple Computers didn't actually start in his garage; it started
even smaller, with Jobs building computers in his bedroom.[417]
Had the company stayed in his bedroom, there would be no
costly overhead, no stacks of compliance paperwork, no bureaucracy. But he never intended for it to stay in his bedroom.
Its growth into something that required leaving the bedroom
for the garage and then for ever-increasing buildings wasn't a
mark that the company had been lost, but that it was flourish-
ing. So, too, with Jobs's shift away from the work of actually
building computers and into the work of running a massive
computer company. Something similar is true for the Church.
It starts out small, capable of meeting in a single room, but it's
tasked with the mission to "go therefore and make disciples
of all nations" (Matt. 28:19), not to stay in the Upper Room
to make sure it never has to grow. Is there more infrastructure
now than there was in the early Church? Absolutely, and for
the same reasons why there's more infrastructure at Apple today than in 1976.

In fact, it would be a serious problem if the Church today
looked like the Church of the first century. Imagine a family
whose seven-year-old son goes missing. They put up post-
ers, even put his picture on the side of milk cartons, but for
twenty years, they hear nothing. Then, after two decades, a
neighbor brings them a seven-year-old who looks remarkably
like how their boy used to look. "See," the neighbor says, "I've
found your son!"

But unless this is part of a show about time travel, he *can't
be* their son. That he looks like a seven-year-old disproves the
identification. Twenty years have passed. His parents are not
looking for a seven-year-old boy anymore; they're looking for

a man of twenty-seven. So it is with the Church: any group priding itself on still looking exactly like the first-century Church is announcing to the world that it can't possibly be the true Church. We're looking to find not a first-century Church anymore, but that same Church grown up. Twenty centuries have passed. Likewise, it's no argument against the papacy that Pope Peter doesn't look like a medieval or modern pope. Of course he doesn't: he was never meant to.

A Church in the Center of the World

The analogy of the lost boy doesn't go quite far enough, for the Church was never "lost" in the first place. As St. Paul said in explaining Christianity to King Agrippa, "For the king knows about these things, and to him I speak freely; for I am persuaded that none of these things has escaped his notice, for this was not done in a corner" (Acts 26:26). The history of the Catholic papacy can be traced through history in general. Even before he arrives in Rome, Paul praises the church there, "because your faith is being reported all over the world" (Rom. 1:8). Remember that Rome was the capital of the Roman Empire at the time. The growth of the Catholic Church "was not done in a corner." Indeed, an ancient monument in the middle of the Roman Forum proudly declared itself *umbilicus mundi*, the center of the world (literally, "the navel of the world").[418]

Particularly if folks like Ian Paisley are going to claim that the Catholic Church is a "synagogue of Satan" and "the mother of harlots and the abominations of the earth" of which Revelation 17 warns us, it shouldn't be too much to ask where this imposter church came from, and when and how it replaced the Church Christ founded.[419] I'm reminded here of a meme I came across years ago, warning against "false prophets" and quoting 1 John 4:1 ("Beloved, do not believe every spirit, but test the spirits to see whether they are of God; for many false prophets have gone out into the world"). The meme consisted of six small images, arranged as a collage, depicting the six alleged false prophets and their associated religious systems:

1. "Joseph Smith, Mormonism"
2. "Charles T. Russell, Jehovah (*sic*) Witness"
3. "Mary Baker Eddy, Christian Science"
4. "Ellen G. White, Seventh Day Adventist"
5. "The Papacy, Roman Catholic Church"
6. "Muhammad, Islam"

Clearly, one of these things is not like the others. Five of these "false prophets" were the founders of religious systems, and we can tell the genesis of each of the religions (or denominations) associated with them.[420] So for five of these six religious systems, we can trace them to the "false prophet" who founded them. But that leaves one obvious outlier. For Catholicism, the meme simply blames "the papacy." Where the other five images were of particular religious founders, the image for Catholicism was of a generic pope.[421] But obviously, "the papacy" didn't found the Catholic Church, any more than "the presidency" founded the United States. So whose name belongs here, and when did he start the Catholic Church?

But even Protestants who don't think the Catholic Church is the "synagogue of Satan" tend to think of it as one more manmade denomination. I was reminded of this in reading *Your Church Is Too Small* by John H. Armstrong. Lamenting the scandal of denominationalism, Armstrong says that "denominations are clearly not found in the Bible, and it is time everyone admits this fact."[422] This would seem to be an argument for returning to the visible Church that Christ *did* found, but Armstrong goes in a different direction. Pointing to Paul's admonition to the Corinthians (1 Cor. 1:11–13), in which he warns them not to separate into factions ("I belong to Paul," or "I belong to Apollos," or "I belong to Cephas," or "I belong to Christ"), Armstrong says:

> Perhaps the only biblical analogue that comes close to our current situation is in Paul's discussion about worldliness in the church at Corinth. One could compare Paul's language to our modern context and hear people saying, "I belong to John Calvin. I belong to John Wesley. I belong to Benedict XVI."[423]

But again, one of these is not like the others. John Calvin started Calvinism, and John Wesley started Methodism, but Pope Benedict XVI didn't start Catholicism. So once more, who *would* be an analogous denominational founder for Catholics?

As I said, the growth of the Catholic Church didn't happen in a corner. It happened in the heart of the empire. St. Irenaeus, bishop of Lyons, explains that while St. Matthew was writing his Gospel, "Peter and Paul were preaching at Rome, and laying the foundations of the Church."[424] This corresponds to what we know of even earlier authorities: in St. Ignatius's letter to the Roman church, which dates to c. A.D. 107, he includes the caveat, "I do not, as Peter and Paul, issue commandments unto you," as if this church was used to being instructed by those two apostles.[425] And although Paul eventually comes to Rome, he is delayed in doing so because of his desire "to preach the gospel, not where Christ has already been named, lest I build on another man's foundation" (Rom. 15:20–22). So who was the "other man" who laid the foundation of the Church of Rome? Peter, of course. This is reflected in Acts 2, where the listeners converted by Peter's Pentecost sermon include "visitors from Rome, both Jews and proselytes" (Acts 2:10).

Nor does our knowledge of the early history of the Church stop there. Irenaeus also says that "we are in a position to reckon up those who were by the apostles instituted bishops in the churches" and to trace "the succession of these men to our own times."[426] Despite being the bishop of Lyons, he chooses to trace the apostolic lineage of a different church, "the very great, the very ancient, and universally known Church founded and organized at Rome by the two most glorious apostles, Peter and Paul," and he explains that his reasoning is because "it is a matter of necessity that every Church should agree with this Church, on account of its pre-eminent authority."[427] And so he does, tracing each successor of St. Peter from his immediate successor Linus (who died c. A.D. 76) all the way down to Eleutherius, who was pope in the year A.D. 180, the time that Irenaeus is writing. To give you some sense of how early this is, Irenaeus is writing about a year before the word *Trinity* "is first found in the writings of Theophilus, Bishop of Antioch, in the year 181 A.D."[428]

D.A. Carson argues that there are "insuperable exegetical and historical problems" with believing that Christ built the papacy to last, particularly the fact that "after Peter's death, his 'successor' would have authority over a surviving apostle, John."[429] So what does history have to say on this score? Irenaeus tells us that Sts. Peter and Paul, "having founded and built up the Church, committed into the hands of Linus the office of the episcopate. . . . To him succeeded Anacletus; and after him, in the third place from the apostles, Clement was allotted the bishopric."[430] It's Clement whom we want to give a closer look. Irenaeus says that "this man, as he had seen the blessed apostles, and had been conversant with them, might be said to have the preaching of the apostles still echoing [in his ears], and their traditions before his eyes."[431] Around the year A.D. 95, while the apostle John is still alive, Clement writes a letter to the Corinthians, settling an internal dispute that the local church there was having about its clergy.[432]

Speaking on behalf of the Roman church, Clement begins by admitting that, owing "to the sudden and successive calamitous events which have happened to ourselves, we feel that we have been somewhat tardy in turning our attention to the points respecting which you consulted us."[433] Clement's response makes clear that both he and the Corinthians view the episcopal structure of the Church as established by the apostles, and he describes rebelling against the legitimate clergy as "shameful and detestable."[434] But in some ways, the most striking thing about the letter isn't what he says, but that he's saying anything at all. While the apostle John is alive, and not terribly far from Corinth, the Corinthian church faces "sedition" in the form of lawless laity. To address this problem, they write a letter to the pope in Rome and await his reply. And this happened so early in the life of the Church that a response in A.D. 95 could be considered "somewhat tardy."

How do the other early Christians respond to this? If they were Protestants, they would probably denounce the papal intrusion into the affairs of the local church, or into affairs that could be left to an apostle. But instead, the ensuing conversation is over whether or not Clement's letter (the first known papal encyclical after 1 and 2 Peter) should be regarded as Scripture. Even by the time of St. Jerome, centuries later, we find that the encyclical "in some places is publicly read" within the liturgy.[435]

It's easy to mythologize the distant past, but it's a lot harder to invent a recent past, for the simple reason that living people were there for it. This is one of the reasons why we believe in the historicity of the Resurrection. And it's the reason why we should believe what these same Christians tell us about the history of the church in Rome. Ignatius in particular has little room to invent the story of Peter and Paul being in Rome, since he's writing *to the Christians of Rome*, only about forty years after the martyrdom of the apostles. So there's a fair amount of historical evidence that the episcopal governance of the Roman church was founded by Peter, alongside Paul, and not a whole lot of evidence of any kind to support the Protestant argument (or more often, the Protestant *assumption*) that someone else started it.

The DNA of the Church

Returning to the image of the mustard tree, we're not looking for a body that still looks like the first-century Church, but we are looking for a body that *is* that Church, all grown up. To put it another way, we're looking for a Church with the same structure built by Christ, a sort of "DNA" of the Church. There's a parallel here to the debates over the nature and meaning of marriage. Back in chapter 2, I compared this to marriage. Just as our job is not to invent new forms of marriage, but to discover God's own design, so, too, our job is not to invent new forms of "Church," but to discover God's own design.

There's another parallel between marriage and the Church as well. In explaining why Christian marriage views the husband as the "head," C.S. Lewis begins by asking why there needs to be a head at all. He explains that marital disputes can ultimately be resolved in only one of two ways:

Either they must separate and go their own ways or else one or other of them must have a casting vote. If marriage is permanent, one or other party must, in the last resort, have the power of deciding the family policy. You cannot have a permanent association without a constitution.[436]

Spouses will not always agree, so the only effective deterrent is for there to be headship. This doesn't mean the husband should be imperious. In calling the husband "the head of the wife," St. Paul calls upon husbands to "love your wives, as Christ loved the church and gave himself up for her" (Eph. 5:25). And we've already seen what that looks like: self-sacrificial love from the one who said that he came "not to be served but to serve, and to give his life as a ransom for many" (Mark 10:45). But this is servant *leadership*: the buck stops with the husband.

This plan of headship, of having the buck stop with one person, turns out to be God's design throughout history. It starts with Adam, the head of the first family, and it continues onward through Abraham and the Patriarchs. Moses has an entire administrative and judicial structure underneath him that handles small cases, but he's the highest authority and the court of last appeal (Exod. 18:25–26). Not long after this, Israel descends into anarchy, for "in those days there was no king in Israel; every man did what was right in his own eyes" (Jdg. 17:6, 21:5). But this isn't God's design or desire, and so he raises up a whole series of judges, individuals he calls to lead his people. Eventually, we get to the monarchy: to Saul, David, Solomon, and the rest. By this point, both the priesthood (with the high priest) and the royal governance of Israel (with the king) have some one individual who is finally accountable for doing things according to God's design.

In other words, God's design for a healthy marriage looks an awful lot like his design for a healthy tribe, or a healthy nation, or a healthy kingdom. This is also God's design for a healthy church: that the Church built by Christ has one individual who is ultimately accountable when things go well or when they go poorly. We see this repeatedly through the New Testament. To take just one example, when all of the apostles fall asleep in the Garden, only one of them is called to task for it (Matt. 26:40). The Reformed theologian D.A. Carson concedes that the "rock" of Matthew 16 is Peter but argues that "the text says nothing about Peter's successors, infallibility, or exclusive authority."[437] The weakness of this argument should be clear: why would God go to all the trouble of setting up this structure repeatedly if he wanted us to abandon it as soon as the apostles died? And if the papal structure of the Church was intended to be destroyed with the death of the apostles, then perhaps Christ would have been better off promising that the gates of Hades *would* prevail and were intended to.

At the very least, it must be conceded that the Church maintaining the structure Christ established is the safest and most faithful course of action. We see from history that it did, in fact, maintain this structure, and apparently thought of it as necessary. St. Optatus, a North African bishop writing against the Donatist heresy around the year 370, reminds his readers that "you cannot then deny that you do know that upon Peter first in the City of Rome was bestowed the Episcopal *Cathedra*"—that is, seat of authority—so that "in this one *Cathedra*, unity should be preserved by all, lest the other apostles might claim—each for himself—separate *Cathedras*," since anyone doing so "would already be a schismatic and a sinner."[438] Optatus's argument for the Church is the same as Lewis's argument for the family: if it is going to survive, there needs to be one person in a position of headship.

If you were to make an argument for the traditional, biblical understanding of marriage, you would be foolish to begin by pretending every marriage is healthy, that all husbands love their wives "as Christ loved the church and gave himself up for her" and that all wives are "subject in everything to their husbands" (Eph. 5:24–25). Not only is that untrue, but you would be setting your listener up for disappointment when he discovered the sometimes painful truth about what marriage can be like, in real life. Instead, you would hopefully confine yourself to a simpler goal: to show that the sacrament of matrimony is established by Jesus Christ, for the good of his people, and that it's better than any of the alternatives we've found.

So it is here. The Church right now is going through a period of crisis at least in part *because of* bad papal and episcopal leadership. The "household of God, which is the church of the living God" (1 Tim. 3:15), is going through the roughest patch it's seen in centuries. Pretending otherwise is dishonest, and it sets non-Catholics up for disappointment. Not every pope or bishop lives up to his calling, just as not every parent does. But the truth is, as with the sacrament of matrimony, the papal structure of the Church is founded by Jesus Christ. It exists for the good of his people. And it is better than any alternative.

ABOUT THE AUTHOR

Previously a litigator in Washington D.C. and then a semi-narian for the Archdiocese of Kansas City, Joe Heschmeyer now works as a religious instructor at Holy Family School of Faith, whose mission is to lead people to Jesus through Mary by means of friendship, good conversation, and the rosary. He blogs at *Shameless Popery* and co-hosts *The Catholic Podcast*. He is also the author of *Who Am I, Lord?: Finding Your Identity in Christ*. He lives in Kansas City with his wife and daughter.

ENDNOTES

1   Andrew Jacobs, "The Zika Virus Is Still a Threat. Here's What the Experts Know," *New York Times*, July 2, 2019.

2   "Full text of Pope Francis' in-flight interview from Mexico to Rome," *Catholic News Agency*, February 18, 2016.

3   Ibid.

4   Joshua J. McElwee, "Francis allows for discernment on contraception in emergency cases, spokesman says," *National Catholic Reporter*, February 22, 2016.

5   Laurie Goldstein, "Catholic Leaders Say Zika Doesn't Change Ban on Contraception," *New York Times*, February 13, 2016.

6   Simon Romero and Jim Yardley, "Francis Says Contraception Can Be Used to Slow Zika," *New York Times*, February 18, 2016 (emphasis added).

7   Barbara Ellen, "If condoms are OK for Zika, why not Aids, Pope Francis?," *The Guardian*, February 20, 2016.

8   Cf. Edward Pentin, "Pope's Words on Contraception in Accord with Magisterium, Philosophers Say, but Context Is Key," *National Catholic Register*, February 19, 2016.

9   Cf. Emily Rauhala, "Stop Breeding Like Rabbits? The Pope Misses the Point on Contraception," *Time Magazine,* January 20, 2015.

10 John Henry Newman, *An Essay on the Development of Christian Doctrine* (London: Basil Montagu Pickering, 1878), pp. 149–50.

11 Ibid., p. 150.

12 Pew Research Center, "Chapter 2: Religious Switching and Intermarriage," *America's Changing Religious Landscape*, May 12, 2015.

13 Ryan P. Burge, "Where Protestants and Catholics Go When They Leave Their Churches," *Christianity Today*, February 28, 2018.

14 Ibid.

15 *Rhode Island v. Massachusetts*, 37 U.S. 657, 718 (1838).

16 C.S. Lewis, "Christian Reunion: An Anglican Speaks to Roman Catholics," in *C.S. Lewis Essay Collection and Other Short Pieces* (New York: HarperCollins, 2000), p. 396.

17 Kurt Vonnegut, *God Bless You, Dr. Kevorkian* (New York: Washington Square Press, 1999), pp. 9–10.

18 C.S. Lewis, *Mere Christianity* (New York, NY: HarperOne, 2001), p. 52.

19 C.S. Lewis, *Collected Letters*, vol. 2, ed. Walter Hooper, p. 646.

20 St. Anselm, *Proslogium*, in *Basic Writings*, 2nd ed. (Peru, IL: Carus Publishing Co., 2001), p. 48.

21 Matt Slick, "Which church is the one true church?," *Christian Apologetics and Research Ministry (CARM)*, available online at https://carm.org/questions/about-church/which-church-one-true-church.

22 J.C. Ryle, *Holiness* (Peabody, MA: Hendrickson Publishers, 2007), p. 273.

23 Kermit Rainman, "Revisionist Gay Theology: Did God Really Say...?," *Focus on the Family*, 2014. Available online at https://www.focusonthefamily.com/socialissues/sexuality/homosexuality-theology-and-the-church/revisionist-gay-theology-did-god-really-say.

24 Cf. Bob Jackson, *Hope for the Church: Contemporary Strategies for Growth* (London, UK: Church House Publishing, 2002), p. 141 ("The springing up of new groups of Christians and of new ways of being Christians together may be what we are aiming for in these changing times. . . . Many examples of new forms and new ways of being church already exist, either independently or as part of one denomination or another").

25 Cf. Carlos Miguel Buela, *Catechism for Youth* (New York, NY: IVE Press, 2008), p. 129.

26 Quoted in John Wycliffe, *Tractatus de Ecclesia*, trans. Johann Loserth (London: Wyclif Society, 1886), p. iv (emphasis added).

27 Martin Luther, *Schmalkald Articles*, trans. William R. Russell (Minneapolis, MN: Fortress Press, 1995), p. 32.

28 Martin Luther, *On the Papacy in Rome Against the Most Celebrated Romanist in Leipzig*, in *Luther's Works*, vol. 39, eds. Jaroslav Pelikan and Helmut T. Lehmann (Philadelphia, PA: Fortress Press, 1970), p. 69.

29 Luther, p. 69.

30 John Calvin, *Institutes of the Christian Religion*, Book IV, trans. Henry Beveridge (Edinburgh: T. & T. Clark, 1863), p. 288.

31 Slick, "What is the Christian church?," *CARM*, available online at https://carm.org/what-the-christian-church.

32 Eugene F. Rice, Jr., *The Foundations of Early Modern Europe, 1460–1559*, 2nd ed. (New York, NY: W. W. Norton & Co., 1971), p. 129.

33 Rice, p. 129.

34 John Bright, The Kingdom of God (Nashville, TN: Abingdon Press, 1981), pp. 258, 256.

35 John MacArthur, *The Master's Plan for the Church* (Chicago, IL: Moody Publishers, 2008), p. 86.

36 James Bannerman, *The Church of Christ*, vol. 1, ed. D. Douglas Bannerman (Edinburgh: T. & T. Clark, 1868), p. 29.

37 Ibid., p. 30.

38 Ibid.

39 "The Westminster Confession of Faith," in *The Creeds of Christendom*, vol. 3, trans. Philip Schaff (New York: Harper & Bros., 1877), pp. 657–58.

40 "The Second Helvetic Confession," in *The Creeds of Christendom*, vol. 3, trans. Philip Schaff (New York: Harper & Bros., 1877), p. 874.

41 Robert Verlarde, "What Is the Church?" Focus on the Family, January 1, 2009.

42 The translation is mine. His original words: "And as Judas was a þef and no mebre of Crist, ne pert of holy Churche, þouȝ he mynistride þe ordre of bischopod, but was a devel of helle, as Crist seiþ in þe gospel, so ȝif þes worldly clerkis schullen be dampned for here cursed synnes, as coveitise ypocrisie symonye and dispeir, as Judas was, þei ben fendis of helle and no Cristene men, ne membris of Crist, ne pert of holy Chirche." John Wycliffe, *The Great Sentence of the Curse Expounded*, 19, in *Select English works of John Wyclif, Volume 3*, ed. Thomas Arnold, M.A., 315. Oxford: Clarendon Press, 1871.

43 John Calvin, *Institutes of Christian Religion*, Book III, 22, trans. Henry Beveridge, vol. 2 (Edinburgh: Calvin Translation Society, 1845), pp. 551–52.

44 Bryan Cross, "Ecclesial Deism," *Called to Communion,* July 6, 2009.

45 Neil S. Wilson, *The Handbook of Bible Application* (Wheaton, IL: Tyndale House Publishers, 2000), p. 89.

46   Carl Sagan, *Cosmos* (New York, NY: Ballantin Books Trade Paperbacks, 2013), p. 134.

47   Bastien D. Gomperts, Ijsbrand M. Kramer, and Peter E.R. Tatham, *Signal Transduc-tion* (San Diego, CA: Elsevier Academic Press, 2003), p. 335.

48   Thomas Aquinas, *Summa Theologica*, I, 76, 1, trans. Fathers of the English Dominican Province, no. 3 (London, U.K.: R. & T. Washbourne, 1912), p. 22.

49   Albert Torbet, *True Christian, True Church, True Teachings* (Boston: The Gorham Press, 1917), p. 20.

50   Harald Hegstad, *The Real Church* (Cambridge, U.K.: James Clark & Co., 2013), p. ix.

51   Ibid., p. 16.

52   Ibid.

53   Bannerman, p. 30.

54   Athanasius, *On the Incarnation of the Word*, §15, in *St. Athanasius: Selects Works and Let-ters* in *A Select Library of Nicene and Post-Nicene Fathers of the Christian Church (NPNF)*, 2nd series, vol. 4, eds. Philip Schaff and Henry Wace (New York: The Christian Literature Co., 1892), p. 44.

55   Ibid.

56   The Protestant Church in Switzerland (PCS) is a coalition of 25 Reformed and Methodist organizations, representing about 2 million Swiss Protestants. Prior to heading the PCS, Locher was head of its predecessor organization, the Federation of Swiss Protestant Churches.

57   Gottfried Wilheim Locher, *Sign of the Advent: A Study in Protestant Ecclesiology* (Fri-bourg, Switzerland: Academic Press, 2004), p. 149.

58   Ibid., p. 150.

59   Thomas White, "The Universal and Local Church," in *Upon This Rock: The Baptist Understanding of the Church*, eds. Jason G. Duesing, Thomas White, and Malcolm B. Yarnell III (Nashville, TN: B&H Academic, 2010), p. 239.

60   So-called "Landmark Baptists" believe that these visible Baptists congregations have existed for two thousand years. We'll explore this claim in chapter 11.

61   Charles Lemuel Dibble, "The Holy Nation," *Anglican Theological Review*, vol. 6, no. 3 (December 1923), pp. 184–85.

62   Ibid., pp. 185–86.

63   Miroslav Volf, *After Our Likeness* (Grand Rapids, MI: Wm. B. Eerdmans Publishing Company, 1998), p. 136 (emphasis in original).

64   Cf. John Winthrop, "A Model of Christian Charity," in *The Puritans in America*, eds. Alan Heimert and Andrew Delbanco (Cambridge, MA: Harvard University Press,1985), p. 91;

65   Richard Gamble, *In Search of the City on a Hill: The Making and Unmaking of an Ameri-can Myth* (London, U.K.: Continuum, 2012), pp. 53–54.

66   Ibid.

67   Abraham C. Van Engen, *City on a Hill: A History of American Exceptionalism* (Yale University, 2020), p. 50.

68   Ibid.

69   Abraham C. Van Engen, "Claiming the Higher Ground: Puritans, Catholics, and the City on a Hill," in *American Literature and the New Puritan Studies*, ed. Bryce Traister (New York, NY: Cambridge University Press, 2017), p. 215.

70   Ibid. ("By emphasizing particular places as *like* a city upon a hill, Protestants em-
      braced an interpretation of Matthew 5:14 that might, in time, slip from an identifica-
      tion of individual churches or godly communions into towns and territories, then
      perhaps a nation, and maybe someday America itself")

71   John MacArthur, *The Master's Plan for the Church* (Chicago, IL: Moody Publishers,
      2008), p. 86.

72   Robert Bellarmine, *De Ecclesia Militante*, quoted in Joseph Clifford Fenton, *The
      Catholic Church and Salvation* (Westminster, MD: Newman Press, 1958), pp. 172.

73   Ibid., pp. 171–72.

74   Ibid., p. 172.

75   Christian Salenson, *Christian de Chergé: A Theology of Hope*, trans. Nada Conic (Col-
      legeville, MN: Liturgical Press, 2012), pp. 96–97.

76   Hans Küng is frequently put forward by certain Protestant or liberal Catholic authors
      to point out that "even" Catholic priests agree on some Protestant point or reject
      some point of Catholic theology. But Küng's heterodoxy is well established, and
      in 1979, the Sacred Congregation for the Doctrine of the Faith (the modern CDF)
      warned that his teachings "are a cause of disturbance in the minds of the faithful"
      and that "Professor Hans Küng, in his writings, has departed from the integral truth
      of Catholic faith, and therefore he can no longer be considered a Catholic theologian
      nor function as such in a teaching role." Sacred Congregation for the Doctrine of the
      Faith, "Declaration," Dec. 15, 1979.

77   Hans Küng, *The Church* (New York, NY: Burns and Oates, 2001), p. 37.

78   Ibid., p. 363.

79   As Pope Benedict XVI has said, his work serves as a still valid "reference point" for
      ecclesiology, particularly "on questions concerning Revelation, the nature of the
      Church, the sacraments and theological anthropology." Benedict acknowledges that
      Bellarmine emphasizes "the institutional aspect of the Church," but this is due to
      "the errors that were then circulating on these issues," and he never does so at the
      expense of the spiritual dimension. Instead, using the analogy of body and soul, "he
      described the relationship between the Church's inner riches and the external aspects
      that enable her to be perceived." Benedict XVI, General Audience, Feb. 23, 2011.

80   Bellarmine, p. 172.

81   This is why the Catholic Church recognizes the marriages of baptized Protestants as
      sacramental, even when those Protestants deny it.

82   For instance, "desirous of promoting the cause of ecumenism, the council fathers, in the
      dogmatic constitution *Lumen Gentium*, decided to emphasize the notion of the People
      of God. They did not by any means set aside the image of the body of Christ, but the
      notion of the People of God allowed them to disengage from the improper restriction
      of the term 'Church of Christ' to 'the Catholic Church,' thus opening up the position
      of previous magisterial documents." Salenson, p. 97. Contrary to Salenson's description,
      the Second Vatican Council actually declared that "the Holy Catholic Church, which is
      the Mystical Body of Christ, is made up of the faithful who are organically united in the
      Holy Spirit by the same faith, the same sacraments and the same government and who,
      combining together into various groups which are held together by a hierarchy, form
      separate churches or rites." Pope Paul VI, *Orientalium Ecclesiarum,* §2, Nov. 21, 1964.

83 Fourth Lateran Council (1215), Constitution 1, in *Reading the Middle Ages*, vol. 2, 3rd ed., ed. Barbara H. Rosenwein (Toronto, Canada: Unviersity of Toronto Press, 2018), p. 368.

84 "If any one shall say, that the baptism which is also given by heretics in the name of the Father, and of the Son, and of the Holy Ghost, with the intention of doing what the Church doth, is not true baptism; let him be anathema." Council of Trent, Canon 4 concerning Baptism, in *Canons and Decrees of the Council of Trent*, trans. Theodore Alois Buckley (London: George Routledge and Sons, 1851), p. 53.

85 Bellarmine couldn't have been ignorant of this dynamic, having experienced it personally. Bellarmine was from Montepulciano in Tuscany but entered the Jesuit novitiate in Rome, before being sent to Mondovì, in Piedmont, part of the Duchy of Savoy. After this, he went to the University of Padua in the Republic of Venice. From there, he was sent to the University of Leuven in the Duchy of Brabant, part of the Habsburg Netherlands. Much of his later life was spent in Rome (where he would eventually die), although he also served as theologian to the papal legate to Paris. Surely, he knew what it was like to belong to one visible society but not to live within its bounds.

86 Jeffrey VanderWilt, *A Church Without Borders* (Collegeville, MN: Liturgical Press, 1998), p. 40.

87 Eugene E. Carpenter and Philip W. Comfort, *Holman Treasury of Key Bible Words* (Nashville, TN: Holman Reference, 2000), p. 40.

88 At the time, this seems to have been part of the standard *haftarah*, the second reading in the Jewish equivalent of what Christians call the Lectionary (the first reading, the *parashah*, is always taken from the Torah). In researching this book, I discovered that now "Isaiah 61:1 is deliberately not read in the synagogue," because "generally speaking, Jews excluded from the haftarah those verses on which Christians based the principles of their religious faith." Hananel Mack, "What Happened to Jesus' Haftarah?," *Haaretz*, Aug. 12, 2005. Other excluded Old Testament passages include Isaiah 7:14, prophesying the Virgin Birth, or Hosea 11:1, which St. Matthew applies to the return of the Holy Family from Egypt (Matt. 2:15).

89 James A. Sanders, *The Monotheizing Process* (Eugene, OR: Cascade Books, 2014), p. 48.

90 Joseph B. Tyson, *Marcion and Luke-Acts: A Defining Struggle*, p. 126 (Columbia, SC: University of South Carolina Press, 2006). ("Marcion took his inspiration from the letters of Paul, most notably Galatians. He was deeply impressed with Paul's contrast of law and grace and concluded that these must be the domains of two Gods. One God is revealed in the Hebrew Bible as the Creator, law-giver, and judge of humankind. This God thus is identified with the created order, Torah, and the Jews, his chosen people. The second God is the Father of Jesus Christ, the God of grace, love, and mercy, who was completely unknown in this world before the appearance of Jesus. The work of Jesus was to release people from the Creator-God and deliver them into the domain of the God of grace.")

91 Richard Dawkins, *The God Delusion*, p. 51.

92 Friedrich Nietzsche described the Old Testament as "the book of divine justice" and the New Testament as "the book of grace" and lamented that to have "bound up the New Testament (a sort of *rococo* of taste in every respect) along with the Old Testament into a single book, as the 'Bible,' and 'the Book in Itself,' is perhaps the

greatest act of audacity and 'sin against the Spirit' which literary Europe has upon its conscience." Friedrich Nietzsche, *Beyond Good and Evil*, part III, aphorism 52, trans. Helen Zimmern, p. 71 (New York: MacMillan Co., 1907).

93   *West Wing*, Season 6, Episode 20, "In God We Trust," script available online at http://westwing.bewarne.com/sixth/620wetrust.html.

94   St. Epiphanius of Salamis, *Panarion*, Book 1, trans. Frank Williams, p. 303. (Leiden, The Netherlands: Koninkijke Brill, 2009)

95   Timothy Weber, "Dispensational Premillennialism: The Dispensationalist Era," *Christian History*, no. 61 (1999).

96   John A. D'Elia, *A Place at the Table* (New York, NY: Oxford University Press, 2008), p. xxiii.

97   Ibid.

98   C.I. Scofield, *Rightly Dividing the Word of Truth*, pp. 3–4 (Danville, IL: Grace & Truth, Inc., 1996).

99   Ibid., p. 28.

100 James Borland, "Church in Prophecy," *The Popular Encyclopedia of Bible Prophecy*, eds. Tim LaHaye, Edward E. Hindson, Wayne A. Brindle (Eugene, OR: Harvest House Publishers, 2004), pp. 54–55.

101 "The traditional *dispensational* view holds that Israel and the church have separate and distinct identities, destinies, and promises. During the so-called Church age, Israel as a nation has been set aside, and the program of God has gone into a parenthesis and intercalation. After this church age parenthesis comes to an end, God will resume relations with the nation Israel once again and restore the Davidic kingdom to its greatest height ever." Walter C. Kaiser, Jr., "An Epangelical Response," in *Dispensationalism, Israel and the Church: The Search for Definition*, eds. Craig A. Blaising and Darrell L. Bock, pp. 360–376 (Grand Rapids, MI: Zondervan, 1992). Cf. Paul D. Miller, "Evangelicals, Israel and US Foreign Policy," *Survival: Global Politics and Strategy*, Vol. 56, No. 1, pp. 7–26 (February–March 2014) ("Dispensationalists interpret the Bible as stating that Israel and the Church are separate bodies; that the dispensation given to Israel was not canceled or dissolved by the advent of Christianity; and that God's promises thus apply to Jews around the world today").

102 Thomas Ice, "Church Age," *The Popular Encyclopedia of Bible Prophecy*, eds. Tim LaHaye, Edward E. Hindson, Wayne A. Brindle (Eugene, OR: Harvest House Publishers, 2004), pp. 51, 54.

103 Mark R. Amstutz, *Evangelicals and American Foreign Policy* (New York: Oxford University Press, 2014). Cf. David D. Kirkpatrick, "For Evangelicals, Supporting Israel is 'God's Foreign Policy," *New York Times* (November 14, 2006). This is not to suggest that *only* dispensationalists are pro-Israel or that this is the only reason for their support.

104 Augustine, *Sermon 341*, in *Sermons 341–400 on Liturgical Seasons*, trans. Edmund Hill, vol. 3, no. 10 of *The Works of Saint Augustine*, ed. John E. Rotelle (Hyde Park, NY: New City Press, 1995), p. 26.

105 J. Dwight Pentecost, "Kingdom of God," *The Popular Encyclopedia of Bible Prophecy*, eds. Tim LaHaye, Edward E. Hindson, Wayne A. Brindle (Eugene, OR: Harvest House Publishers, 2004), p. 189.

106 As the Second Vatican Council explains, "although the Church is the new people

of God, the Jews should not be presented as rejected or accursed by God, as if this followed from the Holy Scriptures." Pope Paul VI, *Nostra Aetate* 4, October 28, 1965. The transition from the Old to New Covenant is not one of rejection, but ongoing growth, "building up the body of Christ, until we all attain to the unity of the faith and of the knowledge of the Son of God, to mature manhood" (Eph. 4:12–13).

107 John MacArthur, Sermon: "The Scandal of the Catholic Priesthood," *Grace to You*, May 1, 2002.

108 Don Stewart, "Did Jesus Give Peter the Unique Authority to Speak for Him? (Papal Authority)," from *Is the Bible the Ultimate Authority?*, available online at https://www.blueletterbible.org/Comm/stewart_don/faq/bible-ultimate-authority/question5-did-jesus-give-peter-authority-to-speak.cfm.

109 William A. Stephens, *Papal Infallibility, as seen in the light of Catholicism, stated and defended by Rev. M. J. Ferguson;. and as seen in the light of Revelation, examined and exhibited by William A. Stephens* (Owen Sound, ON: John Rutherford, 1871), p. 14.

110 Craig A. Evans, *From Jesus to the Church* (Louisville, KY: Westminster John Knox Press, 2014), p. 27.

111 James MacDonald, *Vertical Church* (Colorado Springs, Co: David C Cook, 2012), p. 86.

112 Renaut van der Riet, "Soli Deo Gloria," *Acts29*, available online at https://www.acts29.com/soli-deo-gloria/.

113 Michael B. Buckley, "Sermon the Immaculate Conception of the Blessed Virgin Mary," in *Catholic Oratory: A Compilation of Sacred and Sublime Orations* (New York, NY: Murphy & McCarthy, 1891), p. 623.

114 John MacArthur, *The Master's Plan for the Church* (Chicago, IL: Moody Publishers, 2008), p. 160.

115 Peter Kreeft, *Catholic Christianity: A Complete Catechism of Catholic Church Beliefs Based on the Catechism of the Catholic Church* (San Francisco, CA: Ignatius Press, 2011), p. 98.

116 David Guzik, "Luke 22—The Last Supper; Jesus Is Betrayed," *Enduring Word Biblical Commentary*, available online at https://enduringword.com/bible-commentary/luke-22/. This error is common for English-speaking commentators. Cf. Charles Stanley, "Satan's Strategy," *In Touch Ministries* (September 13, 2017), available online at https://www.intouch.org/read/magazine/daily-devotions/satans-strategy ("The Enemy wanted to shake Peter's faith hard in hopes that he'd fall away from Jesus like chaff").

117 Keith Mathison, *The Shape of Sola Scriptura* (Moscow, ID: Canon Press, 2001), p. 193.

118 John Calvin, *Commentary on a Harmony of the Evangelists, Matthew, Mark, and Luke*, vol. III, trans. William Pringle (Edinburgh, Scotland: Calvin Translation Society, 1846), p. 221.

119 Charles Ellicott (1819–1905), an Anglican bishop and theologian, takes a slightly different interpretation, arguing that "the head Christian of the world, and writing from the thick of the persecution already begun in Rome, the Asiatic elders cannot set his advice down as that of some easy layman who is untouched by the difficulty. It can hardly be said, therefore, that this is an example of St. Peter's *humility*, as though he recognized in himself no higher office than that of these presbyters. The effect is, on the contrary, to make the recipients of the Letter feel that he is using a strong argument *a fortiori*." Charles Ellicott, *Ellicott's Commentary on the Whole Bible*, Vol. 8 (Eugene, OR: Wipf & Stock, 1959), p. 432.

120 Michael S. Wilder and Timothy Paul Jones, *The God Who Goes before You: Pastoral Leadership as Christ-Centered Followership* (Nashville, TN: B&H Academic, 2018).

121 Matt Slick, "Is Peter supreme among the Apostles?," *CARM (Christianity Apologetics & Research Ministry)*, available online at https://carm.org/catholic/peter-supreme-among-apostles.

122 Joseph Benson, *The New Testament of Our Lord and Saviour Jesus Christ*, vol. 2 (New York, NY: Carlton & Phillips, 1856), p. 625.

123 To take a particularly striking example, the biblical scholar Ronald Youngblood argued that "thus led (as we believe) by divine Providence, scholars during the latter half of the fourth century settled for all time the limits of the New Testament canon. The twenty-seven books of Matthew through Revelation constitute that New Testament, which possesses divine authority equal to that of the Old." Youngblood, "The Process How We Got Our Bible," *Christianity Today*, 32:2 (February 5, 1988) 27; cited in M. James Sawyer, "Evangelicals And The Canon Of The New Testament," *Grace Theological Journal*, vol. 11, no. 1 (1991), p. 43. But the Third Council of Carthage doesn't separately set the New and Old Testament canons. Instead, it says, "It was also determined that besides the Canonical Scriptures nothing be read in the Church under the title of divine Scriptures. The Canonical Scriptures are these . . ." and proceeds to list the *entire* Catholic canon. To take half of this declaration as divinely inspired and the other half as erroneous is unabashed special pleading.

124 Brooke Foss Westcott, *A General Survey of the History of the Canon of the New Testament*, 6th ed. (Cambridge, UK: MacMillan and Co., 1889), p. 440.

125 From the start, presbyters were understood as priests in the Church. Indeed, the English word "priest" likely comes from the Latin *prester*, an abbreviated form of *presbyter*.

126 9Marks was founded by Mark Dever, senior pastor at Capitol Hill Baptist Church, which "has been described as the epicenter of the new Calvinism sweeping across many evangelical churches today, including the Southern Baptist Convention." Timothy George, "Puritans on the Potomac," *First Things*, May 2, 2016. 9Marks's self-proclaimed mission is to "help pastors, future pastors, and church members see what a biblical church looks like, and to take practical steps for becoming one." "Who We Are." 9Marks, available online at https://www.9marks.org/about/.

127 "Does a pastor have to be 'called' by God?," 9Marks, available online at https://www.9marks.org/answer/does-pastor-have-be-called-god/. Other than arguments from silence, 9Marks's view is based on a single misunderstood Bible verse, 1 Tim. 3:1, which says that "if any one aspires to the office of bishop, he desires a noble task." They explain, "Paul doesn't say, 'If anyone wants to be a pastor, he must have a special, supernatural, subjective call from God,' but rather, 'If anyone wants to be a pastor, he desires a good thing. Now here are the qualifications.'" But Paul isn't saying that the desire is a good thing, only that the task being desired is a good thing. The desire itself may well be *sinful* (e.g., a man pursues ordination out of pride and ambition, or a lust for power), and is more often *misplaced* (e.g., a man mistakes a call to holiness as a call to ordination). St. Augustine argues that Paul's meaning in 1 Tim. 3:1 is that "it is not the honors or power of this life we should covet, since all things under the sun are vanity, but we should aim at using our position and influence, if these have been honorably attained, for the welfare of those who are under us" and that "it is unseemly to

covet the high position requisite for governing the people, even though that position be held and that government be administered in a seemly manner." Augustine, *City of God*, Book IX, chapter 19, trans. Marcus Dods (Peabody, MA: Hendrickson Publishers, 2009), pp. 360–61. Precisely because the thing being desired is holy and noble, it needs to be protected from men who would seek it unworthily, and so Paul gives some criteria about qualities a bishop must possess. But Paul's list isn't exhaustive, nor was it meant to be (he gives a slightly different list of criteria to look for in Titus 1:7–9). There are plenty of men in the Church who meet all of the criteria listed, the vast majority of whom aren't bishops and aren't called to be.

128 Moody Church is perhaps best known for *Moody Church Hour*, its broadcasted Sunday service.

129 Erwin Lutzer, *Pastor to Pastor: Tackling the Problems of Ministry*, rev. ed. (Grand Rapids, MI: Kregel, 1998), p. 11.

130 "Occupation," *Etymology Dictionary*, available online at https://www.etymonline.com/word/occupation; "Vocation," *Etymology Dictionary*, available online at https://www.etymonline.com/word/vocation.

131 Since both "Christ" and "Christian" derive from the Greek (*khristós*), meaning "the anointed one," it is significant that we find God's calling at work in the selection of priests, prophets, and kings, as these are the three offices within Israel that received an anointing. St. Peter connects each of these offices to the Church in describing Christians as "a royal priesthood" who "declare the wonderful deeds of him who called you out of darkness into his marvelous light" (1 Pet. 2:9).

132 Lutzer, pp. 11–13.

133 Francis de Sales, *The Catholic Controversy*, trans. Henry Benedict Mackey (Rockford, IL: Tan Books and Publishers, 1989), p. 13.

134 Ibid, p. 19.

135 Martin Luther, Pentecost Tuesday homily, in *The Precious and Sacred Writings of Martin Luther*, ed. John Nicholas Lenker, vol. 12 (Minneapolis, MN: Lutherans in All Lands Co., 1907), p. 374.

136 Gregory the Great, *Epistle XX, to Mauricius Augustus*, *NPNF* 2/12:170. (Emphasis in original.)

137 Augustine, *Sermon XCVI, Sermons On Selected Lessons Of The New Testament*, vol. 2 (Oxford: John Henry Parker, 1845), p. 683.

138 St. John Chrysostom, *On the Priesthood*, Book II, *NPNF* 1/9:39.

139 For instance, the section headers in the NIV and many other Bibles label this passage as "Jesus reinstates Peter." Several authors also explicitly argue (or more often, presume) that this passage is about Peter being reinstated. See, e.g., Colin G. Kruse, *The Gospel According to John: An Introduction and Commentary, Tyndale New Testament Commentaries* (Grand Rapids: Eerdmans, 2003), p. 392.

140 Leon Morris, *The Gospel According to John*, rev. ed., *The New International Commentary on the New Testament* (Grand Rapids: Eerdmans, 1995), p. 772.

141 D.A. Carson, *The Gospel According to John* (Grand Rapids: Wm. B. Eerdmans Publishing Co., 1991), p. 679.

142 John Calvin, *Commentary on the Gospel According to John*, vol. 2, trans. William Pringle (Edinburgh: Calvin Translation Society, 1847), pp. 287–288.

143 Ibid., p. 290.

144 Cyril of Alexandria, *Commentary on John*, vol. 2, trans. David R. Maxwell, ed. Joel C. Elowsky, *Ancient Christian Texts* (Downers Grove, IL: InterVarsity Press, 2015), p. 383.

145 Augustine, *Tractate CXXIII on the Gospel of St. John*, *NPNF* 1/7:445. (Emphasis added).

146 Cyril of Alexandria, *A Commentary on the Gospel of Luke*, vol. 2, trans. R. Payne Smith (Oxford: University of Oxford Press, 1859), p. 677.

147 St. John Chrysostom, "Homily XXXVIII," in *The Homilies on First and Second Corinthians,* trans. Talbot W. Chambers (Loschberg 9, Germany: Jazzybee Verlag, 2017), p. 269.

148 John Calvin, *Commentary on the Gospel According to John*, vol. 2, trans. William Pringle (Edinburgh: Calvin Translation Society, 1847), p. 290.

149 D.A. Carson, *The Gospel According to John* (Grand Rapids: Wm. B. Eerdmans Publishing Co., 1991), p. 679.

150 John Calvin, *Commentary on the Gospel According to John*, vol. 2, trans. William Pringle (Edinburgh: Calvin Translation Society, 1847), p. 290.

151 St. Matthew lists Capernaum, alongside Chorazin and Bethsaida, as one of "the cities where most of his mighty works had been done" (Matt. 11:20–24).

152 The silver half shekel was, on average, about 110 grains troy. William Smith, *A Dictionary of the Bible*, Vol. 2 (London: John Murray, 1863), p. 408. As "the shekel and the didrachmon were of the same weight," the ancient translators converted the monetary units accordingly when translating the Hebrew texts of the Old Testament into the Greek Septuagint. Ibid. at 409. Today, that amount of silver would be worth only a few dollars, but precious metals were rarer (and thus more valuable) in ancient Israel: for instance, the prophet Jeremiah purchased a field for only 17 shekels (Jer. 32:9).

153 Balthasar Bickel and Johanna Nichols, "Inclusive-exclusive as person vs. number categories worldwide," in *Clusivity: Typology and Case Studies of Inclusive-Exclusive Distinction*, ed. Elena Filimonova (Amsterdam: John Benjamins Publishing Co., 2005), p. 49.

154 St. John Chrysostom (c. 349–407) suggests that the "we" to which Jesus speaks refers either to "himself and His Father, or concerning himself alone." John Chrysostom, "Homily 26," in *Works of St. Chrysostom: Homilies on the Gospel of St. John and the Epistle to the Hebrews (NPNF* 1/14), p. 92. The use of "we" to refer just to the speaker is not unheard-of in the New Testament (cf. 2 Cor. 10, when St. Paul switches between first-person singular and plural in defending his ministry).

155 "Fremut und Gehorsam" in *Das Neue Volk Gottes* (Düsseldorf, 1969) 249–66, quoted in Heinrich Fries, *Fundamental Theology*, trans. Robert J. Daly, S.J. (Washington, D.C.: Catholic University of America Press, 1996), p. 473.

156 The Jerusalem Talmud is "one of the earlier rabbinic sources, with material probably stemming from the end of the Second Temple period [530 B.C.–A.D. 70] and compiled at the latest in the early fifth century." Sebastian Selvén, "The Privilege of Taxation: Jewish Identity and the Half-shekel Temple Tax in the Talmud Yerushalmi," *Svensk Exegetisk Årsbok*, Vol. 81, p. 63.

157 Ibid., p. 70. It is somewhat surprising that the Levites (the tribe from which the priests came) were taxed. The half-shekel tax was connected to the first census (Exod. 30:13, "each who is numbered in the census shall give this: half a shekel according to the shekel of the sanctuary"), and the tribe of Levi was exempted from the census (Num. 1:48–50).

158   All priests were Levites, but not all Levites were priests. "The Hebrew Bible presumes the existence of two clerical classes, both of which are inherited from father to son. The first, larger, class is that of the Levites, presumed to be the lineal descendants of Levi, one of the twelve sons of the patriarch Jacob. Moses and Aaron were both Levites. Aaron's descendants, though, gain a new status—that of priest, or *kohen*. Throughout the history of biblical Israel, the status and role of both of these classes was highly contested, although by the fifth century BCE they had more or less stabilized. The priests primarily administered the sacrificial system at the temple and the Levites assisted them in a variety of ways. The Levites had a position subordinate to the priests." Michael L. Satlow, "Markets and Tithes in Roman Palestine," *Gift Giving and the "Embedded" Economy in the Ancient World*, eds. Filippo Carlà and Maja Gori (Heidelberg: Universitätsverlag Winter, 2014), p. 316. The trifold high priest, priest, Levite structure prefigured the trifold Christian structure of bishop, presbyter, and deacon, as we see from 1 Clement 40.

159   Satlow, p. 319, fn. 16.

160   Under the Levitical law, the sin offering was required only of women who "had received seed" and given birth. St. Bede the Venerable (672–735) points this connection out in an ancient homily: "Mary, God's blessed mother and a perpetual virgin, was, along with the Son she bore, most free from all subjection to the law. The law says that a woman who "had received seed" [Lev. 12:2] and given birth was to be judged unclean and that after a long period she, along with the offspring she had borne, were to be cleansed by victims offered to God. So it is evident that the law does not describe as unclean that woman who, without receiving man's seed, gave birth as a virgin. Nor does it teach that she had to be cleansed by saving sacrificial offerings. But as our Lord and Savior, who in His divinity was the one who gave the law, when he appeared as a human being, willed to be under the law[.] . . . So too His blessed mother, who by a singular privilege was above the law, nevertheless did not shun being made subject to the principles of the law for the sake of showing us an example of humility." St. Bede the Venerable, *Homilies on the Gospels I.18* in "Luke," *Ancient Christian Commentary* (Downers Grove, IL: InterVarsity Press, 2003), p. 47.

161   John Calvin, *Bible Commentaries on the Harmony of the Gospels*, Vol. 2, trans. William Pringle and John King (Altenmünster, Germany: Jazzybee Verlag, 2017), p. 300.

162   Ibid.

163   Ibid., 301.

164   Ibid.

165   Andy M. Reimer, *Miracle and Magic: A Study in the Acts of the Apostles and Philostratus' Life of Apollonius*, (Sheffield: Sheffield Academic Press, 2002), p. 5. Reimer is critical of this sharp distinction, arguing (on the basis of the varying, even contradictory ways the terms "miracle" and "magic" are used in antiquity) that "'miracle' and 'magic' are simply empty labels that competing religious groups use for their own convenience." While other religions approach the question of "magic" differently (a fact that Exodus 7 confirms), the manipulative-supplicative distinction is the view that most accords with the Biblical depiction of magic vis-à-vis miracles. Cf. Howard Clark Kee, *Medicine, Miracle and Magic in New Testament Times* (Cambridge, UK: Cambridge University Press, 1986), p. 3.

166 Thomas 4:1–2, quoted in Reidar Aasgaard, *The Childhood of Jesus: Decoding the Apocryphal Infancy Gospel of Thomas* (Cambridge, UK: James Clarke & Co., 2010), p. 17.

167 Augustine, *Tractate XLIX on John (John 11:1–54)*, in *The Works of St. Augustin* 49.2 (trans. John Gibb and James Innes, *NPNF* 1/7:270).

168 Sometimes, the meaning is simple enough, as when Jesus heals a blind man and then has a conversation about spiritual blindness (John 9), or when he miraculously multiplies bread and then has a conversation about the spiritual bread of the Eucharist (John 6). Other times, as St. Augustine notes, "to find out [the deeper meaning] in regard to such deeds is a somewhat harder task than to read or hear of them." Ibid.

169 Bertrand Russell, *Why I Am Not a Christian*, ed. Paul Edwards (New York, NY: Simon & Schuster, 1957), p. 19.

170 C.S. Lewis, "Miracles," in *The Grand Miracle*, ed. Walter Hooper (New York, NY: Ballantine Books, 1970), p. 5.

171 Charles Spurgeon, *The Soul Winner* (New York, NY: Cosimo Classics, 2007), p. 232 (emphasis in original).

172 Tim Challies, "How Evangelism Is Kind of Like Fishing," January 28, 2019. Available online at https://www.challies.com/articles/how-evangelism-is-kind-of-like-fishing/.

173 Luke has already presented Jesus as using Peter's house as a sort of base of operations in Galilee from which to heal "any that were sick with various diseases," including Peter's own mother-in-law (Luke 4:40), but the Gospels of Matthew and Mark present those healings as occurring *after* the calling of Peter and the other disciples (cf. Matthew 4:18–22, 8:14–17; Mark 1:16–20, 29–39). The ordering in Matthew and Mark is more likely the historical order, as Luke occasionally inverts the order of events to make theological points. For instance, Luke "structures his gospel as to build attention and suspense directed towards that final crisis and decision at Jerusalem" by presenting approximately forty percent of his Gospel (Luke 9:51–19:44) as a single journey to Jerusalem. Floyd V. Filson, "The Journey Motif in Luke-Acts," in *Apostolic History and the Gospel: Biblical and Historical Essays Presented to F.F. Bruce*, eds. W. Ward Gasque & Ralph P. Martin (Exeter: The Paternoster Press, 1970), pp. 70–71. This should be understood in a similar way to how we understand the autobiography of Senator Daniel Inouye, *Journey to Washington*. It is true on the order of intention, not geography. Luke begins the great travel narrative by saying that "when the days drew near for him to be received up, he set his face to go to Jerusalem" (Luke 9:51). From this point on, every step is toward Calvary. Luke appears to be comfortable organizing the events of Christ's life thematically rather than chronologically, even changing the order of the three temptations to show the superiority of the Temple to the world (cf. Matt. 4:1–11; Luke 4:1–13).

174 C.S. Lewis, "Miracles," in *The Grand Miracle*, ed. Walter Hooper (New York, NY: Ballantine Books, 1970), p. 5 (emphasis in original).

175 St. Jerome believed that the number 153 referred to the number of known species of fish at the time, suggesting that the haul included every nation and people on earth. The fascination with the 153 fish may also suggest Johannine authorship, since St. John appears to have been keenly interested in numbers, and particularly "triangular numbers" like 153. A triangular number is a number that corresponds to objects arranged in an equilateral triangle. If it helps, imagine how many billiard balls could

be arranged into an equilateral triangle: 3, 6, 10, 15, 21, 28, and so on, with the space between the numbers going up by one each time. If you were to do this ten more times, you would have 153. If you were to do it another fourteen times, you would have 496, and John has 496 syllables in his Prologue, and 496 words in his Epilogue. Richard Bauckham, "The 153 Fish and the Unity of the Fourth Gospel," *Neotesta-mentica*, vol. 36, no. 1/2 (2002), p. 82. Five more times, and you would have 666, the number of the Beast (Rev. 13:18).

176 Augustine, *Tractate CXXII on John (John 20:30–21:11)*, in *The Works of St. Augustin* 122.1 (trans. John Gibb and James Innes, *NPNF* 1/7:439).

177 This point should not be overstated. Earlier critical scholars exaggerated the differences between John 1–20 and John 21, arguing that the former is Christology and the latter is ecclesiology (study of the Church), but bifurcation ignores Christ's teaching in John 10 and elsewhere about the Church. Finn Damgaard, *Rewriting Peter as an Intertextual Character in the Canonical Gospels* (London, UK: Routledge, 2016), p. 90.

178 Paul S. Minear, "The Original Functions of John 21," *Journal of Biblical Literature*, vol. 102, no. 1 (Mar. 1983), p. 94.

179 St. Augustine saw the relationship between the first multiplication as about the Church "as it exists in this world" and this final miracle as about the Church "as it shall be in the end of the world"; hence, "the one accordingly took place before, and the other subsequently to the resurrection of the Lord." Augustine, *Tractate CXXII on John (John 20:30–21:11)*, in *The Works of St. Augustin* 122.7 (trans. John Gibb and James Innes, *NPNF* 1/7:441).

180 Gregory the Great, *Homily 24*, in *Reading the Gospels with Gregory the Great: Homilies 21–26*, trans. Santha Bhattacharji (Petersham, MA: St. Bede's Publications, 2001), p. 61.

181 Cyril of Alexandria, *Commentary on John*, vol. 2, trans. David R. Maxwell, ed. Joel C. Elowsky (Downers Grove, IL: InterVarsity Press, 2015), p. 381

182 F.F. Bruce, *The Gospel of John,* (Grand Rapids, MI: William B. Eerdmans Publishing Company, 1983), p. 402.

183 This interpretation of the "sheep" and "lamb" distinction of John 21:15–17 can be found in the writings of Theophylact of Ohrid, an eleventh-century Byzantine commentator. Theophylact of Ohrid, *The Explanation of the Holy Gospel by Blessed Theophylact* (House Springs, MO: Chrysostom Press, 2007), p. 309. Theophylact is quoted by St. Thomas Aquinas, in his own *Catena Aurea* ("Golden Chain"), an assemblage of Biblical commentaries, mostly from the Church Fathers, on every part of the four Gospels.

184 I omit here the particularly absurd mis-readings of John 21, as when the nineteenth-century Anglican theologian Sir Edwyn Hoskyns accused the disciples of "complete apostasy" for going fishing. Cf. Edwyn Hoskyns, *The Fourth Gospel*, ed. Francis N. Davey (London: Faber and Faber, 1947), p. 552.

185 Kevin Quast, *Reading the Gospel of John: An Introduction* (New York, NY: Paulist Press, 1991), p. 142.

186 "Protestant Pastors Name Graham Most Influential Living Preacher," *LifeWay Research*, February 2, 2010. Available online at https://lifewayresearch.com/2010/02/02/protestant-pastors-name-graham-most-influential-living-preacher/.

187 D.A. Carson, *The Gospel According to John* (Grand Rapids, MI: William B. Eerdmans Publishing Company, 1991), p. 673. For MacArthur's indebtedness to Carson, see

John MacArthur, *The MacArthur New Testament Commentary: John 12–21* (Chicago, IL: Moody Publishers, 2008), p. 394.

188   MacArthur, p. 394. Carson's approach is humbler, noting that the number may be symbolic but that "if the Evangelist has some symbolism in mind connected with the number 153, he has hidden it well." Carson, p. 673.

189   Martin Luther, *Luther's Church Postil Gospels: First to Twelfth Sunday After Trinity*, vol. 4, trans. John Nicholas Lenker, in *The Precious and Sacred Writings of Martin Luther* (Minneapolis, MN: Lutherans in All Lands, 1904), p. 165. I have been unable to find any commentaries by Luther on John 21:1–14, since he omitted this portion of Scripture from the lectionary he created.

190   Charles Spurgeon, *The Metropolitan Tabernacle Pulpit*, vol. 8 (London: Passmore and Alabaster, 1863), pp. 202–3.

191   Luther, p. 137; Patrick Spencer, "Narrative Echoes in John 21: Intertextual Interpretation and Intratextual Connection," *Journal for the Study of the New Testament [JSNT]*, vol. 22, no. 75 (1999), p. 58. But see J. Michael Miller, *The Divine Right of the Papacy in Recent Ecumenical Theology* (Rome: Gregorian University, 1980), p. 101 ("Whereas Luther and Melanchton both interpreted the Petrine texts in such a way that Peter personally received no special commission from Christ, this reading of the Scriptures is no longer normative. Even prior to 1960, many [Lutheran] theologians recognized that a certain Petrine primacy was testified to in the New Testament. In recent years this interpretation has gained ground").

192   Randy Poon, "John 21: A Johannine Model of Leadership," *Journal of Biblical Perspectives in Leadership*, vol. 1, no. 1, p. 53 ("The disciple, Peter, is referred to 13 times in this text. He is called Peter, Simon Peter, and Simon son of John. As a group, the disciples are referenced six times. The author also refers to "the disciple whom Jesus loved" six times [once as one of the sons of Zebedee]").

193   John Calvin, *John* (Wheaton, IL: Crossway Books, 1994), p. 465.

194   John MacArthur, sermon entitled "Audacious Disobedience," *Grace to You*, November 13, 2016. Available online at https://www.gty.org/library/sermons-library/43-115/audacious-disobedience.

195   Carson, p. 672.

196   Charles Spurgeon, *The Metropolitan Tabernacle Pulpit*, vol. 8 (London: Passmore and Alabaster, 1863), p. 203.

197   Carson, p. 668; MacArthur, p. 390.

198   Ibid., p. 679.

199   MacArthur, pp. 390, 402.

200   Charles Spurgeon, "Feed My Sheep," *The Sword and the Trowel*, no. 3211 (July 1877).

201   Gregory the Great, *Forty Homilies Homily 24*, in *John 11–21*, ed. Joel C. Elowsky, *Ancient Christian Commentary on Scripture* (Downers Grove, IL: InterVarsity Press, 2007), p. 382.

202   On the implausibility of the "Q source" theories, see generally William R. Farmer's *The Gospel of Jesus: The Pastoral Relevance of the Synoptic Problem* (Louisville, KY: Westminster / John Knox Press, 1994).

203   John MacArthur, *Twelve Ordinary Men* (Nashville, TN: Thomas Nelson, 2002), pp. 29–30.

204   These two titles may mean the same thing; the word translated as "Cananaen" is *Kananaios*, which is "probably a Hellenized form of the Aramaic *qannāyā*, 'zealot,'" but the

word is "obscure" and the meaning ultimately unclear. David Bentley Hart, *The New Testament: A Translation* (New Haven, CT: Yale University Press, 2017), p. 68, fn. e.

205 Acts doesn't end with Judas's name, as Judas is dead by this point (cf. Acts 1:13).

206 Cf. "Apostle" in *A Dictionary of Religious Knowledge*, ed. Lyman Abbott (New York: Harper & Brox. Publishers, 1885) ("Peter and John were the only remarkable men among them, and constituted the natural leaders of the band. For the rest, the disciples were plain, common, matter-of-fact men, whose prosaic nature perpetually stumbled over Christ's enigmatical sayings"); W. H. Griffith Thomas, *The Apostle John: Studies in His Life and Writings* (CrossReach Publications, 2016), p. 22 ("Peter is the natural leader, no doubt because of his greater age and experience").

207 William Dexter Wilson, *The Papal Supremacy* (New York: James Pott & Co., 1889), p. 138.

208 James B. Jordan, "Peter as High Priest," *Biblical Horizons*, no. 66 (December 1994).

209 Ibid.

210 John Calvin, *Bible Commentaries on the Harmony of the Gospels*, vol. 3, trans. William Pringle and John King (Altenmünster, Germany: Jazzybee Verlag Jürgen Beck, 2017), p. 284.

211 It's true, as started above, that Luke sometimes rearranges the order of events in his Gospel to make a theological point, but there's no question that the replacement of Judas occurs prior to the Twelve (including Matthias, Judas' replacement) being sent on Pentecost.

212 John Calvin, *Bible Commentaries on the Harmony of the Gospels*, vol. 3, trans. William Pringle and John King (Altenmünster, Germany: Jazzybee Verlag Jürgen Beck, 2017), p. 284.

213 Ibid.

214 Ibid., p. 193.

215 Rolland Wolfe, *Studies in the Life of Jesus: A Liberal Approach* (Lewiston, NY: Edwin Mellen Press, 1990), p. 80. Professor Wolfe gets many things wrong in his interpretation of Scripture, but his geography is correct.

216 A. Edward Siecienski, *The Papacy and the Orthodox* (Oxford, UK: Oxford University Press, 2017), p. 126. For more on the Church Fathers' positions, see the debate between Webster and Ray generally. William Webster, *The Matthew 16 Controversy* (Battleground, WI: Christian Resources, Inc., 1996); Steve Ray, *Upon This Rock: St. Peter and the Primacy of Rome in Scripture and the Early Church* (San Francisco: Ignatius Press, 1999). It would be easy to get lost in the dueling litanies, but Ray makes a crucial point that Webster concedes: there are no Church Fathers "who denied the primacy of Peter or of his successors." Ray, p. 12.

217 Augustine, *The Retractions*, trans. M. Inez Bogan (Washington, D.C.: Catholic University of America Press, 1968), pp. 90–91.

218 Norman L. Geisler, "An Evaluation of John Henry Newman's *Essay on the Development of Christian Doctrine*" (2016), available at https://normangeisler.com/evaluation-jhnewman-dev-christian-doctrine/; Michael A. Field, "Is the Roman Catholic Church the Only Church of Christ?" (August 2007), available at https://normangeisler.com/is-the-rcc-the-only-church/.

219 Dave Hunt, *The Woman Rides the Beast* (Eugene, OR: Harvest House Publications, 1994), p. 145.

220 Keith Mathison, *The Shape of Sola Scriptura* (Moscow, ID: Canon Press, 2001), p. 184.

221 Ibid.

222 For more on the theology and importance of name-changing, see Joe Heschmeyer, *Who Am I, Lord?* (Huntington, IN: Our Sunday Visitor, 2020), pp. 143–163.

223 Joseph Fleishman, "On the Significance of a Name Change and Circumcision in Genesis 17," *Journal of the Ancient Near Eastern Society*, vol. 28 (2001), p.22.

224 D.H. Williams, "Response to Michael Root's John 21," in *The Gospel of John: Theological-Ecumenical Readings*, ed. Charles Raith II (Eugene, OR: Cascade Books, 2017), pp. 234–35.

225 John MacArthur, *The MacArthur Study Bible*, 2nd ed. (Nashville, TN: Thomas Nelson Publishers, 2019),p. 1293.

226 Ibid.

227 Richard France, *The Gospel According to Matthew* (Grand Rapids, MI: William B. Eerdmans Publishing Co., 2002), p. 254.

228 John Calvin, *Bible Commentaries on the Harmony of the Gospels*, vol. 2, trans. William Pringle and John King (Altmünster, Germany: Jazzybee Verlag Jürgen Beck), p. 234.

229 Some Biblical manuscripts have these four instances as "son of Jonah" rather than "son of John," but this is most likely an attempt by copyists to "correct" what they incorrectly regarded as an error.

230 Michael Hilton, *Bar Mitzvah: A History* (Philadelphia, PA: The Jewish Publication Society, 2014), p. 23.

231 CSC Williams, *A Commentary on the Acts of the Apostles* (New York: Harper's, 1957), p. 152. Another to notice is Robert W. Wall, "Peter Son of Jonah: The Conversion of Cornelius in the Context of Canon," *Journal for the Study of the New Testament* vol. 29 (1989), pp. 79–90.

232 R.T. France claims that this new name "is not now given for the first time, for Matthew has used it throughout ... and Mark 3:16 and John 1:42 indicate that it was given at an earlier stage." Richard France, *The Gospel According to Matthew* (Grand Rapids, MI: William B. Eerdmans Publishing Co., 2002), p. 254. This argument is odd. The examples from Matthew and Mark are of the Gospel *narrators* referring to Simon by the name we now know him by, just as one might say, "Mark Twain was born in Hannibal, Missouri" without suggesting that Samuel Clemens was already known as Mark Twain at birth. As for John 1:42, Jesus tells Simon in the future tense, "You *shall be* called Cephas." This also answers Protestant scholars like David Bivin, who suggest that Simon just already happened to be nicknamed Peter. See, for instance, David N. Bivin, "Jesus' *Petros-petra* Wordplay (Matthew 16:18): Is It Greek, Aramaic, or Hebrew?" *The Language Environment of First Century Judaea* (Leiden, Netherlands: Brill, 2014), pp. 380–81. Brill says that "apparently, Jesus' most prominent disciple bore two Hebrew names," with *Petros* being "Simon's nickname, or second name, with which contemporaries could distinguish him from the many other Simons in the population." But Matthew 16 clearly appears to be Jesus changing Simon's name (or bestowing of a second name), with John 1:42 placing this name change in the future, rather than treating Simon as already having a second name.

233 The first time we see the name Peter among non-Christians is in A.D. 170. Other allegedly earlier texts containing the name "Peter" actually date to long after the New Testament. Cf. Joseph Fitzmeyer, *To Advance the Gospel*, 2nd ed. (Grand Rapids, MI: Wm. B. Eerdmans Publishing Co., 1998), pp. 119–120.

234 D.H. Williams, "Response to Michael Root's John 21," in *The Gospel of John: Theological-Ecumenical Readings*, ed. Charles Raith II (Eugene, OR: Cascade Books, 2017), pp. 235.

235 The radio host and author Ron Rhodes goes so far as to claim that "it is critical to note that the entire context of Matthew 16:13–20 is all about Jesus, not Peter." Ron Rhodes, *Reasoning from the Scripture with Catholics* (Eugene, OR: Harvest House, 2000), p. 104. Hopefully, no one who has read this far takes such an assertion seriously.

236 Chrys C. Caragounis, *Peter and the Rock* (Berlin: Werner Hildebrand, 1989), pp. 1–3.

237 A.T. Robinson, *Commentary on the Gospel According to Matthew* (New York: Macmillan Company, 1911), p. 191. Obviously, I'm not suggesting that ordinary Protestants are reading A.T. Robinson, but rather that he neatly captures the sort of "anything but that" exegesis that is still in vogue at a popular level.

238 A.T. Robinson, *Commentary on the Gospel According to Matthew* (New York: Macmillan Company, 1911), p. 191 (emphasis added).

239 Marvin Richardson Vincent, *Word Studies in the New Testament*, Vol. 1 (New York: Charles Scribner's Sons, 1906), pp. 91–92.

240 Dave Hunt, *The Woman Rides the Beast* (Eugene, OR: Harvest House Publications, 1994), p. 148; Todd D. Baker, *Exodus from Rome, Vol. 1* (Bloomington, IN: iUniverse, 2014), p. 16.

241 Joseph Benson, *The Holy Bible, Containing the Old and New Testaments . . . with Critical, Explanatory, and Practical Notes,* Vol. 3 (New York: G. Lane & C.B. Tippett, 1846), p. 252.

242 D.A. Carson puts the argument best: "Here Jesus build his church; in 1 Corinthians 3:10, Paul is 'an expert builder.' In 1 Corinthians 3:11, Jesus is the church's foundation; in Ephesians 2:19–20, the apostles and prophets are the foundation (cf. Rev. 21:14), and Jesus is the 'cornerstone.' Here Peter has the keys; in Revelation 1:18; 3:7, Jesus has the keys. In John 9:5, Jesus is 'the light of the world'; in Matthew 5:14, his disciples are. None of these pairs threatens Jesus' uniqueness. They simply show how metaphors must be interpreted primarily with reference to their immediate contexts." D.A. Carson, *Matthew and Mark*, vol. 9 of *Expositor's Bible Commentary*, eds. Tremper Longman III and David E. Garland (Grand Rapids, MI: Zondervan, 2010), p. 419.

243 John MacArthur, *The MacArthur New Testament Commentary: Matthew 16–23* (Chicago: Moody Publishers, 1988), p. 28.

244 John MacArthur, *Strange Fire: The Danger of Offending the Holy Spirit with Counterfeit Worship* (Nashville, TN: Nelson Books, 2013), pp. 96–97.

245 Mike Lynch, "Barack Obama's Big Data won the US election," *CIO*, Nov. 13, 2012.

246 Gregg Allison, "What Does 'This Rock' Refer to in Matthew 16:18?," *The Gospel Coalition*, Jan. 16, 2020.

247 Ibid.

248 Thomas R. Schreiner, *New Testament Theology* (Grand Rapids, MI: Baker Academic, 2008), p. 682

249 Martin Luther, *Luther's Explanatory Notes on the Gospel*, ed. E. Mueller, trans. P. Anstadt (York, PA: P. Anstadt & Sons, 1899), p. 97.

250 Ibid.

251 Calvin, p. 235.

252 There is ongoing scholarly debate over whether "Peter" was Simon's new personal

name, nickname, or title. In favor of it being a personal name are the repeated instances of it being used as such: "Now Peter was sitting outside in the courtyard" (Matt. 26:69), etc., and the fact that Luke says Jesus "named" him Peter (Luke 6:14). Mark's verbiage is vaguer: he uses the same verb for Jesus' calling Simon "Peter" as he does for Jesus' calling James and John "the sons of thunder" (Mark 3:16–17). Against its being a personal name are the fact that Peter is still sometimes called Simon or Simon Peter afterward and the fact that it is translated into Greek (which is how we end up with both the Aramaic transliteration *Cephas* and the Greek translation *Petros*). Cullmann suggests that "the fact of translation supports the contention that Cephas was not a proper name, since one does not translate proper names. In order to bring out the power of the nickname as the authors and early readers of the NT felt it, we ought perhaps to follow the NT practice and reproduce the name as 'Simon Rock.'" Oscar Cullmann, *Theological Dictionary of the New Testament*, Vol. 6, eds. Gerhard Kittel and Gerhard Friendrich, trans. Geoffrey W. Bromiley (Grand Rapids, MI: Wm. B. Eerdmans Publishing Co., 1968), p. 101. Perhaps the closest answer is that Peter was both a personal name and a title and that the New Testament authors took pains to let it be known that the name meant "rock" by having it translated rather than simply transliterated. An analogue may be found in the modern practice of papal names. Joseph Ratzinger became Pope Benedictus XVI but was known in English as "Benedict the Sixteenth" and was sometimes still referred to as "Ratzinger."

253 Outside mainstream Protestantism, this same *petros-petra* argument is regularly made by other non-Catholics, including Mormon/LDS and Adventist theologians and apologists. Cf. Matthew L. Bowen, "Founded Upon a Rock: Doctrinal and Temple Implications of Peter's Surnaming," *Interpreter: A Journal of Mormon Scripture*, Vol. 9 (Orem, UT: Interpreter Foundation, 2014), p. 9 (quoting BYU professor and Mormon apologist Eric Huntsman: "*Petros*, the name Jesus gave Peter at his initial call means an isolated rock or stone, where *Petra*, a feminine noun, means bedrock, the type of rock of which a tomb was hewn or the foundation of an impregnable position or rocky fortress"); Sidney B. Sperry, "The Meaning of Peter's Confession," *The Improvement Era* [LDS], vol. 52 (1949), p. 496 (claiming that "*petros* and *petra* are two distinct words, as distinct in Greek as pebble and boulder are two distinct English words"); Reinder Bruinsma, *The Body of Christ: An Adventist Understanding of the Church* (Review and Herald Publishing Association, 2009), pp. 37–38 ("Protestants—Adventists among them—point to the play on words" wherein "*petra* is used to denote a large solid rock and *petros* refers to a small stone"); Catherine Taylor, "On Becoming a Pebble: The Name God Gave Simon," *Spectrum Magazine* [Adventist], Vol. 45, No. 2 ("*Petros* describes a small individual stone, a pebble. Linguistically, the term can be used in contrast to *petra*, the bedrock").

254 William Cathcart, *The Papal System: From Its Origin to the Present Time* (Aurora, MO: Menace Publishing Company, 1872), p. 76.

255 John MacArthur, "Empty Hearts," *Grace to You*, June 8, 1980. Online, available at https://www.gty.org/library/sermons-library/2256/empty-hearts.

256 John MacArthur, *The MacArthur New Testament Commentary: Matthew 16–23* (Chicago, IL: Moody Publishers, 1988), p. 28.

257 MacArthur, *Matthew 16–23*, p. 28.

258 Ibid.

259 Recounted in William A. Edmundson, *John Rawls: Reticent Socialist* (Cambridge, UK: University of Cambridge Press, 2017), p. 119.

260 Oscar Cullmann, *Theological Dictionary of the New Testament*, Vol. 6, eds. Gerhard Kittel and Gerhard Friendrich, trans. Geoffrey W. Bromiley (Grand Rapids, MI: Wm. B. Eerdmans Publishing Co., 1968), p. 101.

261 Cullman, p. 108.

262 D.A. Carson is a well-respected theologian in Protestant circles. He is the founder and president of The Gospel Coalition, "a fellowship of evangelical churches in the Reformed tradition." The Reformed Baptist theologian John Piper describes him as "secondarily a great defender of Christ, but mainly a joyful advocate and witness." John Piper, "Tribute to Don Carson," *The Gospel Coalition National Conference*, April 12, 2011.

263 D.A. Carson, *The Expositor's Bible Commentary, Vol. 9: Matthew and Mark*, eds. Tremper Longman III and David E. Garland (Grand Rapids, MI: Zondervan, 2010), p. 418.

264 Ibid., p. 418.

265 Apollonius Rhodius, *The Argnoautica*, Book III, trans. R.C. Seaton (New York: The Macmillan Co., 1912), p. 287.

266 Apollonius of Rhodes, *The Argnoautica*, Book III, ed. R.L. Hunter (Cambridge: Cambridge University Press, 1989), p. 93, line 1365.

267 Chrys C. Caragounis, *Peter and the Rock* (Berlin: Werner Hildebrand, 1989), p. 116.

268 Cullman, p. 106.

269 A transliteration is the conversion of one text to another. For example, the city that the Chinese call 北京 used to be transliterated as "Peking," and is now transliterated as "Beijing." The name didn't change in Chinese—it was simply an attempt to more accurately represent in English what was being said in Chinese. A translation of 北京, in contrast, would be "Northern Capital," which is what the name means. *Cephas* is the Greek transliteration of כֵּיפָא; *Petros* is the translation.

270 Carson, p. 418. He adds that "the underlying Aramaic in this case is unquestionable, and most probably *kēpā'* was used in both clauses (you are *kēpā'*, and on this *kēpā'*) . . . The Peshitta (written in Syriac, a language cognate with Aramaic) makes no distinction between the words in the two clauses."

271 Cullman, p. 106. Several scholars have suggested that the wordplay would not work in Aramaic, precisely because the two words are the same. For instance, Bivin thinks that wordplay requires "a contrast between two different though related words" and argues that this would point to Jesus speaking in Greek, rather than Aramaic. Bivin, p. 382. I can only say such arguments misunderstand both wordplay (some of the best puns, like the "eats, shoots, and leaves" one about pandas and the "right to bear arms" one about bears involve wordplay with identical-sounding words) and the nature of the blessing going on here.

272 Nigel Turner explains that calling Peter *Petros* "cannot be connected directly with [*petros*], since this was out of general use," and instead was simply a masculinizing of [*petra*]." Nigel Turner, *A Grammar of New Testament Greek: Syntax*, ed. James Hope Moulton (Edinburg, UK: T. & T. Clark, 1963), p. 22. In other words, just as in the case where, if one were to jokingly refer to a female governor as "governess," he may be trying to feminize a common word, rather than using an antiquated word, the same seems to be happening here.

273 The RSV-CE, for some reason, has "the power of death" here, noting Jesus' actual expression ("the gates of Hades")

274 James Leo Garrett, Jr., "The Congregation-Led Church," in *Perspectives on Church Government*, ed. Chad Owen Brand and R. Stanton Norman (Nashville, TN: Broadman & Holman Publishers, 2004), p. 157.

275 Terence L. Nichols, "Participatory Hierarchy" in *Common Calling: The Laity and Governance of the Catholic Church*, ed. Stephen J. Pope (Washington, D.C.: Georgetown University Press, 2004), p. 124.

276 Joan S. Gray and Joyce C. Tucker, *Presbyterian Polity for Church Officers*, 3rd ed. (Louisville, KY: Geneva Press, 1999), p. 2.

277 Ibid., p. 4.

278 Paul F.M. Zahl, "The Bishop-Led Church," in *Perspectives on Church Government*, ed. Chad Owen Brand and R. Stanton Norman (Nashville, TN: Broadman & Holman Publishers, 2004), p. 213.

279 Ibid., p. 234.

280 Aristotle, *Politics*, Book III, 2nd ed., trans. Carnes Lord (Chicago, IL: University of Chicago Press, 2013), p. 73.

281 Robert Booth Fowler, Allen D. Hertzke, Laura R. Olson, and Kevin R. den Dulk, *Religion and Politics in America*, 5th ed. (Boulder, CO: Westview Press, 2014), p. 42

282 Paul Lakeland, *Church: Living Communion* (Collegeville, MN: Liturgical Press, 2009), p. 176.

283 Martin Luther, *The Bondage of the Will*, trans. Henry Cole (London: T. Bensley, 1823), p. 17.

284 Craig D. Atwood and Roger E. Olson, "Religion in America," in *Handbook of Denominations in the United States*, 14th ed., eds. Roger E. Olson, Craig D. Atwood, Frank S. Mead, and Samuel S. Hill (Nashville, TN: Abingdon Press, 2018).

285 Alcuin of York, letter to Charlemagne (c. 798), in *Vox Populi: Essays in the History of an Idea* (Baltimore, MD: Johns Hopkins University Press, 1969), pp. 3–38, doi:10.1353/book.72158.

286 C.S. Lewis, "Equality," in *Present Concerns,* ed. Walter Hooper (San Diego, CA: Harcourt, Inc., 1986), p. 17. ("I am a democrat because I believe in the Fall of Man. I think most people are democrats for the opposite reason. . . . Mankind is so fallen that no man can be trusted with unchecked power over his fellows.")

287 Aristotle, *Politics*, Book III, 2nd ed., trans. Carnes Lord (Chicago, IL: University of Chicago Press, 2013), p. 73.

288 Timothy Ware (Bishop Kallistos of Diokleia), *The Orthodox Church* (London, UK: Penguin Books, 1993), p. 7.

289 Ibid.

290 Eugen J. Pentiuc, *The Old Testament in Eastern Orthodox Tradition* (Oxford, UK: Oxford University Press, 2014), p. 109.

291 Stanley S. Harakas, "The Stand of the Orthodox Church on Controversial Issues," *Greek Orthodox Archdiocese of America*, Aug. 12, 1985. Available online at https://www.goarch.org/-/the-stand-of-the-orthodox-church-on-controversial-issues.

292 Gayle Kassing, *History of Dance* (Champaign, IL: Human Kinetics, 2007), p. 56.

293 For the underlying Hebrew and Aramaic, see Ramesh Kathry, *The Authenticity of the Parable of the Wheat and Tares and Its Interpretation* (Ph.D. diss., Westminster College, 1991; Dissertation.com, 2000), pp. 136–37.

294 David McCracken, *The Scandal of the Gospels: Jesus, Story, and Offense* (New York, NY: Oxford University Press, 1994), p. 34. ("The figurative sense of 'stone' in *skandalon* stands in direct contrast to Peter as "rock" and foundation of the church.")

295 Joseph Ratzinger, *Das neue Volk Gottes*, pp. 80ff., in Joseph Ratzinger, *Co-workers of the Truth: Meditations for Every Day of the Year*, trans. Mary Francis McCarthy and Lothar Krauth (San Francisco, CA: Ignatius Press, 1992), p. 208.

296 Ibid.

297 John Calvin, *The Institutes of the Christian Religion*, Book III, trans. Henry Beveridge (Peabody, MA: Hendrickson Publishers, 2009), p. 758.

298 Joe Heschmeyer, "St. Peter: Rock or Stumbling-Stone?," *Catholic Answers Magazine Online*, Feb. 21, 2018.

299 Carmel McCoubrey, "Don't Quote Them on It," *New York Times*, Feb. 14, 2017.

300 Robert H. Gundry, *Peter—False Disciple and Apostate According to Saint Matthew* (Grand Rapids, MI: William B. Eerdmans Publishing Co., 2015), p. 24. Gundry, who was chair of biblical studies at Westmont College, advances the bizarre claim that St. Matthew presents "Peter as a false disciple and apostate" and that "in his Gospel Peter appears to be headed for hell, whereas in Luke-Acts and John 21 Peter appears on the contrary to be rehabilitated." Gundry, pp. 103–04.

301 Ibid.

302 Joseph Benson, *The Holy Bible, Containing the Old and New Testaments (according to the Present Authorized Version) with Critical, Explanatory, and Practical Notes* (New York, NY: G. Lane & C.B. Tippett, 1846), p. 147.

303 Paul V.M. Flesher and Bruce Chilton, *The Targums: A Critical Introduction* (Leiden, The Netherlands: Brill, 2011), pp. 8, 6 (emphasis in original).

304 Quoted in Bruce Chilton and Craig A. Evans, *Jesus in Context: Temple, Purity, and Restoration* (Leiden, The Netherlands: Brill, 1997), p. 257.

305 Josephus, *Antiquities of the Jews*, Book X, in *The Works of Flavius Josephus*, vol. 2, trans. William Whiston (London, U.K.: Lackington, et al, 1820), p. 146. The *Midrash Rabbah* says that Shebna, the man Eliakim was replacing, was also high priest. Cf. Michael Patrick Barber, "Jesus as the Davidic Temple Builder and Peter's Priestly Role in Matthew 16:16–19," *Journal of Biblical Literature*, vol. 132, no. 4 (2013), p. 944.

306 The recorder here is Joah, not his father Asaph. "Joah the son of Asaph" (Joah bar-Asaph) is a patronymic.

307 Frederik Poulsen, *The Black Hole in Isaiah: A Study of Exile as a Literary Theme* (Tübingen, Germany: Mohr Siebeck, 2019), pp. 195–196.

308 Barber, p. 945.

309 Poulsen, pp. 195–196.

310 Along alternate lines, the Protestant theologian James B. Jordan argues that the New Testament presents Peter in the role of the high priest – for example, in his role in the Transfiguration and in the entrance to the Empty Tomb. The argument is an intriguing one, and fits in neatly with the idea of Peter as the new Eliakim. James B. Jordan, "Peter as High Priest," *Biblical Horizons* 68 (December 1994).

311 Kauffman Kohler, "Binding and Loosing," in *The Jewish Encyclopedia*, vol. 3 (New York: Funk and Wagnalls Co., 1907), p. 215.

312 Mark Allan Powell, "Binding and Loosening: Asserting the Moral Authority of Scrip-

ture in Light of a Matthean Paradigm," *Ex Auditu*, vol. 19 (2003), p. 82. He adds that "the words are used in this regard by Josephus and in targumic materials. Jewish rabbis 'bound' the law when they determined that a commandment was applicable to a particular situation, and the 'loosed' the law when they determined that a word of Scripture (while eternally valid) was not applicable under certain specific circumstances."

313 Flavius Josephus, *The Jewish War*, 5.2, in *The Works of Flavius Josephus*, vol. 2, trans. William Whiston (Philadelphia: J.B. Lippincott & Co., 1856), p. 174.

314 Chagigah 3b, *A Translation of the Treatise Chagigah from the Babylonian Talmud*, trans. A.W. Streane (Cambridge, Cambridge University Press, 1891), p. 9.

315 Robert H. Gundry, *Matthew*, 2nd ed. (Grand Rapids, MI: William B. Eerdmans Publishing Co.,1994), p. 336.

316 Richard H. Hiers, "'Binding' and 'Loosing': The Matthean Authorizations," *Journal of Biblical Literature*, vol. 104, no. 2 (June 1985), p. 233.

317 Ibid., p. 235.

318 Joel Marcus, "The Gates of Hades and the Keys of the Kingdom (Matt 16:18–19)," *The Catholic Biblical Quarterly*, Vol. 50, No. 3, p. 450 (adding that "in the end Hiers admits that his interpretation of binding and loosing does not hold for Matt 16:19 and 18:18 in their *Matthean* contexts").

319 Malcolm B. Yarnell III, "'Upon This Rock I Will Build My Church' A Theological Exposition of Matthew 16:13–20," in *Upon This Rock: The Baptist Understanding of the Church*, eds. Jason G. Duesing, Thomas White, and Malcolm B. Yarnell III (Nashville, TN: B&H Academic, 2010), p. 48.

320 Luther, *Against the Papacy*, 315–16, quoted in Yarnell, p. 48.

321 Benjamin L. Merkle, *Exegetical Gems from Biblical Greek* (Grand Rapids, MI: Baker Academic, 2019), pp. 104–105.

322 Jonathan Leeman, *Political Church* (Downers Grove, IL: InterVarsity Press, 2016), p. 344.

323 Ernest DeWitt Burton, *Syntax of the Moods and Tenses in New Testament Greek*, 3rd ed. (Edinburgh, U.K.: T. & T. Clark, 1898) p. 45.

324 Ibid. In Luke 12:52, it's used to say that "henceforth in one house there will be five divided, three against two and two against three;" and in Hebrews 2:13 it's used to say "I will put my trust in him," not to say that the house "will have been" divided, or "I will have placed my trust in him." The other two cases are the ones in dispute here (Matt. 16:19 and 18:18). So there are no clear cases of the periphrastic future perfect ever being used to refer to a future past action, two cases where it seems not to mean that, and then the two cases before us.

325 Grant R. Osborne, *Exegetical Commentary on the New Testament* (Grand Rapids, MI: Zondervan, 2010), p. 629.

326 Yarnell III, "'Upon This Rock I Will Build My Church' A Theological Exposition of Matthew 16:13–20," in *Upon This Rock: The Baptist Understanding of the Church*, p. 48-49.

327 D.A. Carson, *Matthew*, in *Matthew and Mark*, revised edition, vol. 9 of *The Expositor's Bible Commentary with the New International Version*, eds. Tremper Longman III and David E. Garland (Grand Rapids, MI: Zondervan, 2010), p. 423.

328 Ibid., p. 422.

329 Regarding the debate over the tense of the verbiage, perhaps we should follow the advice of St. Paul, who calls us to "avoid disputing about words, which does no good,

but only ruins the hearers" (2 Tim. 2:14).

330 Ibid., p. 426.

331 Rousas John Rushdoony, *The Institutes of Biblical Law*, vol. 1 (Vallecito, CA: Chalcedon Foundation, 2012), Kindle version 1.0.

332 Merkle, p. 106.

333 Tord Fornberg, "Peter—the High Priest of the New Covenant?," *East Asia Journal of Theology*, vol. 4, no. 1 (1986), p. 113.

334 Hans Bayer, *Peter as Apostolic Bedrock* (Eugene, OR: Wipf & Stock, 2019), p. 61.

335 Kauffman Kohler, "Binding and Loosing," in *The Jewish Encyclopedia*, vol. 3 (New York: Funk and Wagnalls Co., 1907), p. 215 (internal citations omitted).

336 In Leviticus 23:2, God says, "Say to the people of Israel, The appointed feasts of the Lord which you shall proclaim as holy convocations, my appointed feasts, are these." The *halakhic midrash* to the Book of Leviticus explains the "which you shall proclaim" by saying that "if you call them, they are My festivals. If not, they are not My festivals." Sifra Emor, Section 9.2, trans. Shraga Silverstein, Sefaria, available online at https://www.sefaria.org/Sifra%2C_Emor%2C_Section_9.2?lang=en&with=all&lang2=en. Whether or not this is a good understanding of Leviticus is beside the point. The point here is simply that the Jewish people believed (and believe) that God has left certain earthly authorities with the ability to determine disputed matters.

337 Barber, p. 948 ("prior to the temple's destruction, definitive interpretation of the Law was especially associated with the priests, who clearly held an authoritative role as interpreters of the Torah").

338 *The International Standard Bible Encyclopedia*, vol. 4, ed. Geoffrey W. Bromley (Grand Rapids, MI: William B. Eerdmans Publishing Co., 1988), p. 332 ("In number the Sanhedrin consisted of seventy members and the high priest as president").

339 Keith Mathison, "To Be Deep in History," *Tabletalk Magazine*, Sept. 1, 2010.

340 Ben Witherington, III, *John's Wisdom* (Louisville, KY: Westminster John Knox Press, 1995), p. 275.

341 Ovid, *Metamorphoses*, Book VIII, trans. Rolfe Humphries (Bloomington, IN: Indiana University Press, 1983), p. 208.

342 Emma Green, "Why Can't Christians Get Along, 500 Years After the Reformation?" *The Atlantic*, Oct. 29, 2017.

343 Witherington, p. 274.

344 Martin Luther, *Bondage of the Will*, trans. Henry Cole (London: T. Bensley, 1823), p. 17.

345 Ibid.

346 "Making Sense of Christian Denominations," *Focus on the Family*, 2010. Available online at https://www.focusonthefamily.com/family-qa/making-sense-of-christian-denominations/.

347 Martin Luther, *Sermon on the Mount and the Magnificat*, vol. 21 of *Luther's Works*, ed. Jaroslav Pelikan (St. Louis, MO: Concordia Publishing House, 1956), p. 68.

348 Jerome, *Dialogue against the Luciferians*, in *Jerome: Letters and Select Works*, trans. W.H. Fremantle (New York, NY: The Christian Literature Co., 1893), NPNF 2/6:233.

349 "Making Sense of Christian Denominations," *Focus on the Family*, 2010. Available online at https://www.focusonthefamily.com/family-qa/making-sense-of-christian-denominations/.

350 Prior to his conversion to Catholicism, my friend Doug Beaumont compiled a list of some 75 doctrines that were viewed as "major" or non-negotiable by some Protestants and rejected or treated as non-essential by other Protestants. You can find the full list at https://douglasbeaumont.com/2013/04/24/on-protestant-abstrusity/.

351 C.S. Lewis, "Christian Reunion: An Anglican Speaks to Roman Catholics," in *C.S. Lewis Essay Collection and Other Short Pieces* (New York: HarperCollins, 2000), p. 396.

352 Keith Mathison, *The Shape of Sola Scriptura* (Moscow, ID: Canon Press, 2001), pp. 217–18.

353 Quoted in Ross Douthat, "A Time for Contrition," *New York Times*, Mar. 28, 2010.

354 Quoted in Robert Speaight, *The Life of Hilaire Belloc* (London: Hollis & Carter, 1957), p. 383.

355 Cf. John Ford and Germain Grisez, "Contraception and the Infallibility of the Ordinary Magisterium," *Theological Studies*, vol. 39, no. 2 (June 1978), pp. 258–312.

356 Ibid., 61.

357 "Is papal infallibility biblical?," GotQuestions.org, available at https://www.gotquestions.org/papal-infallibility.html.

358 Quoted in Martin Brecht, *Martin Luther: His Road to Reformation 1483–1521*, trans. James L. Schaaf (Minneapolis: MN: Fortress Press, 1993), p. 460.

359 Keith Mathison, *The Shape of Sola Scriptura* (Moscow, ID: Canon Press, 2001), p. 261.

360 Ibid.

361 R.C. Sproul, *Now, That's a Good Question!* (Wheaton, IL: Tyndale House Publishers, 1996), p. 82.

362 John H. Hayes, "Historical Criticism of the Old Testament Canon," in *Hebrew Bible, Old Testament: The History of Its Interpretation*, vol. 2, ed. Magne Sæbø (Göttingen, Germany: Vandenhoeck & Ruprecht, 2008), p. 989.

363 Ibid.

364 Mathison, p. 316.

365 Albert C. Sundberg, Jr., "The 'Old Testament': A Christian Canon," *The Catholic Biblical Quarterly*, vol. 30, no. 2 (April 1968), p. 143.

366 Benedict T. Viviano and Justin Taylor, "Sadducees, Angels, and Resurrection (Acts 23:8–9)," *Journal of Biblical Literature*, vol. 111, no. 3 (Autumn 1992), p. 496.

367 Cf. *The Israelite Samaritan Version of the Torah*, trans. Benyamin Tsedaka, eds. Benyamin Tsedaka and Sharon Sullivan (Grand Rapids, MI: Wm. B. Eerdmans Publishing Co., 2013), pp. 173–77.

368 Matthias Henze, *Biblical Interpretation at Qumran* (Grand Rapids, MI: Wm. B. Eerdmans Publishing Co., 2005), p. 2.

369 Timothy H. Lim, *The Formation of the Jewish Canon* (New Haven, CT: Yale University Press, 2013), p. 182.

370 Mathison, for instance, claims that "the assertion of Paul that the Jews were entrusted with the oracles of God (the Old Testament) would largely resolve the question of the so-called 'Apocryphal' books were it not for Rome's insistence on her own autonomy and infallibility." Mathison, p. 316. This is a bastardization of Romans 3:2, which refers to the historical reality that God revealed himself to the Jewish prophets. To interpret it to say that the true Jews are the ones outwardly, and that they have a perpetual ability to determine which books do and don't belong in the Bible, could

scarcely be more alien from the theology Paul advances in the epistle. Mathison's reading is tenable only by reducing "the oracles of God" to the books of the Old Testament, and nothing else.

371 Viktor Potapov, "Primacy and 'Infallibility' of the Roman Pope," Russian Orthodox Cathedral of St. John the Baptist, 1998. Available online at https://stjohndc.org/en/orthodoxy-foundation/primacy-and-infallibility-roman-pope.

372 Ibid.

373 David Bentley Hart, "Saint Origen," *First Things* (October 2015). A few months prior to this article, in the comments of the blog *Eclectic Orthodoxy*, he argues against the Fifth Ecumenical Council that if "you consult the (very dubious) records of the council, you will find something called Origenism condemned. But no authentic finding of the council condemns universalism as such." But he then added, "Not that I would care if it did. That very imperial 'ecumenical' council is an embarrassment in Christian history, and I sometimes think it a mercy that such a hash was made of its promulgation that we literally do not know what was truly determined there. For my money, if Origen was not a saint and church father, then no one has any claim to those titles. And the contrary claims made by a brutish imbecile emperor are of no consequence." Comments under the post "Readings in Universalism," *Eclectic Orthodoxy*, available online at https://afkimel.wordpress.com/essential-readings-on-universalism/.

374 Timothy Kallistos Ware, *The Orthodox Church* (London, UK: Penguin Books, 1993), p. 252.

375 "Encyclical of the Eastern Patriarchs," quoted in *Russo-Greek Papers, 1863–1874*, eds. Edward Kasinec and J. Robert Wright (New York, NY: Norman Ross Publishing, 2001), p. 259.

376 Quoted in Reinhard Flogaus, "Inspiration—Exploitation—Distortion: The Use of St. Augustine in the Hesychast Controversy," *Orthodox Readings on Augustine*, eds. George E. Demacopoulos and Aristotle Papanikolaou (Crestwood, NY: St. Vladimir's Seminary Press, 2008), p. 69.

377 Ernest Honigmann, "The Original Lists of the Members of the Council of Nicaea, the Robber-Synod and the Council of Chalcedon," *Byzantion*, vol. 16, no. 1 (1942–1943), p. 34.

378 Alain Besançon, *The Falsification of the Good* (London, UK: Claridge Press, 1994), p. 44.

379 Cara Berkeley, *Some Roman Monuments in the Light of History*, vol. 2 (London, U.K.: Sheed & Ward, 1927), p. 248.

380 Gaddis, p. 40.

381 Besançon, p. 44.

382 Matthew B. Koval, "Council of Chalcedon," in *Great Events in Religion*, vol. 1, eds. Florin Curta and Andrew Holt (Santa Barbara, CA: ABC-CLIO, 2017), p. 290.

383 Ibid.

384 Olivier Clément, You Are Peter: *An Orthodox Theologian's Reflection on the Exercise of Papal Primacy* (Hyde Park, NY: New City Press, 2003), p. 49.

385 Quoted in J.I. Packer, *A Quest for Godliness: The Puritan Vision of the Christian Life* (Wheaton, IL: Crossway Books, 1990), p. 224.

386 "Treatise on the Power and Primacy of the Pope," in *The Book of Concord*, trans. Theodore G. Tappert (Philadelphia, PA: Fortress Press, 1959), p. 327.

387 Ibid., p. 330.

388 Quoted in David Hawkes, *John Milton: A Hero of Our Times* (Berkeley, CA: Counterpoint, 2009), p. 116.

389 Quoted in Jean-Louis Quantin, *The Church of England and Christian Antiquity* (Oxford, UK: Oxford University Press, 2009), p. 257.

390 Stanley Hauerwas, "The Reformation is over. Protestants won. So why are we still here?" *Washington Post*, Oct. 27, 2017.

391 Gavin Ortlund, "Searching for Gospel-Centered Theology Before the Reformation," *The Gospel Coalition*, May 9, 2013.

392 Gregory L. Jackson, *Catholic, Lutheran, Protestant* (Glendale, AZ: Martin Chemnitz Press, 2007), p. 17.

393 John Henry Newman, *An Essay on the Development of Christian Doctrine*, 7th ed. (London, UK: Longmans, Green, and Co., 1890), p. 7.

394 Ibid.

395 John Milton, *Paradise Lost*, Book II: 230–37 (New York, NY: Thomas Y. Crowell & Co., 1892), p. 225.

396 Jack P. Lewis, "'The Gates of Hell Shall Not Prevail Against It' (Matt 16:18): A Study of the History of Interpretation," *Journal of the Evangelical Theological Society*, vol. 38, no. 3 (1995), pp. 355–56.

397 The account found 1 Maccabees is corroborated by Greek testimonies as well. The Greek historian Diodorus Siculus recounts that after subduing the Jews, he "entered into the temple of God, into which none was allowed to enter by their law except the priest." Once there, he waged war directly on Israel's God: "Antiochus therefore, abhorring their antagonism to all other people, tried his utmost to abolish their laws. To that end he sacrificed a great swine at the image of Moses, and at the altar of God that stood in the outward court, and sprinkled them with the blood of the sacrifice. He commanded likewise that the books, by which they were taught to hate all other nations, should be sprinkled with the broth made of the swine's flesh. And he put out the lamp (called by them immortal) which burns continually in the temple. Lastly he forced the high priest and the other Jews to eat swine's flesh." Diodorus Siculus, *Historical Library*, book 34, in *The Historical Library of Diodorus the Sicilian*, vol. 2, trans. G. Booth (London: W. McDowell, 1814), p. 544.

398 Paul Niskanen, *The Human and the Divine in History* (London, UK: T&T Clark International, 2004), p. 117.

399 Jerome, *Jerome's Commentary on Daniel*, trans. Gleason L. Archer (Eugene, OR: Wipf & Stock, 2009), pp. 31–32.

400 John Bergsma and Brant Pitre, *A Catholic Introduction to the Old Testament* (San Francisco: Ignatius Press, 2018), p. 880.

401 Thomas F.X. Noble, "Narratives of Papal History," in *A Companion to the Medieval Papacy*, eds. Keith Sisson and Atria A. Larson (Leiden, The Netherlands: Brill, 2016), p. 17.

402 Norman Fox, *Christ in the Daily Meal* (New York, NY: Fords, Howard & Hulbert, 1898), p. 105.

403 Ibid.

404 James E. Talmage, *The Great Apostasy* (Salt Lake City, UT: Deseret News, 1909), p. 159.

405 Ibid., p. 160.

406 Alister E. McGrath, "Forerunners of the Reformation? A Critical Examination of the Evidence for Precursors of the Reformation Doctrines of Justification," *The Harvard Theological Review*, vol. 75, no. 2 (April 1982), pp. 224, 241–42.

407 Randall Balmer, "Landmark Movement," in *Encyclopedia of Evangelicalism* (Waco, TX: Baylor University Press, 2004).

408 J.M. Carroll, *The Trail of Blood* (Corunna, MI: The Bible Nation Society, 2017), p. 70.

409 Lisa M. Bitel, *Women in Early Medieval Europe, 400–1100* (Cambridge, UK: Cambridge University Press, 2002), p. 14.

410 Jan de Vries, "Population," in *Handbook of European History 1400–1600*, vol. 1, eds. Thomas A. Brady, Jr., Heiko A. Oberman, and James D. Tracy (Leiden, The Netherlands: E.J. Brill, 1994), p. 13.

411 David d'Avray, "The Cathars from Non-Catholic Sources," in *Cathars in Question*, ed. Antonio Sennis (York, UK: York Medieval Press, 2016), p. 184.

412 James Leo Garrett, Jr., *Baptist Theology: A Four-Century Study* (Macon, GA: Mercer University Press, 2009), p. 6.

413 Martin Luther, *Bondage of the Will*, trans. J.I. Packer and O.R. Johnston (Grand Rapids, MI: Baker Academic, 1957), p. 121.

414 Bernard Nathanson, *The Hand of God* (Washington, D.C.: Regnery Publishing, 2013), p. 129.

415 Michael S. Gazzaniga, "Facts, Fictions, and the Future of Neuroethics," in *Neuroethics: Defining the Issues in Theory, Practice, and Policy*, ed. Judy Illes (Oxford: Oxford University Press, 2006), p. 144.

416 Nathanson, p. 151.

417 Michael B. Becraft, *Steve Jobs: A Biography* (Santa Barbara, CA: Greenwood, 2017), p. 36.

418 Kathy Lavezzo, *Angels on the Edge of the World* (Ithaca, NY: Cornell University Press, 2006), p. 108.

419 Ian Paisley, *Roman Catholic Priests*, 13, quoted in Joshua T. Searle, *The Scarlet Woman and the Red Hand: Evangelical Apocalyptic Belief in the Northern Ireland Troubles* (Eugene, OR: Pickwick Publications, 2014), p. 206.

420 To wit, Joseph Smith founded Mormonism in the 1820s, during an American Protestant religious movement called the Second Great Awakening. Charles Taze Russell founded the Bible Student movement in the 1870s, renamed the Jehovah's Witnesses by his successor Joseph Franklin Rutherford (1869–1942). The Bible Student movement was an offshoot of the Millerites, a fringe Protestant group who believed that Christ's return would be in 1843 (they were wrong). Mary Baker Eddy founded the Church of Christ, Scientist, better known as Christian Science, in 1879. It was part of the "New Thought" religious movements that blended liberal Protestantism and spiritualism (Eddy was a patient of the hypnotist Phineas Quimby, one of the founders of the New Thought movement). Ellen Gould White founded Seventh Day Adventism in 1863. Like Russell, White was a disillusioned Millerite. Muhammad founded Islam around 622.

421 More specifically, the image was taken from Vittore Carpaccio's painting *The Meeting of the Pilgrims with the Pope* (1497–98), and the pope depicted is probably Pope Siricius, who reigned from 384 to 399, succeeding Pope Damasus I. It's improbable (and illogical) that anyone would claim that Pope Siricius was the first pope.

422 John H. Armstrong, *Your Church Is Too Small: Why Unity in Christ's Mission Is Vital to the Future of the Church*, p. 134 (Grand Rapids, MI: Zondervan, 2010).

423 Ibid.

424 Irenaeus, *Against Heresies*, 3, 1, in *The Apostolic Fathers with Justin Martyr and Irenaeus*, trans. (New York: Charles Scribner's Sons, 1905), *ANF* 1:414. St. Peter alludes to his presence in Rome in his letter to the universal Church, when he says, "She who is at Babylon, who is likewise chosen, sends you greetings; and so does my son Mark" (1 Pet. 5:13). From the earliest days of the Church, this was understood as a symbolic reference to Rome, not a literal reference to the city of Babylon, which had gone "into terminal decline" after the death of Alexander the Great, and was by this time "completely in ruins." Jacqueline Griffin, "Babylon (Babylon, Iraq)," *International Dictionary of Historic Places*, vol. 4, eds. K.A. Berney, Trudy Ring, and Noelle Watson (Chicago, IL: Fitzroy Dearborn Publishers, 1996), p. 104.

425 Ignatius of Antioch, *The Epistle of Ignatius to the Romans*, *ANF* 1:73.

426 Irenaeus, *ANF* 1:415.

427 Ibid.

428 Bernard Reynolds, *Handbook to the Book of Common Prayer* (London: Rivingtons, 1903), p. 203.

429 Carson, p. 419.

430 Irenaeus, *Against Heresies*, book 3, *ANF* 1:416.

431 Ibid.

432 On the dating of 1 Clement, see David G. Horrell, *The Social Ethos of the Corinthian Correspondence: Interests and Ideology from 1 Corinthians to 1 Clement* (Edinburgh, UK: T&T Clark, 1996), p. 239 ("although a precise and irrefutable dating of 1 Clement is impossible, there is widespread agreement that it was written in the last decade of the first century, perhaps around 95–96 CE."). An early dating of 1 Clement is also consistent with the internal evidence; for instance, referring to the martyrdoms of Peter and Paul as "noble examples furnished in our own generation." Clement of Rome, *1 Clement* 5, *ANF* 1:6. On the dating of the death of the Apostle John, we know from Irenaeus that the Book of Revelation was written "towards the end of Domitian's reign" (which was in A.D. 96). Irenaeus, *Against Heresies* 5.30.3, *ANF* 1:560. St. Clement of Alexandria (not the same Clement) says that after Domitian's death, John "returned to Ephesus from the isle of Patmos, he went away, being invited, to the contiguous territories of the nations, here to appoint bishops, there to set in order whole Churches, there to ordain such as were marked out by the Spirit." Clement of Alexandria, *Who Is the Rich Man That Shall Be Saved?* 42, *ANF* 2:603.

433 Clement of Rome, 1 Clement 1, *ANF* 1:5.

434 Ibid., 42, 1, *ANF* 1:16, 5.

435 Jerome, *De Viris Illustribus* (New York, NY: Scriptura Press, 2015), p. 15.

436 C.S. Lewis, "Christian Marriage," in *The Complete C.S. Lewis Signature Classics* (New York, NY: HarperOne, 2007), p. 96.

437 D.A. Carson, *Matthew and Mark*, vol. 9 of *Expositor's Bible Commentary*, eds. Tremper Longman III and David E. Garland (Grand Rapids, MI: Zondervan, 2010), p. 419.

438 Optatus of Milevis, *The Work of St. Optatus Bishop of Milevis Against the Donatists*, trans. O.R. Vassall-Phillips (re-published through CreateSpace Independent Publishing Platform, 2013), pp. 66-67.

Share the Faith | Defend the Faith

Catholic Answers

MAGAZINE

The premier magazine of Catholic apologetics and evangelization for more than two decades, *Catholic Answers Magazine* helps build your faith—and your ability to defend it. Its lively articles are written by some of the best thinkers in the U.S. Church.

Six times a year, the magazine's 48 eye-catching, full-color pages will hit your mailbox with articles explaining the Faith or answering objections from other points of view.

You'll find clear-to-understand critiques of non-Catholic positions, exchanges between Catholics and non-Catholics on key religious issues, and personal conversion stories.

Don't miss another issue—subscribe now.

catholic.com/magazine

Join Us in the Vineyard!

Catholic Answers is in the business of saving souls.

We need your help to do that, because we're an independent, non-profit organization. We don't ask for or receive financial support from any diocese.

Instead, Catholic Answers is supported by the generosity of individual Catholics who understand the value of the work that we do explaining and defending the Faith.

Your donations make our soul-saving work possible.

Won't you join us? For your convenience, there are several ways to make your tax-deductible donation.

You can:

Visit give.catholic.com/donate
Call 888-291-8000
Mail Send checks to:

Catholic Answers
2020 Gillespie Way
El Cajon, CA 92020

Catholic Answers is a 501(c)3 non-profit organization.

Catholic Answers
TO EXPLAIN & DEFEND THE FAITH